Y0-DKL-663

CHICAGO PUBLIC LIBRARY
HAROLD WASHINGTON LIBRARY CENTER

R0004064129

CHICAGO PUBLIC LIBRARY

FOR

REFERENCE USE

ONLY

NOT TO BE TAKEN FROM THIS ROOM

Minority Group Participation in Graduate Education

A Report with Recommendations of the
NATIONAL BOARD ON
GRADUATE EDUCATION

Washington, D.C.

Number Five • June 1976

REF

REF
LB
2371
'N27
1976

Cop. 1
Sc.

Library of Congress Cataloging in Publication Data

National Board on Graduate Education.
  Minority group participation in graduate education.

  (Board reports—National Board on Graduate Education; no. 5)
  Bibliography: p.
  1. Universities and colleges—United States—Graduate work. 2. Minorities—Education (Higher)—United States. I. Title. II. Series: National Board on Graduate Education. Board reports—National Board on Graduate Education; no. 5.
LB2371.N27   1976   378.1'553'0973   76–16850
ISBN 0–309–02502–8

Available from

Printing and Publishing Office
National Academy of Sciences
2101 Constitution Avenue, N.W.
Washington, D.C. 20418

Printed in the United States of America

80 79 78 77 76   10 9 8 7 6 5 4 3 2 1

Foreword

In implementing its mandate from the Conference Board of Associated Research Councils,* the National Board on Graduate Education (NBGE) early identified the subject of this report as having high priority in any thorough analysis of graduate education and its relation to American society in the future. In the Preface to the first report of the Board, *Graduate Education: Purposes, Problems, and Potential* (November 1972), access for and recruitment of minority group members and women was listed as a topic for Board study and recommendation. The report stated:

> The overwhelming majority of faculty members in the United States are white males. It is unlikely that this accurately reflects the distribution of talents required for teaching and research in the population. Conditions must be created to assure access to graduate education for minority members and for women. In addition to access, these individuals must have the financial resources and the type of graduate environment that provide them with a reasonable opportunity to complete the degree program. Those who join college and university faculties must be assured equal opportunity for professional advancement. (p. 14)

In the Board report, *Federal Policy Alternatives toward Graduate Education* (January 1974), *"Ensuring the responsiveness of graduate education*

* Composed of the American Council on Education, the Social Science Research Council, the American Council of Learned Societies, and the National Research Council. General financial support for the National Board on Graduate Education has come from: Carnegie Corporation of New York, The Ford Foundation, The Andrew W. Mellon Foundation, the National Institute of General Medical Sciences, and the National Science Foundation. Financial support for special studies and technical reports has come from Carnegie Corporation of New York, The Ford Foundation, Lilly Endowment, Inc., and the National Science Foundation.

to the needs of society" was listed (p. 26) as one of the fundamental action goals in enabling graduate education to contribute most effectively to society now and in the future. A main means to that end would be "Ensuring that graduate education contributes to the national commitment to eliminate discrimination based on race, sex, age, and socioeconomic status."

At that point, in the preliminary preparation of the report on federal policy alternatives, it was intended to analyze the issues and outline the conditions relevant to eliminating the barriers to access to graduate education that appear to affect members of minority groups. However, after a period of further study, it became apparent that the issues involved in promoting successful access to and completion of graduate study by minority group individuals were of such complexity that a thorough analysis was not possible within the time constraints upon the completion of the federal policy alternatives report. It was then determined that because of the importance of the topic, NBGE would issue a separate report on the subject, which would include specific policy recommendations directed to the federal government, to other agents and agencies concerned, and to the general public (p. 37).

An advisory panel of experienced and informed students of the subject, under the chairmanship of Frederick Thieme, was established to work with NBGE in the preparation of the present report. Sharon C. Bush, staff associate of NBGE, was asked to work with the panel, draft the report, and assume responsibility for editorial direction.

The members of the advisory panel were:

Frederick Thieme,* Professor of Anthropology, University of Colorado (*Chairman*)

Herman Branson,* President, Lincoln University

Elias Blake, President, Institute for Services to Education

W. Donald Cooke,* Vice President—Research, Cornell University

Joseph Cosand, Director, Center for the Study of Higher Education, University of Michigan

Eugene Cota-Robles, Vice Chancellor—Academic Affairs, University of California, Santa Cruz

Cyrena Pondrom, Assistant Chancellor, University of Wisconsin, Madison

Lois Rice, Vice President, College Entrance Examination Board

Kenneth Tollett, Director, Institute for the Study of Educational Policy, Howard University

Leonard Spearman, Acting Associate Commissioner for Student Assistance, U.S. Office of Education

---

* NBGE member.

iv

The members of NBGE are exceedingly grateful to the panel members for the time, effort, and dedication that made the report possible. The skillful and careful search for material, the scholarly analysis, and the effective organization and presentation by Sharon C. Bush are also gratefully acknowledged, as well as her commitment to the importance of the endeavor.

We also wish to express our appreciation to The Ford Foundation and the Carnegie Corporation of New York for providing financial support to assist in publication of this report.

NBGE hopes that this study will assist in policy formulation, program planning, and specific actions designed to reduce barriers confronting minority group members as they seek graduate education and to develop a hospitable academic environment that will encourage the success of those who enroll. Data and experience to undergird such outcomes have been fragmentary, scattered, and of recent origin. The National Board believes that the material presented here will be useful in continuing research on the problems involved and their dimension in higher education. However, Board members believe that generalizations are now in order, even within the present focus, and that the recommendations contained in the report merit the attention of institutions, of government, and of the general public as well.

DAVID D. HENRY, *Chairman*
National Board on Graduate Education

June 1976

Preface

The past decade has witnessed the emergence of equality of educational opportunity as one of the most prominent—and controversial—questions facing higher education. At the graduate level the issue is clear; few minority men and women hold advanced degrees. Pressures for affirmative action in employment, the national commitment to improved access, and an underlying concern with social justice have called attention to the need to increase minority participation in graduate study. Yet despite widespread concern, there has been surprisingly little systematic examination of this subject and even fewer proposals for action. Two considerations are pertinent.

First, the very magnitude and complexity of the topic are formidable. Data with which to assess the current status of minority persons in graduate education have been wholly inadequate. Moreover, the causes of deficient participation are rooted in mutually reinforcing economic, social, and cultural factors that cannot be fully understood if viewed in isolation. Similarly, sensible solutions require a pluralistic program approach. The sensitivity, expertise, and resources required will be forthcoming only through the combined efforts of institutions, government, and the private sector.

Second, individual values, opinions, and beliefs affect how a problem is perceived and the importance attached to its resolution. They also shape the fundamental premises from which analysis must proceed. Clearly, intense emotions and ideologies surround this subject and, as such, have often frustrated thoughtful inquiry.

In light of the above, the National Board on Graduate Education (NBGE) concluded that this study must adopt a broad perspective, recognizing the interrelated character of the problems, as well as the practical constraints imposed on institutions and agencies that attempt to resolve them. The basic goals and values that underly the report are expressed at the outset; however, strong commitment to the fundamental goals does not assure unanimity with respect to appropriate courses of action for their attainment. The conclusions and recommendations set forth in this report represent a broad consensus of the Board, although individual members offered separate views on specific points.

Early in development of this report, the NBGE determined that broad input from various sectors of society interested and involved in minority education was critical to development of a perceptive and balanced report. Accordingly, we undertook extensive consultation with a wide range of faculty and staff within institutions, representatives of government agencies, congressional staff, and researchers. We especially sought to involve minority faculty and administrators and individuals from numerous minority organizations in order to obtain their insights and counsel throughout this effort. To those many individuals, institutions, agencies and organizations that provided us with valuable data and materials, responded to our inquiries and surveys, and offered constructive advice during the course of this study, we express our deep appreciation.

A number of persons and organizations deserve special mention. Bernard Khoury of the Association of American Universities served as consultant for discussion of selected topics, and Kenneth Tollett of the Institute for the Study of Educational Policy prepared an excellent background paper on the legal issues. Frank Atelsek of the Higher Education Panel of the American Council on Education compiled the results of the survey of minority baccalaureates.

The cooperation of the Institute for Services to Education, Institute for the Study of Educational Policy, Association of American Universities, American Council on Education, and U.S. Office of Education enabled effective implementation of various activities.

We are grateful to representatives of the Conference of Deans of Black Graduate Schools for the time and work they gave in developing the Supplement to this report, "Mission, Status, Problems, and Priorities of Black Graduate Schools," and to Atlanta University for hosting a meeting on this subject. We express our special thanks to Henry E. Cobb of Southern University for his leadership in preparing the Supplement.

The report benefited greatly from the advice and comments of Elizabeth Abramowitz, Institute for the Study of Educational Policy, Howard University; Henry J. Casso, University of New Mexico; John Chase, U.S. Office of Education; Henry E. Cobb, Southern University; Leroy Falling,

Bureau of Indian Affairs; Miles Mark Fisher IV, National Association for Equal Opportunity in Higher Education; Franklin Hale, The Ohio State University; I. Bruce Hamilton, Educational Testing Service; Phillip E. Jones, University of Iowa; Mary Lepper, University of North Carolina; Theodore A. Miles, Howard University; Merritt Norvell, Jr., University of Wisconsin, Madison; Robert O'Neil, Indiana University; Rodney Reed, University of California, Berkeley; Thom Rhue, Stanford University; Carmen Scott, Educational Testing Service; Langley Spurlock, American Council on Education; Sheldon Steinbach, American Council on Education; and Louis Venuto, U.S. Office of Education.

David Breneman, staff director of NBGE, provided strong support and valuable criticism throughout development of the report. Edward Dolbow, René Licht, and Charles Sherman provided research assistance, and Sandra Matthews and Mark Nixon of the NBGE staff and Lawrence Carter were responsible for preparation of the final manuscript. Muriel Quinones compiled the doctoral statistics from the files of the National Research Council.

General administrative support was provided to NBGE by the Commission on Human Resources of the National Research Council, under the direction of William C. Kelly.

SHARON C. BUSH, *Staff Associate*
National Board on Graduate Education

National Board on Graduate Education

JOSEPH BEN-DAVID
Professor of Sociology
The Hebrew University of
　Jerusalem

HERMAN R. BRANSON
President
Lincoln University

ALLAN M. CARTTER
Professor in Residence
University of California,
　Los Angeles

PAUL F. CHENEA
Vice President
Research Laboratories
General Motors Technical Center

W. DONALD COOKE
Vice President, Research
Cornell University

JOHN P. CRECINE
Dean
College of Humanities and
　Social Sciences
Carnegie-Mellon University

JUDITH BLAKE DAVIS
Professor
Graduate School of Public Policy
University of California, Berkeley

EVERETT W. FERRILL
Professor of History
Ball State University

MARTIN GOLAND
President
Southwest Research Institute

NORMAN HACKERMAN
President
Rice University

DAVID D. HENRY (*Chairman*)
President Emeritus
University of Illinois

HANS LAUFER
Professor
The Biological Sciences
University of Connecticut

SOL M. LINOWITZ
Attorney
Coudert Brothers

ROBERT LUMIANSKY
President
American Council of Learned
   Societies

MAURICE MANDELBAUM
Professor of Philosophy
The Johns Hopkins University

JOHN PERRY MILLER
Chief Executive Officer
The Campaign for Yale
   University

JOHN D. MILLETT
Vice President and Director
Management Division
Academy for Educational
   Development, Inc.

HANS NEURATH
Chairman
Department of Biochemistry
University of Washington

ROSEMARY PARK
Professor of Higher Education
University of California,
   Los Angeles

MARTHA PETERSON
President
Beloit College

RICHARD C. RICHARDSON, JR.
President
Northampton County Area
   Community College

TERRY SANFORD
President
Duke University

STEPHEN H. SPURR
Professor
Lyndon B. Johnson School of
   Public Affairs
University of Texas, Austin

ROBERT STROTZ
President
Northwestern University

FREDERICK THIEME
Professor of Anthropology
University of Colorado

xi

Contents

Summary, Conclusions, and Recommendations   1

1. Introduction   27

2. Patterns of Minority Participation   30
   The Not Too Distant Past, 30
   Present Participation, 34
       Definitions of minority groups, 34; How many minorities?, 37; Significance of citizenship status in assessing minority representation, 40
   Enrollments and Degree Attainment, 42
   A Note on Native American Participation, 45
   Distribution among Disciplines, 46
   Measures of Time to Degree in Doctoral Study, 55
   Distribution among Graduate Schools, 55
   The Contribution of the Black Graduate Schools, 59
   Relative Impact of Law and Medical School Enrollments, 60
   The Status of Women Minority Students, 61
   Prospects for Future Participation, 64

3. Barriers to Participation   76
   Financial Barriers, 77
   Educational Barriers, 87
       The educational pyramid, 96
   Psychosocial Barriers, 100
   Cultural Barriers, 103

4. Present Context of Graduate Education and Impact on Minority Participation   107
   The Labor Market for Advanced-Degree Holders, 110
   Implications of Affirmative Action in Higher Education, 113
   Legal Issues, 129

5. Activities and Concerns of Graduate Schools   141
      Structural Contrasts between Graduate Schools and Professional Schools, 142
      Patterns of Activities, 145
      Recruitment, 149
      Admissions, 152
      Supportive Services, 154
      Financial Aid, 156

6. Current Efforts to Promote Minority Participation   161
      The Federal Role, 161
          Federal mission-oriented agencies, 166
      Professional Societies, 174
          Current responses, 175; Surveys, 175; Committees, 176; Fellowship programs, 177
      Other Efforts: The States, Philanthropic Foundations, and Business and Industry, 179
          The states, 179; Business and industry, 183; Foundations, 185

   Supplement: Mission, Status, Problems, and Priorities of Black Graduate Schools   189
      Introduction, 191
      The Mission of Black Graduate Schools, 192
      Current Status of Black Graduate Schools, 195
      Special Problems and Alternatives, 205
      Priorities for Black Graduate Schools, 212
      Contributors, 216

   Appendix A: Reference Tables   219
   Appendix B: Survey Forms   249
   Bibliography   261

Summary, Conclusions, and Recommendations

This nation has made a commitment to ensure equality of opportunity for all persons. In graduate education that promise has not yet been realized for minority men and women. Inequalities in the participation of blacks, Chicanos, Puerto Ricans, and American Indians in advanced study are clear. While minority men and women comprise more than 16 percent of the total population, they represent less than 6 percent of all students enrolled in master's and doctorate programs in U.S. colleges and universities. Minority persons born in this country earned less than 5 percent of the doctorates awarded in 1973–74. We believe this situation is inconsistent with the societal goal of equal opportunity and that positive action is required to improve the participation of minority persons in graduate study.

Graduate and professional education provide a major avenue for entrance into leadership and professional positions in this society. As scientists, professionals, and members of higher education faculties, minority men and women can bring a wealth of intellectual talent and skills for the benefit of all persons. As role models for future generations, they become change agents for society and for the socioeconomic mobility of their own groups. As minorities are enabled to participate more fully in the political, social, and economic institutions of this country, the very fact of their participation will contribute to a more just and humane society by signifying the diminution of past inequities. We affirm our belief that:

Increased minority participation in graduate education is an important national goal to be realized for the social, economic, intellectual, and cultural well-being of all persons. It is for the collective benefit of society

1

that the representation of minority group persons among those earning advanced degrees be increased.

Individual equity is a fundamental concern. Distinctions that confer opportunity and status according to race, religion, sex, or national origin must be removed so that minority persons may be afforded a full opportunity to pursue graduate study according to individual motivation and intellectual potential.

The establishment of goals toward which to strive and by which to measure progress in realizing equal opportunity in graduate education is essential. The Carnegie Commission on Higher Education has stated that:

> The transcendent goal is that inequality in one generation should not, inevitably, be a legacy of succeeding generations. Each young person should have a full chance to demonstrate his intellectual ability and respond to his motivations to excel in constructive endeavor. From a national point of view, we cannot afford the domestic brain drain of able young persons who, through no fault of their own, are handicapped in making valuable contributions to the life of society.[1]

We concur. The long-range goal should be elimination of barriers that determine the extent of an individual's participation in higher education according to racial or ethnic identity. Minority men and women should participate in all levels of education in numbers roughly approximating their population proportion. We recognize, however, that cultural traditions specific to certain minority groups may influence the feasibility of attaining this goal. Therefore, while affirming its desirability and utility in assessing progress, a degree of tentativeness is necessary in stating this goal. We propose a series of measures to be used as indices of progress in moving toward equality of educational opportunity:

- Enrollment in graduate education proportional to the share of baccalaureates received by minority men and women.
- Parity in award of Ph.D.'s to minority persons proportional to baccalaureates awarded.
- Enrollment in graduate education approximating the distribution of minority individuals in the pertinent age cohort of the U.S. population.
- Parity in award of Ph.D.'s to minority persons approximating their distribution in the pertinent age cohort of the total population.

Some may interpret goals premised on a parity concept to mandate equality of educational outcome. We do not find *approximate* equality to be an unreasonable objective—for persons of equivalent intellectual potential, motivation, and aspiration. We do reject prediction of educational

---

[1] Carnegie Commission on Higher Education, *A Chance to Learn: An Action Agenda for Equal Opportunity in Higher Education* (New York: McGraw-Hill, 1970), p. 3.

achievement based on racial or ethnic identity (as well as economic status and sex). This is clearly unacceptable.

Others may worry that the issue of equal participation may be carried to an extreme. Precise arithmetic distribution of persons by age, race, income level, ethnic identity, and sex in every discipline specialty, type of school, and degree level is both impractical and unnecessary. Distinctions must be made among differences that are acceptable or a matter of choice and those that are unjust. We also do not intend to imply quotas wherein it might be inferred that certain groups are overrepresented and thereby should be denied further educational opportunity. Common sense and reasonable judgments must prevail.

Attention to broad numerical targets should not be allowed to detract from the more fundamental goal of setting into motion a self-sustaining process wherein minority participation is the accepted norm rather than the result of special effort. As such, our proposed set of actions should be viewed as serving in the role of a catalyst. Their very success should obviate the need for their existence. While a broad range of activities will be required in the coming years to assist minority students, the long-run outcome should be creation of an educational environment conducive to minority student access and achievement.

* * *

The existence of barriers specific to minority students in graduate education is reflected by the low levels of participation. Present disparities are striking. Minorities (excluding Orientals) comprise only 6–7 percent of total graduate enrollments and less than 5 percent of doctorates awarded to native-born U.S. citizens. In 1973–74, the proportion of (U.S. native-born) doctorates awarded to blacks was 3.5 percent, while Puerto Ricans earned 0.2 percent and Chicanos and other Spanish Americans received 0.6 percent. Persons identified as American Indians comprised 0.5 percent of total doctorates. Minority women, as is true of nonminority women, are also underrepresented in doctorate study. For every Ph.D. degree awarded to a minority woman, four were conferred on minority men (pp. 30–34, 42–46, 61–64).

The patterns of minority enrollments among disciplines differ from those of nonminority students. In 1973–74, black, Hispanic, and American Indian persons received 2.6 percent of natural science doctorates awarded to native-born U.S. citizens yet comprised almost 5 percent of doctorates in all disciplines. The apparent "overconcentration" of minority students in the field of education is often considered problematic. In 1973–74, 59 percent of the black Ph.D.'s earned degrees in education, compared with 25 percent of all students. Yet blacks received only 8 percent of all doctorates conferred in education. While a 100 percent increase in the number

3

of minority doctorates in education is needed to bring minority participation to the level attained by nonminority persons, a sixfold increase over current levels would be required in the natural science fields. This problem should not be viewed as one of overrepresentation in certain disciplines, but rather as one of varying degrees of inadequate participation in all fields. A more balanced distribution among disciplines compatible with realistic career opportunities should be encouraged.

There is a pronounced shift among disciplines as black students move to higher levels of education, with many who received baccalaureates in science fields switching to other disciplines for graduate work. For example, 52 percent of the 1973–74 black Ph.D.'s who had majored in the life sciences in college continued in that field for doctoral study, while 80 percent of white Ph.D.'s with undergraduate training in the life sciences earned a Ph.D. in the same field. Education is the preferred choice of those black students who change disciplines. While only one-third of the 1973–74 black doctorates had earned a bachelor's degree in education, 59 percent received education doctorates. This pattern of field-switching is greatly accentuated for black students relative to majority students. These data suggest that efforts to encourage a broader distribution of black students among fields of study may also be effective through altering the causes for these shifts at the graduate level (pp. 46–53).

While expansion of the numbers of minority persons entering and completing graduate study is a high priority, the quality of the student's educational experience is an overriding concern. Since the quality of graduate programs varies among institutions, as do curricular offerings and emphases, the choice of institution attended by a student is key. There is no significant difference in the proportions of minority and nonminority students enrolled in public *vis-à-vis* private Ph.D.-granting institutions, although minorities are less likely to have earned a doctorate from one of the major research universities. In 1973–74, 24 graduate schools conferred 50 percent of the doctorates earned by blacks. About one-fifth of black graduate students attend predominantly black institutions, most of which do not offer doctoral study (pp. 55–60).

While the last decade has witnessed a rapid growth in minority participation in higher education, current evidence concerning the continuation of these increases is equivocal. Data reported by the U.S. Bureau of the Census show a steady convergence in the proportions of white and black high school graduates entering college and increases in the total number of blacks enrolled in college. However, the figures for blacks are characterized by large year-to-year fluctuations, and many have questioned the reliability of these data for pinpointing annual enrollment levels. Moreover, other evidence indicates the persistence of black/white disparities in college entrance and overall college participation; in 1974, 22 percent of blacks

4

between the ages of 18 and 21 years were enrolled in college compared with 32 percent of whites in the corresponding age group (pp. 64–67).

The availability of minority persons with bachelor's degrees is critical to the outcome of efforts to enroll minority students in graduate education. In 1973–74, black, Hispanic, and American Indian persons earned about 7 percent of all bachelor's degrees. Blacks received 5.3 percent of total baccalaureates, a lower figure than some observers had previously estimated. Since most black students attend nonminority colleges and universities, it has been assumed that this distribution would also be reflected in degree attainment. However, black colleges graduated almost one-half of all black baccalaureates. These data indicate the need to examine the influence of different types of institutions on the educational achievement of black students (pp. 67–69).

The past few years have witnessed sharp increases in doctoral attainment by blacks. Minority persons (including Asians) comprised 3.3 percent of the doctorates conferred by the major research universities during the period 1969–72 but accounted for 5.8 percent in the following 3 years. The percentage of total doctorates awarded to U.S. native-born blacks rose from 2.8 percent in 1972–73 to 3.5 percent the following year, although comparable figures for Hispanics and American Indians showed little change.

Under the assumption that increases in graduate enrollments should precede changes in doctoral attainment, it is useful to contrast graduate enrollments in Ph.D.-granting institutions with the number of doctorates conferred the same year. Comparison of 1973 figures reveals that black enrollment proportions exceed degree achievement, whereas Hispanic and American Indian proportions are about equal. From this, some expansion in the number of black doctorates in the next few years might be predicted, but no increase could be forecast for Spanish-surnamed or American Indian Ph.D.'s.

Asian participation follows a different pattern. Persons of Asian origin comprise about 1 percent of total graduate enrollments but receive more than 4 percent of the doctorates. Their apparent "overrepresentation" in doctoral attainment may stem from a choice of doctoral in preference to master's study or greater persistence in degree achievement.

Minority persons are typically older than nonminorities upon completion of their doctoral work. This fact has stimulated speculation that the recent expansion in graduate minority enrollments may be attributed, in part, to a one-time phenomenon. The opening up of opportunities for minorities in graduate education has encouraged many older individuals to return to school for advanced study. Certainly, various federal and private programs in the 1960's and early 1970's focused on assisting black college faculty to upgrade their academic credentials. Hence, once the initial influx of

5

students from this source has ceased, the growth in Ph.D. attainment may level off. Following this line of reasoning, recent trends may be inappropriate predictors of the long-run outlook.

An informal survey of 66 graduate institutions on recent changes in first-year minority graduate enrollments suggests a shift in the distribution of minority students among graduate schools. While data limitations necessarily preclude extrapolation to national trends, certain patterns emerged. Institutions that had recently implemented special efforts to encourage minority participation, as well as schools located in the South, reported increases in first-year minority enrollments from 1973 to 1974. Several other schools noted a stabilization or decline in minority participation. Lack of financial assistance and preference for professional study were two factors among those cited to explain this development. The availability of qualified applicants did not appear to be a major factor, since more than one-half of the graduate schools indicated that the academic qualifications of the minority applicants had improved, while only one institution indicated a contrary experience. For various reasons, it appears that the process has not been set into motion wherein increased minority participation is the rule at all institutions (pp. 70–75).

* * *

An understanding of the population distribution of minority persons is essential to assessment of minority participation. Blacks, Hispanics, and American Indians presently comprise 16 percent of the U.S. population, but this proportion is rising, reflecting their higher birth rates. Minority persons will represent an increasing share of the total college-age population in the future; in 1990, minority persons 20–24 years old will constitute more than 22 percent of all persons in that age-group.

Access, choice, and achievement are the most widely accepted measures of educational participation. Unfortunately, available data by which to assess these measures are, at best, incomplete and often no more than gross estimates. Definitional problems in identification of minority groups— categories that are ambiguous or overlapping—often confuse collection and interpretation of data. For this reason:

We endorse the aims of the Federal Interagency Committee on Education and the U.S. Office of Management and Budget in coordinating development of common definitions for racial and ethnic groups for use by federal agencies in the collection and reporting of data. We further recommend that nongovernmental organizations and institutions use common definitions whenever such use is compatible with their individual purposes in collecting data on race and ethnicity (pp. 34–40).

Careful specification of citizenship status is required for accurate assessment of the status of the principal minority groups. The educational

6

backgrounds of noncitizens often differ from those of the resident U.S. population; the effect of merging data on citizens and noncitizens may obscure the educational characteristics of U.S. minority persons. In 1973–74, minority men and women, including noncitizens, received 12 percent of the Ph.D.'s conferred by the nation's universities, but only 6 percent were conferred to U.S. citizen minorities. Orientals obtained 60 percent of all doctorates awarded to minority persons, but only 6 percent of Oriental Ph.D.'s were born in the United States. We believe that:

While provision of opportunity in graduate study for foreign citizens is a worthwhile goal, it should not be confused with equal educational opportunity for U.S. citizens. We recommend that citizenship status be specified in the collection and reporting of data pertaining to the educational status of minority persons, whenever pertinent and feasible to do so (pp. 40–42).

Accurate data for use in monitoring minority group participation in higher education in the coming years is needed. Information about the availability of minority persons holding higher education degrees is essential to formulation of affirmative action plans required by the federal government. Present data-collection activities are fragmented, lack comparability, are often inaccurate, and are neither sufficiently sensitive nor comprehensive to meet these needs. Moreover, the multiplicity and duplication of sporadic sample surveys impose an enormous administrative burden on institutions providing such information. There is a need to consolidate, improve, and expedite the collection, analysis, and dissemination of racial and ethnic data in order to provide a regular assessment of minority access and achievement in higher education.

We recommend that the Secretary of the Department of Health, Education, and Welfare direct the National Center for Educational Statistics (NCES) with the cooperation and support of the Office for Civil Rights (OCR) to collect, on an annual basis, enrollment figures and degrees conferred to individuals by race and ethnic identity in higher education institutions. These data would be collectible under the legal obligation of the Civil Rights Act of 1964 and made available to OCR for this purpose.

*   *   *

To many, attainment of a bachelor's degree signifies that, at last, socioeconomic, educational, and cultural disparities among persons of various income, racial, and ethnic backgrounds have been overcome. We believe, however, that many minority men and women still face special handicaps that disadvantage them relative to nonminority students. All students may be affected by individual circumstances, such as financial constraints, family obligations, and poor undergraduate preparation that prevent

7

graduate school attendance, but for minorities such handicaps are more frequent and mutually reinforcing.

Minority students typically experience difficulty in financing undergraduate study. They must rely more on scholarship, work–study, and loan programs in contrast to nonminority students, who receive greater family support. Whereas in 1974–75 black and Hispanic college-bound high school seniors estimated that their parents would contribute about $200 toward college expenses, the median figure for whites was over $1,100. That same year minority students comprised one-third of the persons assisted through the major U.S. Office of Education aid programs. Upon graduation from college, immediate employment opportunities may appear more rewarding than advanced study in view of the prospect of further financial difficulties, the academic risk of graduate study (about one-half of all doctoral candidates fail to complete the Ph.D. degree), and labor market uncertainties (pp. 76–87).

Award of a bachelor's degree clearly does not certify equality of educational background. Some institutions provide better academic preparation for graduate study than others, since colleges differ as to curricular emphases, degree requirements, and standards for evaluating achievement. Further, the type of institution attended may influence a student's interest in postgraduate training. Current evidence suggests that the distribution of minority students among institutions differs from that of nonminority students. For example, blacks are more likely to attend 2-year and less-prestigious 4-year colleges. In 1973–74, slightly less than one-half of the bachelor's degrees earned by blacks were conferred by the predominately black schools.

Apart from differences among institutions, the quality of undergraduate education also varies *within* individual institutions. In some instances, minority students may be counseled into a form of "tracking" that is inappropriate training for graduate study. Others have entered special programs designed to remedy secondary education deficiencies, but such programs may not provide the intensive preparation necessary for advanced study. As a consequence, many talented students have uneven academic backgrounds that may lower performance in graduate study. Therefore:

We urge undergraduate institutions to sustain, and strengthen where necessary, their commitment to the education of minority students— whether admitted through "open admissions" processes, or enrolled in Educational Opportunity Programs or regular academic programs—to ensure that such students obtain an education comparable in quality to that of all students in the institution. Any compromise in standards for evaluation of academic performance and curricula does a disservice both to the student and society (pp. 87–91).

Other access problems exist. Minority student admissions has been the subject of extensive debate. The basic dilemma is how to identify those students with strong academic promise despite uneven records of achievement. Many minority students are "late bloomers," having entered college with a poor high school background, and do not realize their academic potential until late in their undergraduate careers. The widespread (and controversial) use of standardized tests presents another hurdle, since minority students typically receive lower test scores relative to other students. Apart from questions concerning their differential impact on minorities, there is broad agreement that tests are only modest predictors of Ph.D. attainment for all students. Attrition in graduate school is high and influenced by a host of other factors that are not measured by tests, such as motivation, persistence, and compatibility with departmental expectations and resources.

Advanced study in the scientific disciplines presents added barriers. The problem of "automatic tracking" is primary. For certain fields of study—for example, chemistry, physics, and engineering—extensive preparatory coursework is required. The long time period needed to obtain these prerequisites almost precludes advanced study if a student does not decide to study a scientific discipline in high school. Low academic self-confidence, combined with intimidating impressions of the rigors of scientific study, the scarcity of minority scientists and engineers to serve as visible success models, and the lack of cultural support for pursuit of scientific careers, may further discourage minority students (pp. 92–96).

In addition to barriers to access, other factors affect performance during graduate study. Attitudes are an elusive yet significant influence on the quality of the educational experience. Minority students may perceive insensitivity or indifference on the part of the faculty, while faculty may be uncomfortable or naive in responding to minority styles and aims. The unfamiliarity of many graduate schools with the education of minority students may reinforce the unease of students, while intentional or unintentional biases can demoralize the student. The lengthy "apprenticeship" relation in doctoral study may be perceived as constraining for the minority person for whom newly realized social and individual autonomy may be an important consideration. Moreover, the research interests of the minority student may be grounded in a strong ethnic consciousness and thus differ from the academic and professional concerns of departmental faculty (pp. 100–106).

Although the educational aspirations of minority students are as high as or higher than those of white students, minorities are less likely to receive the thoughtful advice and guidance necessary to realize those aspirations. This circumstance underscores the importance of diversifying the ethnic and racial composition of college and university faculty to provide appropriate role models for minority youth and to reassure potential applicants that an institution is receptive to minority students.

Efforts to increase access are constrained by high attrition in elementary, secondary, and undergraduate education. If educational progress is viewed as successive levels of a pyramid, it is clear that minorities cluster at the bottom but are scarce at the apex—graduate and professional education. The success of efforts at the graduate level is related to development of an adequate pool of minority baccalaureates qualified to proceed to advanced study. In 1973, 85 percent of white persons 20 or 21 years of age had completed high school, compared with 68 percent of black and 58 percent of Hispanic persons in that age group. However, despite the failures of successive levels of the educational pyramid, we suggest that substantial gains in minority participation can be achieved now by focusing on the existing pool of high school seniors and students already enrolled in college. Mounting evidence indicates that minority students experience much higher attrition during college relative to the overall student body. Efforts to improve college entrance and retention rates could significantly augment the pool of minority candidates for graduate study (pp. 96–99).

*   *   *

The present is not the best of all possible worlds for higher education, especially when compared with the expansionary decade of the 1960's. Efforts to promote minority participation in graduate education are both helped and hindered by recent developments.

Financial difficulties are obvious. Federal support of graduate students has plummeted. Institutions faced with the prospect of declining enrollments in the coming decade, a leveling off of research support, and uncertainties in state appropriations feel hard-pressed to maintain current expenditure levels. Special efforts for minority graduate students compete directly with other program priorities for a shrinking pool of resources. The sudden, strong emergence of the women's movement has caused many to express concern that minority interests are being overshadowed. Although the problems and situation of minorities and women differ in many respects, attention to the needs of these groups is often merged, and they are frequently forced to compete for public visibility, resources, and employment opportunities.

The development of nontraditional and more flexible programs to meet the needs of new groups of students in innovative learning environments offers expanded opportunities for minorities. Moreover, as the forecast declines in higher educational enrollments are realized, universities may be encouraged to look beyond their traditional recruitment areas for a broader range of student interests, backgrounds, and educational objectives (pp. 107–110).

The pessimistic outlook for the academic labor market and uncertainties in the nonacademic sector have caused many to question the wisdom of

10

encouraging minority students to pursue doctoral study. In our view, employment uncertainties should not serve as a rationale for limiting efforts to increase minority participation. However, careful counseling to inform potential students of realistic career opportunities—all students, not only minorities—must be given the highest priority. Moreover, the labor market experience of minorities may differ from that of nonminorities in two respects. First, employment openings for minority graduates in certain disciplines, especially those with a professional orientation, may arise from manpower needs related to the minority community. The field of education is one example; the demand for minority educators with advanced degrees is stimulated, in part, by bilingual–bicultural programs mandated by the federal government. Second, other disciplines, such as economics, psychology, and the health sciences, may have applications specific to minority concerns. The impact of affirmative action regulations on employment prospects for minorities is widely contested. While affirmative action efforts will definitely expand the representation of minority persons in the pool of candidates considered for employment, we are uncertain as to the effect of ethnic or racial status in selection of the individual to be hired in a position requiring an advanced degree (pp. 110–113).

*　　*　　*

While most agree about the desirability of increasing minority participation, considerable controversy exists about the legality of various programs designed to achieve this goal. The immediate debate centers on issues raised in the well-known *DeFunis* v. *Odegaard* case, in which an applicant to the University of Washington law school claimed that he was denied admission while less-qualified minority persons were given preference by virtue of their minority status.

Since the U.S. Supreme Court did not rule on the merits of this case, the fundamental legal questions remain unresolved. The basic precepts of the "equal protection" clause of the Fourteenth Amendment presume the unconstitutionality of racial classifications, although the courts have ruled that race-conscious policies may be permitted to overcome prior discrimination. The key question, crystallized by the *DeFunis* case, and for which there is no clear judicial guidance, is when and for what purpose may use of a race-conscious policy be allowed? This issue concerns not only admission decisions but also a wide range of programs that are "targeted" to minorities, such as financial aid, summer institutes, and supportive services.

While many agencies and institutions have implemented minority programs, others have been reluctant to do so for fear of legal complications. Although similar cases are likely to be presented to the U.S. Supreme

Court in the near future, it is uncertain if and when the Court will choose to rule on the substantive issues. In the meantime, questions about the constitutionality of a broad spectrum of "targeted" activities remain unanswered. As long as such legal uncertainties exist, initiation of special programs for minority students will continue to be inhibited; but, on the other hand, sincere, thoughtful efforts need not be precluded (pp. 129–140).

*   *   *

Few minority men and women are members of the academic faculties of colleges and universities; in 1975 blacks represented only 2 percent of the faculties at major research universities. Expansion of career opportunities for minority persons in higher education institutions is a desirable social and educational goal; moreover, current civil rights legislation and regulations have strong implications for the academic employment of minority doctorates. Executive Order 11246 requires colleges and universities holding federal contracts to take affirmative action to ensure that institutions do not discriminate in their employment practices on the basis of race, color, religion, sex, or national origin. But the requirements of the Executive Order are premised on a static concept; the employment targets for minority faculty are derived from the available supply of qualified candidates.

We concur in the objectives of affirmative action in the employment of minority faculty in colleges and universities as required under Executive Order 11246. We emphasize, however, that affirmative action as specified by the federal government will result in increased minority participation on faculties of colleges and universities only if there is an increase in the pool of qualified minority candidates.

The federal government and graduate institutions have a joint responsibility. Neither sector should condition its efforts upon the other. If persons of minority background are to join the faculties of colleges and universities, graduate schools must expand opportunities for minorities to enter and complete graduate study. The federal government, through its obligations to ensure the civil rights of all persons (affirmative action being but one example), must support efforts to promote minority participation in graduate study (pp. 113–129).

*   *   *

Effective commitment to expanding opportunities for minority graduate students requires that such commitment be a publicly articulated institutional and departmental priority. Only through active support from the central campus administration, the graduate school, and faculty can equal opportunity objectives be achieved. In the absence of a strong commit-

12

ment and extensive faculty involvement, it is unlikely that other activities and attitudes will be influenced in ways that create an institutional environment supportive of minority student achievement. We believe that:

Graduate institutions have the primary responsibility for encouraging and assisting minority students in attaining a high-quality graduate education. Initiative must derive from the institutions themselves, since they have the fundamental responsibility for selecting those who will receive the benefits of advanced education and enabling those persons to realize their educational goals. While government and other organizations must provide assistance, such support should be viewed as a complement, not a substitute, to existing institutional activities.

Opinions about the appropriate focus of programmatic efforts are sharply divided. Some hold that such programs should be limited to students believed to have strong academic potential but who, for a variety of reasons, are not competitive with respect to traditional admissions criteria or, if admitted, might be high-risk students without special assistance. This approach assumes that not all minority students require, and thus should not receive, financial or academic support. Others believe that attention should be directed to those students with demonstrated outstanding academic ability, with the goal being to ensure their representation among those qualified to enter top-level academic and professional positions. This debate is reflected in the diversity of recruitment, admissions, supportive service, and financial aid activities implemented by institutions (pp. 141–149).

The feasibility of recruiting graduate trainees is dependent on the adequacy of the pool of students qualified for graduate study. Although a major responsibility must rest at the elementary and secondary levels, substantial gains in the number of eligible candidates can be realized through efforts directed toward minority students already enrolled in undergraduate study. Therefore, we stress that:

Faculty and staff must be active in identifying, motivating, and improving the academic preparation of talented minority students early in their undergraduate careers. For advanced study in some disciplines, such as the natural and quantitative social sciences, this developmental approach is essential. Science internships, undergraduate honors programs, and summer research institutes are possible program models.

Fundamental to any recruitment procedure is the need to identify prospective students, motivate such students to apply to graduate school, and inform them of the basic admissions requirements and the programs available at the institution. A less obvious, but equally important, purpose is to help applicants in evaluating their qualifications and goals in relation to the expectations and resources of individual departments. While most schools and departments engage in the identification, motivation, and

13

information functions, efforts in the second area are less satisfactory and should be improved.

The propriety of giving special attention to minority applicants in the admissions process is widely debated. Some institutions advocate strict nondiscrimination policies, while others pursue affirmative practices. In general, modification of procedures for minority applicants takes the form of permitting flexibility in the interpretation of certain criteria supplemented by information from other sources, such as personal interviews and recommendations. The aim is to liberalize requirements that appear to be inadequate indicators of intellectual ability to enable a broader, often more intensive, examination of academic potential. In most instances, these procedures would be desirable for evaluation of all applicants (minority and nonminority), although they may be more time-consuming and costly.

Ideally, admissions decisions represent the middle link of a coordinated continuum from recruitment, admissions, financial support, and supportive services. If a student is well-acquainted with the resources and requirements for graduate study, and if the department is cognizant of the student's academic background and objectives, then the admissions decision is simplified. A department can decide whether it has the capability to assist a student in strengthening his or her academic background if needed. Clearly, the "sink-or-swim" attitude resulting from a guesswork admissions mode is costly both to the student and school in the event a student fails (pp. 149–154).

Many students, both minority and nonminority, benefit from some form of supportive services. It has been a long-standing practice to provide assistance to students with uneven academic preparation. For example, graduate students often enroll in undergraduate courses, special mathematics courses are offered for students with nonscience college backgrounds, and a 2-year M.B.A. program may offer 1 year of basic work in the field without academic credit. What is generally unacceptable are separate courses geared at a slower-than-normal pace or enrollment in major courses with the expectation that the student will need extensive tutoring or other help. Most graduate schools offer supportive services to minority students similar to those afforded to all students, although they may be provided to the former to a greater extent. For minority students, the availability of counselors to acquaint them with academic resources, advise on realistic career opportunities, aid in social adjustments, and bolster academic self-confidence is essential. Assistance to improve the basic writing and quantitative skills of minority students is another frequently cited need (pp. 154–156).

The inadequacy of financial aid funds for minority students is a pressing institutional concern. Many believe that lack of financial support is the

14

foremost obstacle to increased minority participation. The level of funding allocated to graduate minority student aid varies greatly among institutions—from zero to over $3 million per year. In general, funds come from university operating budgets, although special state appropriations and federal, foundation, and private funds have played a significant role.

Philosophies and attitudes toward "targeting" funds solely for minorities are mixed. Consideration of financial need in the award of aid to minority students is more common than for other students. Minority students tend to be supported with special monies rather than by regular departmental funds, and a central problem is how to motivate departments to commit a proportionate share of their resources—research and teaching assistantships and stipends—to minority students. Mechanisms for financial support that designate minorities as a "second class" or a "free good" and special programs without faculty involvement tend to isolate students and, in the long run, are unsuccessful (pp. 156–160).

The paradox of successful recruitment activities, financial assistance, and programs of supportive services for minorities is that their very success should lead to their self-extinction. However, we are not aware of any institution that has reached the point where minorities are routinely integrated into the mainstream of institutional and departmental activities.

Four recommendations are offered:

1. RELATION OF SELECTION PROCESS TO STUDENT ACHIEVEMENT

Prior to admission, graduate departments and faculty should thoroughly inform prospective students of the available opportunities and expectations of individual departments and the institution in order to ensure a successful match between student interests and educational goals and those of the department. Once a student has been admitted, we believe that the graduate department has a clear obligation to assist that student, in whatever ways necessary and appropriate, to achieve his educational objectives and perform at a level consistent with individual potential and the academic expectations of the department.

2. ASSESSMENT OF ACADEMIC PERFORMANCE

Diversity and flexibility in the selection and evaluation of student applicants are desirable features of the graduate admissions process. However, we also wish to emphasize our belief in the importance of maintaining the highest standards for evaluation of educational achievement and the award of graduate degrees. We firmly oppose any compromise in the standards for academic performance in graduate education.

3. INTEGRATION OF THE STUDENT INTO THE MAINSTREAM OF TEACHING AND RESEARCH ACTIVITIES

Programs that isolate or tend to denote the minority student as "second class" should be avoided. The aim of all institutional efforts must be to

15

bring minority students into the mainstream of teaching, research, and other departmental and institutional activities. Special emphasis should be placed on development of financial support mechanisms that encourage individual departments to "invest" in a commitment to assisting the student to achieve his or her educational goals. Faculty should be encouraged to involve minority students as research and teaching assistants in individual departments.

4. EVALUATION OF MINORITY STUDENT ACCESS AND ACHIEVEMENT

Graduate departments and faculty should monitor the effectiveness of their efforts to promote minority participation in advanced study. Such evaluation should include both academic achievement and the broader experiences of minority students, since failure to complete graduate study may result from intangible factors in the teaching environment and social relationships with other students and faculty that influence academic success.

*   *   *

Since the Higher Education Act of 1965, the federal government has shown a consistent, although uneven, commitment to equalizing opportunity in elementary, secondary, and baccalaureate education. However, this commitment has, at best, had limited impact at the graduate level.

We believe there is a clear federal responsibility to support efforts directed toward improving the participation of minority persons in graduate education. Present support of research and advanced training should be extended to recognize the importance of involving minority persons. The talents of minority men and women as scholars, professionals, scientists, and teachers constitute a valuable national resource. Individual equity is another concern. Distinctions that confer status and opportunity on the basis of race or ethnic identity must be removed. The federal government, through its authority and resources, is best able to redress social inequities. Executive Order 11246, calling for affirmative action in higher education employment, and various directives stemming from the Civil Rights Act of 1964 exemplify the federal government's broad obligation to foster social justice. Yet requirements for affirmative action cannot be achieved without concurrent efforts to increase the number of minority persons with advanced degrees. A strong federal role is critical to attainment of these objectives.

We urge the executive and congressional branches to express a resolution for federal support of and increased concern for minority participation in graduate education. Strong national leadership is essential to achievement of equal opportunity goals in graduate education.

Responsible federal policy must recognize the pluralistic nature of barriers constraining minority participation. While one course of action must be directed toward assisting individual minority students, another concern is creation of an institutional environment that is supportive of minority student achievement. For these reasons, we believe the federal government should channel support to minority students through institutions with the capability and commitment to sustain effective programmatic efforts.

The U.S. Office of Education should implement a program of competitive institutional grants for the purpose of supporting efforts to increase minority participation in graduate education. Funds should be provided for a broad range of activities, including student aid, tuition, supportive services, and administrative costs. Selection of grant recipients should be based on evaluation of institutional commitment and program effectiveness.

The approach embodied in current federal training grant programs is suggested as an appropriate model for implementation of this proposal. Institutional initiative and flexibility as to program scope, emphasis, and organization should be encouraged. Accordingly, funds should be available for a variety of purposes—tuition, student stipends, additional support personnel, special summer programs, and research and evaluation directly related to program effectiveness. An 8 percent administrative allowance should be provided.[2] The federal role should complement, not supplant, institutional efforts; therefore, provision for maintenance of effort should be a condition of the award. Initial grants should cover a 3- to 5-year period, with renewal contingent upon demonstration of program success as measured by student achievement.

An annual appropriation of $50 million would permit support of a total of 6,500 students or about 1,500–2,500 new entrants each year, depending on the number of years students are supported through the program. This figure represents less than 1 percent of total graduate enrollments in U.S. colleges and universities.

The following distribution of funds is suggested as appropriate for implementation of a balanced program of activities, although considerable variation in individual grants should be permitted:

1. Student assistance and tuition — 65-70 percent
2. Special new programs and supportive services — 25-30 percent
3. Research and evaluation — 5 percent

[2] Alternatively, if an institution with ongoing activities only requires funds for student assistance in order to expand minority participation, a cost-of-education allowance of $4,500 per additional full-time student might be allocated. In its report *Federal Policy Alternatives toward Graduate Education,* NBGE urged that cost-of-education allowances accompanying federal fellowships be increased to $4,500 to reflect in part the rapid cost increases of the past decade.

Student assistance should be awarded on the basis of academic merit and financial need. Financial support available through this program should be closely linked with existing institutional mechanisms for student aid, such as departmental fellowships and research and teaching assistantships.

Examples of special, new programs that might be funded through an institutional grant include:

1. Activities designed to identify, motivate, and prepare talented undergraduate students for advanced study;

2. cooperative recruitment, admissions, and financial aid programs involving departments in a specific field of study administered by several graduate institutions; and

3. summer institutes to strengthen preparation for graduate work.

Funds should be available to support research pertinent to minority student achievement. In addition, mechanisms for evaluation by individual institutions of their activities should be required.

Legislative authority for implementation of this program is provided under Title IX of the Higher Education Act of 1965, as amended in 1972. Part A presently authorizes grants to institutions for "(1) faculty improvement; (2) the expansion of graduate and professional programs of study; (3) the acquisition of appropriate institutional equipment and materials; (4) cooperative arrangements among graduate and professional schools; and (5) the strengthening of graduate and professional school administration." Research pertinent to the improvement of graduate programs is also allowed. Authorization for fellowships is specified under Part B of Title IX and stresses "the need to prepare a larger number of teachers and other academic leaders from minority groups." Part C provides public service graduate or professional fellowships, and Part D authorizes fellowships for "persons of ability from disadvantaged backgrounds as determined by the Commissioner, undertaking graduate or professional study." Technical amendment of this legislation would permit implementation of our program as proposed (pp. 161–166).

* * *

The mission-oriented federal agencies have implemented a variety of programs designed to involve more minorities in education and research pertinent to the individual programmatic missions of these agencies. Most agency efforts target funds to minority institutions through programs such as training grants or activities to strengthen the research capabilities of faculties and departments. Only a few target money directly to minority students because of concern about the political and legal implications of doing so.

Programs that assist minority colleges are effective yet necessarily limited in scope. While they may have a significant impact on the undergraduate education of minority students, at the graduate level minority institutions comprise only a small share of total graduate enrollments. Moreover, most minority graduate schools do not possess the capabilities for scientific research comparable to those of the leading research universities in this country, and few offer doctoral work. Consequently, most agency programs have only a minimal impact on minority participation in doctoral-level education and research activities. It is unfortunate that legal uncertainties, compounded by the absence of clear national leadership on these issues, both limit the scope and inhibit the potential for expansion of the efforts of federal agencies—and will continue to do so in the foreseeable future (pp. 166–172).

We believe it fundamental to the national interest to encourage the development and involvement of underutilized minority talent in scientific and research activities. Accomplishment of these goals requires that attention be directed to three broad areas:

1. Early identification, motivation, and preparation of talented undergraduate students for graduate study in science;

2. increased opportunities for advanced (primarily doctoral) training of minority persons leading to careers in science and research; and

3. strengthening the academic credentials and research capabilities of minority scientists and faculty.

Initiative and diversity of approaches in resolving these underlying problems should be encouraged. We urge that a variety of programs such as those described in this report be sustained insofar as their effectiveness is demonstrated and the need for these activities remains. There are, however, striking omissions in the array of programmatic efforts sponsored by the mission-oriented agencies.

First and foremost is the lack of activities directed toward increasing the involvement of minority students in scientific research and training in Ph.D.-granting institutions. We believe that this area deserves the highest priority. Second, greater efforts to prepare and assist talented undergraduates in nonminority institutions for advanced study are essential in view of the extensive curricular prerequisites for graduate work in science.

A number of alternatives are proposed for consideration:

1. As one means of encouraging graduate faculty to identify and involve talented minority graduate students in research projects in universities (primarily at the doctoral level), the federal mission agencies should provide unrestricted supplemental funds to graduate institutions, earmarked to reimburse principal investigators who employ minority students

on research grants. Funds would be allocated as a share of the normal stipend paid to minority students for their services, thus partially reimbursing the project for costs of employing these students. This activity would complement the institutional grants program previously recommended since all institutions and departments would be eligible to receive such reimbursements, given the voluntary, decentralized nature of the program. Combined funding from several agencies at a level of $5 million per year would permit support of 2,000 students with an average reimbursement of $2,500.

2. Cooperative programs between undergraduate and graduate institutions would facilitate a developmental approach in motivating, preparing, and assisting undergraduate minority students to enter and successfully complete advanced study in the scientific disciplines. Mechanisms to gain exposure to and experience in research projects prior to entry in graduate school might be one component of this kind of effort.

3. Early identification of undergraduates who show extraordinary promise in science and engineering, complemented by undergraduate honors or research assistant opportunities, offers another means of increasing the pool of minority students who are interested in, qualified for, and aware of opportunities for graduate study in science and engineering.

4. The consortium model exemplified by existing efforts in the fields of law and business administration may be effectively used for the scientific disciplines. Through this approach, graduate departments in a single discipline or a group of related disciplines may consolidate their identification, recruitment, financial assistance, and supportive service activities. Resources and expertise would be pooled for the benefit of all participating institutions and departments, and the importance of faculty involvement emphasized. Joint summer institutes, research internship experiences, and exchange of undergraduate students among institutions for graduate study are possible features of this activity.

5. Alteration of the tendency for many minorities with undergraduate training in the natural sciences to shift into other fields for doctoral study would sharply expand the supply of new candidates for graduate study in the scientific disciplines. Programs to strengthen and update the scientific background of minority persons—many of whom may have completed their bachelor's degrees some year previously—who wish to undertake graduate work would address this problem (pp. 172–174).

*   *   *

Professional associations have initiated various activities designed to increase minority participation in the professions and in graduate education. Most disciplinary societies have established *ad hoc* committees and surveyed minority representation in graduate study, and a few have implemented small fellowship programs. In general, however, these special activities have been constrained by their *ad hoc,* temporary nature. Programs have been peripheral to the mainstream of association concerns. Consequently, as other program priorities emerge and financial constraints become more severe, these special programs often disappear for lack of support.

We urge professional associations to draw upon the prestige and talents of members and to assign a high priority to promoting increased opportunities for minority men and women in graduate study and in the professions. Associations should facilitate communication and serve in a coordinating role among departments and among faculty to:

1. Disseminate and publicize successful program models designed to promote minority group participation;

2. encourage leadership and commitment from members with the highest standing in the discipline in addressing these concerns;

3. encourage and facilitate cooperation among institutions and departments to implement special programs; and

4. continue to monitor and evaluate the status of minority persons in the discipline.

A variety of activities should be implemented with the encouragement and involvement of professional societies, including short-term summer workshops to strengthen student preparation in specific subject areas prerequisite to work in the major disciplines, i.e., quantitative skills for advanced study in the social sciences, cooperation among institutions and departments for the recruitment and financial support of minority students, and association-sponsored fellowship programs (pp. 174–179).

*   *   *

A recent report on the state role in graduate education and research declared that:

While graduate education with its attendant research, including masters' and doctoral programs, is clearly a national resource, it is also a regional, state, and local resource. Primary responsibility for providing educational opportunity constitutionally and historically rests with the states.[3]

The necessity of a state role in facilitating minority student access and achievement in graduate education is dictated by two broad considera-

___

[3] Education Commission of the States, *The States and Graduate Education,* Report No. 59 (Denver, Colorado: Education Commission of the States, February 1975), p. 1.

tions. First, the specific emphasis and form of advanced training are a function of employment and research needs as well as traditional patterns of support for graduate education within individual states. State and regional manpower requirements also derive, in part, from the skills and training necessary to address concerns pertinent to the resident minority communities. Second, the history, size, composition, education, and socio-economic circumstance of the minority population vary among states and affect participation throughout higher education.

Although equal educational opportunity is a widely accepted goal in postsecondary education, the basic philosophies and programmatic efforts adopted by states are diverse. While direct state programs to assist economically and educationally disadvantaged students are widespread at the undergraduate level, only a few states award aid to graduate students on the basis of financial need. We are not aware of any statewide programs to assist graduate students considered to have educational deficiencies.

State higher education programs that use racial or ethnic criteria in determining eligibility are rare; however, state scholarships for persons of American Indian heritage and grants for black college faculty pursuing terminal degrees are notable examples. Although not restricted to minority individuals, programs to train personnel to implement federal and state bilingual–bicultural requirements benefit the minority population. Several states have undertaken or coordinated surveys of ethnic and racial enrollments in higher education, and many have initiated detailed examination of minority participation in institutions and programs.

There is an important distinction between institutional activities that are supported by state funds and programs and those that are administered on a direct, statewide basis. We believe the former strategy is preferable in view of the decentralized nature of graduate education and research and the importance of involving minority graduate students in the mainstream of departmental research and teaching activities (pp. 179–183).

The states have both an obligation and special capabilities to address issues of minority access and achievement in graduate education. Insofar as master plans have been developed in individual states, such plans should specify a concern about equality of educational opportunity in graduate education. States should encourage and respond to institutional initiatives in development of efforts directed to this end. We recommend that states provide support to institutions for:

1. Financial assistance for disadvantaged graduate students to advance the participation of minority persons;
2. provision of supportive services within institutions; and

3. development of cooperative programs between undergraduate and graduate institutions to identify, encourage, and strengthen the academic preparation of talented minority undergraduates for entry to graduate study.

* * *

Private, nonprofit foundations have demonstrated strong commitment to advancement of equal opportunity objectives. They have supported programs to provide financial assistance to minority students, to strengthen minority institutions, to develop leadership capabilities in the minority community, to undertake relevant research, and to improve the academic preparation of minority students. Foundations have contributed support for innovative programs, provided "seed money" for promising new efforts, and assisted other activities that might not have otherwise been initiated because of the reluctance or inability of institutions and government to act. While minorities have realized significant gains over the past decade, unresolved problems remain. Unfortunately, total foundation support directed to promotion of minority participation in education is projected to decline in the coming years.

We urge foundations to initiate, develop, and sustain commitment to and selective support of programs to improve minority participation in graduate education as an important complement to federal, institutional, and other activities.

Through their involvement in activities to advance the cause of minority education, foundations have developed a high level of expertise and insight as to effective and ineffective ways to address these issues. Yet other organizations involved in minority concerns, institutions, government, and individuals do not normally receive the benefits of the knowledge developed from the experience of foundations. Systematic dissemination of both informal and formal evaluation of significant programs has in general not occurred (pp. 185–187).

We recommend that foundations consider various means of sharing the insights gained through their specific experiences in minority concerns. Two possibilities are suggested:

1. Periodic conferences sponsored either singly or jointly by foundations with relevant activities to exchange information about particular subject areas, with the aim of identifying effective program approaches. The proceedings of such conferences should be published and broadly disseminated.

2. Systematic codification and dissemination of knowledge derived from their activities in order to provide information about productive pro-

23

gram efforts. The availability of such information would be useful to other institutions and individuals who are interested and involved in these concerns.

*   *   *

Minority men and women are severely underrepresented in managerial and professional positions in business and industrial firms. The importance of bringing more minority persons into these positions in the private sector is underscored by federal efforts to ensure equal employment opportunities for them. Business and industry have a fundamental interest in and responsibility for increasing the supply of highly educated minority persons. We suggest two strategies for the private sector to contribute to increased minority participation in graduate education.

Provision of financial support to graduate institutions or a consortium of graduate departments that normally provide personnel with advanced degrees to particular business or industrial firms. One example of productive cooperation between graduate departments and the private sector is the graduate business school consortia which seek to increase the number of minority persons with M.B.A. degrees. Various business firms contribute funds for recruitment, stipends, and other activities.

Identification, encouragement, and financial assistance for promising minority employees to undertake advanced study that will enable them to move into high level positions. This strategy has particular significance in view of the economic forces tending to encourage minority baccalaureates to accept immediate employment upon graduation. Promising minority students may be diverted from graduate study although their long-run career goals may be best served by undertaking advanced study (pp. 183–185).

*   *   *

For almost a half century a number of black institutions have offered programs of graduate study. Presently, 28 schools award the master's degree, including four that confer the doctorate. About one-fifth of all black students pursuing advanced study nationwide attend a predominately black institution. These schools have, moreover, experienced vigorous enrollment growth. In 1967 the black graduate schools enrolled 8,500 students, but 6 years later attendance had risen to almost 20,000.

In view of the significance of these schools, the National Board on Graduate Education concluded that a report on minority group participation in graduate education must give high priority to discussion of the black graduate schools. Several questions emerged for consideration. First, what is the role and mission of the black graduate institutions in light of the rapidly changing context of higher education? Second, what is the current status of

24

the black graduate schools as indicated from a profile of basic data on enrollments, degrees, faculty, and program offerings? With respect to the problems facing these schools, are there distinctions between the problems that are endemic to all sectors of higher education and those that are unique to the black institutions? And finally, what are the needs and priorities of these schools for coming years? A thoughtful discussion of these issues is presented in the Supplement to this report, entitled "Mission, Status, Problems, and Priorities of the Black Graduate Schools," prepared by the Conference of Deans of Black Graduate Schools (pp. 189–218).

1 Introduction

Our nation has made a commitment to equality of opportunity for all persons. In graduate education that promise remains unfulfilled for minority men and women. Today, blacks, Chicanos, Puerto Ricans, and American Indians represent less than 1.4 percent of all U.S. scientists and engineers holding doctoral degrees.[1] Minority persons comprise over 16 percent of the U.S. population yet account for only 6 percent of enrollments in the nation's graduate schools.[2] In 1973–74 minority individuals received 5 percent of the doctorates awarded to native-born citizens.[3] It is self-evident that few minorities have shared in the benefits of graduate study. We believe the importance of effecting change in this situation is twofold.

In an era faced with increasingly complex social and technological problems, the availability of highly educated scientists, scholars, administrators, and professionals is essential to the success of efforts to improve the quality of life in our society. Social advancement requires solutions that are creative, just, and humane. Failure to develop and utilize the talents of certain sectors of our population is to neglect a vital resource.

[1] Special analysis by NBGE of data from National Research Council, National Academy of Sciences, Comprehensive Roster of Doctorate Scientists and Engineers, January 1975.

[2] Elaine H. El-Khawas and Joan L. Kinzer, *Enrollment of Minority Graduate Students at Ph.D. Granting Institutions,* Higher Education Panel Reports, No. 19 (Washington, D.C.: American Council on Education, August 1974), Table 1.

[3] Special analysis by NBGE of data from National Research Council, National Academy of Sciences, Doctorate Records File, June 1975.

If minority persons do not participate fully in the research, scientific, and managerial activities of this nation, the loss will be a loss to all society.

Moreover, justice and fairness must be a goal with regard to all people. The conflict between high ideals and reality, the "American dilemma" posed by Gunnar Myrdal, arising from the circumstance of minority persons in this country, remains a source of social discord. Inequities in educational opportunity stemming from race, religion, sex, or ethnic identity must be abolished. Every individual should have a genuine chance to pursue advanced study according to his or her motivation and intellectual potential. The principle of equal opportunity must become a reality at all levels of education.

We have not attempted to formulate a precise definition of the ever elusive goal of equity with respect to opportunity for minority persons in graduate education. We have, however, suggested broad targets that may serve as indices by which to measure progress. These should not detract from the central objective of setting into motion a self-sustaining process wherein minority participation in the mainstream of graduate education and research is the accepted norm rather than the result of special effort. As such, our proposed set of actions should be viewed as serving in the role of a catalyst. Their very success will obviate the need for their existence. While continued efforts will be required in the coming years to assist individual minority students, the more fundamental outcome should be creation of an educational environment conducive to minority student access and achievement.

The focus of this report concerns the educational status of black, Puerto Rican, Chicano, and American Indian citizens. The situation of persons of Asian origin is not considered here since, in general, they have achieved educational levels well above the national average. Other sectors of the population are also affected by circumstances that constrain educational attainment; persons from rural areas in Appalachia or Filipinos residing in the West might be included in this category. Nonetheless, while some of these groups might be considered "disadvantaged" in a few respects, they are difficult to identify empirically, and typically their disadvantaged status did not originate from negative historical experience—most notably, denial of civil rights. Similarly, while women (minority and nonminority) confront special problems that limit participation, the origin and character of these factors differ from those affecting minority persons. Therefore, the situation of women as a separate group is not examined.

The legacy of past inequities continues to exert an adverse impact on minority participation in graduate education. The problems facing minority men and women are of many dimensions; mutually reinforcing socioeconomic, educational, and cultural handicaps continue to depress achievement and must be alleviated. It is clear, however, that not all minority persons are disadvantaged and that individuals of every ethnic and racial background have been successful in graduate education and the professions. Accordingly, our recommendations are primarily directed toward disadvantaged minority students.

We believe that efforts to encourage minority persons to undertake graduate study are timely. Broad pressures stemming from the civil rights movement of the 1960's and affirmative action in employment have focused attention on these issues, while growing awareness of barriers specific to minorities and of the critical national interest in providing equal educational opportunity have provided stimuli to action. Moreover, the past decade has been marked by a rapid rise in the numbers of minority persons entering postsecondary education, thus creating a substantial pool of minority students eligible for advanced study.

Although many have worked toward expansion of graduate opportunities for minorities, current efforts are fragmented and inadequate. Confusion exists about the legality and appropriateness of specific means to implement this goal, while competing priorities in higher education limit financial resources. Given the pluralistic nature of the problems facing minorities in graduate education, it is clear that their resolution requires extraordinary sensitivity, expertise, commitment, and resources. Only through the combined efforts of government, colleges and universities, professional societies, philanthropic foundations, and the private sector can progress in enlarging educational opportunities for minority men and women be realized. We hope that the conclusions and recommendations embodied in this report will be constructive to this end.

2 Patterns of Minority Participation

THE NOT TOO DISTANT PAST

Minority access to higher education emerged as a visible concern of public policy during the decade of the 1960's. As a first step in addressing this situation, attention was directed toward determining the extent of minority participation in higher education. In graduate education, especially at the doctoral level, it was readily apparent that few minority students were there. Paradoxically, systematic efforts to collect racial and ethnic data on students in higher education were thwarted by the new social propriety of "color blindness" and various state statutes barring racial identification of students in colleges and universities; both were the legacy of earlier decades in which hard-fought battles had been won to abolish invidious systems of racial classification.

Some of the first information on minority participation came from rosters developed from straightforward searches through minority periodicals, personal inquiries and acquaintanceships, affiliations with black colleges, and photographs in professional journals. James M. Jay, utilizing this method to identify blacks who had earned a doctorate, estimated that from 1876 through 1969, only 587 blacks had been awarded a doctorate degree in the natural sciences.[1] This represented only 0.36 percent of the degrees awarded in the natural sciences during this period. At about the same time, Fred E. Crossland asked graduate deans in 105 doctoral institutions to estimate (or simply guess) how many blacks had received doctor-

[1] James M. Jay, *Negroes in Science: Natural Science Doctorates, 1876–1969* (Detroit: Balamp Publishing, 1971).

30

ates in those schools. He reported that only 0.8 percent of all Ph.D.'s awarded in the arts and science fields between 1964 and 1968 had been earned by black Americans.[2] In 1972–73, the comparable annual figure had increased to only 1.4 percent.[3]

Figures do exist for master's degrees awarded in the historically black colleges. These schools awarded 1,213, or 2 percent, of all master's degrees conferred in 1952–53.[4] By 1962–63, these schools accounted for 1,339, or 1.5 percent, of a total of 91,400 master's degrees earned in the United States.[5] While there is no firm estimate of the numbers of master's degrees attained by blacks in white colleges and universities, a minimum of half were earned in black colleges (although 80 percent seems a more likely figure given the population distribution of blacks in the country during the 1950's and early 1960's and admitted discriminatory practices of some higher education institutions).[6] Hence, at best, between 2 and 4 percent of all master's degrees were earned by black Americans in the years prior to the civil rights movement of the 1960's.

The best information available to date on the number of minority persons holding doctorates in science and engineering is provided by the National Academy of Sciences' Comprehensive Roster of Doctorate Scientists and Engineers, which includes the names of all doctoral scientists and engineers in the United States. In 1973 a survey of 59,086 persons (approximately 25 percent of the total included on the roster) provided estimates of the proportion of ethnic and racial minority doctoral scientists and engineers. Table 1 shows that 0.9 percent of the native-born doctoral scientists and engineers are black, while Spanish-speaking and Asian Americans represent 0.5 and 0.6 percent, respectively.[7] Only a few individuals are identified as American Indians.

Although the data may be sparse, the record seems clear; in the past,

[2] Fred E. Crossland, "Graduate Education and Black Americans" The Ford Foundation, November 25, 1968, unpublished.
[3] Special analysis by NBGE of data from National Research Council, National Academy of Sciences, Doctorate Records File, November 1974.
[4] U.S. Department of Health, Education, and Welfare, Office of Education, *Earned Degrees Conferred by Higher Education Institutions, 1952–53* (Washington, D.C.: U.S. Government Printing Office, 1955).
[5] U.S. Department of Health, Education, and Welfare, Office of Education, *Earned Degrees Conferred, 1962–63, Bachelor's and Higher Degrees* (Washington, D.C.: U.S. Government Printing Office, 1965).
[6] See President's Commission on Higher Education, *Higher Education for American Democracy*, Vol. 2, *Equalizing and Expanding Individual Opportunity* (Washington, D.C.: U.S. Government Printing Office, 1947), pp. 29–36; *Sweatt* v. *Painter, U.S. Reports* 629(1950): 633–634; and Theodore Caplow and Reece J. McGee, *The Academic Marketplace* (New York: Doubleday & Co., 1965).
[7] Special analysis by NBGE of data from National Research Council, National Academy of Sciences, Comprehensive Roster of Doctorate Scientists and Engineers, January 1975.

TABLE 1 Doctorate Scientists and Engineers, by Field of Doctorate and Racial/Ethnic Group, U.S. Native-born Citizens, 1973

Field of Doctorate		Total	White	Total Minority	Black	American Indian	Asian	Spanish-Sur-named	Other Minorities
Physical sciences	N[a]	7,149	7,016	133	57	3	36	27	10
	WN[a]	52,886	52,014	872	379	16	269	172	36
		(100.0%)	(98.4%)	(1.6%)	(0.7%)	—	(0.5%)	(0.3%)	(0.1%)
Mathematics	N	1,773	1,743	30	15	1	2	11	1
	WN	10,359	10,199	160	72	1	10	72	5
		(100.0%)	(98.5%)	(1.5%)	(0.7%)	—	(0.1%)	(0.7%)	—
Engineering	N	2,979	2,937	42	9	2	19	11	1
	WN	26,078	25,721	357	79	15	171	82	10
		(100.0%)	(98.6%)	(1.4%)	(0.3%)	(0.1%)	(0.7%)	(0.3%)	—
Biosciences	N	8,684	8,428	256	113	2	83	51	7
	WN	48,373	47,055	1,318	527	8	445	294	44
		(100.0%)	(97.3%)	(2.7%)	(1.1%)	—	(0.9%)	(0.6%)	(0.1%)
Psychology	N	2,858	2,793	65	31	1	12	11	10
	WN	20,256	19,757	499	222	12	87	95	83
		(100.0%)	(97.5%)	(2.5%)	(1.1%)	(0.1%)	(0.4%)	(0.5%)	(0.4%)

32

Social sciences	N	3,193	3,114	79	34	5	15	20	5
	WN	24,912	24,311	601	263	48	120	134	36
		(100.0%)	(97.6%)	(2.4%)	(1.1%)	(0.2%)	(0.5%)	(0.5%)	(0.1%)
Nonsciences	N	1,997	1,954	43	25	—	5	10	3
	WN	7,300	7,146	154	86	—	17	36	15
		(100.0%)	(97.9%)	(2.1%)	(1.2%)	—	(0.2%)	(0.5%)	(0.2%)
Unknown	N	8	8	—	—	—	—	—	—
	WN	17	17	—	—	—	—	—	—
		(100.0%)	(100.0%)	—	—	—	—	—	—
Total	N	28,641	27,993	648	284	14	172	141	37
	WN	190,181	186,220	3,961	1628	100	1,119	885	229
		(100.0%)	(97.9%)	(2.1%)	(0.9%)	(0.1%)	(0.6%)	(0.5%)	(0.1%)

[a] "N" is the number of survey respondents in each tabulated category. "WN" (the weighted N) is an estimate of the number of persons who would have been tabulated in each category if everyone on the entire Roster had been surveyed. Statistical confidence in the WN's and percentage estimates is partly a function of the sample (and population) sizes. Sample sizes are sufficient to compare the "White" and "Total Minority" categories, but figures for individual minority groups are very small and should be regarded only as broad estimates.

The ratio of WN to N varies across the categories tabulated above because of the use of variable sampling ratios in the survey design. The number of persons sampled from a given cell was a function of the size of the cell. Relatively larger proportions were sampled from smaller cells, thereby increasing the accuracy of estimates for graduates of smaller universities and graduates in less populous fields. The sample was not stratified according to racial/ethnic group, since this information was not known for persons on the Roster.

SOURCE: Special analysis by NBGE of data from National Research Council, National Academy of Sciences, Comprehensive Roster of Doctorate Scientists and Engineers, January 1975.

33

few minority group individuals have benefited from opportunities for graduate study.

PRESENT PARTICIPATION

The dynamics of the process of educational achievement requires examination of various patterns of participation. Access, choice, and achievement are the most widely accepted measures of educational participation. Yet available data by which to assess these parameters of participation are at best incomplete and, in many cases, no more than gross estimates. Statistics on enrollments comprise the major share of current empirical evidence on participation, but provide insights into only one measure—access. Systematic information on degrees attained by minorities, as a proxy for achievement, has become available only very recently and it, too, is.fragmentary. Data on attrition and factors influencing completion of education are essentially nonexistent, particularly at the graduate level. Choice is perhaps the most elusive of these three variables. How does one determine whether a student enrolled in a particular school or discipline because it best suited his educational needs and aspirations (a positive choice) or was relegated to a certain institution or field because of limited alternatives, financial and geographic barriers, and past educational inadequacies (a negative choice)?

Compounding the scarcity of data pertinent to assessment of patterns of participation, considerable confusion results from imprecision in definition and enumeration of the minority groups under discussion. In this section we will first review various definitions of the minority group populations. Then the population representation of minority persons by age cohort and the effect of citizenship status on analysis of educational attainment will be examined in order to assist in interpretation of the data subsequently presented in this report.

Definitions of Minority Groups

A major difficulty in enumerating the extent of minority participation through surveys and analyses is the lack of operational definitions for individual minority groups. Some groups are racial; others are based on ethnic characteristics. There is confusion about the geographic coverage of Asian or Oriental groups. The Spanish-surnamed classification overlaps with racial definitions; Spanish-speaking includes other groups, such as Filipinos, who regard Spanish as their native language. There is the complication of peoples of Caribbean background who consist of many racial and ethnic groups. Individuals of mixed racial or ethnic heritage pose a dilemma; this becomes even more problematic when classifying persons who have both a racial or ethnic and a nonethnic white heritage. Mixed ancestry is particularly significant when determining who is or who is not an American Indian.

Definition of blacks is perhaps the most straightforward. Blacks are a racial group, and individuals are classified as black regardless of geographic origin or cultural identity.

The term Oriental refers to the indigenous peoples of the geographic region south and southeast of the Himalayas in Asia, according to formal definition.[8] Asian also incorporates a geographic reference. Yet popular usage of Asian or Oriental often designates all peoples of Asia, including Indians and Pakistanis and persons from the Middle East of both the Mongoloid and Caucasian races. The term Oriental may also refer to peoples of Japanese, Chinese, Korean, and other Far Eastern ancestry, emphasizing the racial character. Polynesians and other Pacific islanders are other groups subject to inclusion or exclusion, depending on the particular definition. In 1972–73, 17 percent of noncitizen doctorate recipients who identified themselves as Orientals were from India. A significant number of persons from Middle Eastern countries such as Syria, Iran, and Iraq also identified themselves as Orientals.[9] However, other persons from India may identify with Indo-European groups, stressing their Caucasian ancestry, in preference to an Asian or Oriental classification.

In this report we will use both Asian and Oriental to refer to peoples of Chinese, Japanese, Korean, and Filipino ancestry, although other groups such as Samoans, Indians, and Pakistanis, who could be broadly classified as Asians, may be included in the various data sources reported.

Peoples variously categorized as Spanish-surnamed, Spanish-speaking, of Spanish heritage, Hispanic, and Latin American are diverse in terms of geographic origin, race, language, and culture. In the recent past, Spanish-surnamed has been used as a rough proxy for identifying persons of Spanish heritage, language, and culture. Today it often refers to some groups of Spanish peoples, but possession of a Spanish surname is only infrequently used as an exclusive criterion for classification [10] and has limited utility for identification purposes.[11] Spanish-speaking incorporates a broad spectrum of racial, ethnic, and cultural groups (such as Filipinos)

[8] *Webster's New Collegiate Dictionary,* 7th ed., s.v. "Oriental."

[9] Special analysis by NBGE of data from National Research Council, National Academy of Sciences, Doctorate Records File, October 1974.

[10] The U.S. Bureau of the Census uses Spanish-surnamed as one factor in enumerating the Spanish heritage population.

[11] Marriage between Spanish and non-Spanish persons is a major source of error in use of this method.

and thus is also imprecise. The U.S. Bureau of the Census employs a variety of definitions in its data collection and reporting activities for these groups. They are not mutually exclusive and exhibit a gerrymandered kind of complexity.[12]

It has been argued that persons from Spain resemble Europeans in culture and socioeconomic status more closely than Latin Americans and thus should be excluded from certain definitions according to the purposes for which a particular taxonomy is developed. In the United States, ethnic and racial classifications are commonly used in assessment of the socioeconomic and educational status of certain groups regarded as disadvantaged relative to the majority of society. Consequently, definition of the Spanish group should be targeted toward those persons with similar characteristics who are disadvantaged. Clearly, persons from Spain, as an identifiable group, would not be included. There is also debate over whether persons of Spanish ancestry in Central and South America should be included.

Numerically, individuals of Puerto Rican and Mexican heritage constitute the most important subgroups of Spanish minority groups in the United States, comprising approximately 70 percent of persons of Spanish origin in this country.[13] Moreover, these groups retain distinct cultural and language identities in the U.S. and have remained outside the mainstream of American society. Puerto Ricans and Mexican Americans (Chicanos) are the main Spanish groups considered in this report and, where possible, data will be separately reported for these two groups.[14] The U.S. Commission on Civil Rights has studied the status of Mexican Americans in the five southwestern states, with the premise that nearly all Spanish-surnamed

[12] Persons are classified as being of Spanish origin if they indicate their origin or descent to be Mexican, Puerto Rican, Cuban, Central or South American, or Spanish. The population of Spanish heritage includes persons in 42 states and the District of Columbia identified as persons of Spanish language, in the five southwestern states as persons of Spanish language or Spanish surname, and in the middle Atlantic states as being of Puerto Rican birth or parentage. The Spanish heritage definition, therefore, excludes non-Puerto Rican Spanish persons in the middle Atlantic states, families of persons of Spanish origin or descent who do not consider Spanish to be their native tongue, and persons of Puerto Rican origin who were not born in Puerto Rico and whose parents were not born in Puerto Rico. Spanish-surname applies only to persons in the five southwestern states. U.S. Bureau of the Census, Census of the Population: 1970, Vol. I, *Characteristics of the Population,* Part 1, "United States Summary," Section 2 (Washington, D.C.: U.S. Government Printing Office, 1973), Appendix, pp. 17–18.

[13] U.S. Bureau of the Census, 1970 Census of Population, Subject Reports, Final Report PC(2)–1C, *Persons of Spanish Origin* (Washington, D.C.: U.S. Government Printing Office, 1973), Table 1.

[14] Cubans, the other significant Spanish-surnamed group residing in the United States, are better educated than Chicanos or Puerto Rican Americans, although their educational levels are not as high as those of nonminority persons.

36

persons in the region are of Mexican ancestry. Data reported by the U.S. Census Bureau show that 87 percent of Mexican Americans reside in those five states.[15] A similar geographic criterion is used in examining the status of Puerto Ricans, 74 percent of whom reside in New York and New Jersey.[16] In many instances, data are available only for groups ambiguously defined as Spanish-surnamed or Spanish-speaking. The terms Spanish-speaking, Spanish-surnamed, and Hispanic will be used interchangeably in this report unless otherwise specified.

Participation of American Indians in graduate education is extremely difficult to examine for a very simple reason—it is not clear who is an American Indian. The U.S. Bureau of the Census reported 793,000 persons classified as American Indians in 1970, 0.37 percent of the U.S. population. The Bureau of Indian Affairs (BIA) specifies that an individual must be at least one-quarter blood Indian and registered on the tribal roster of a federally recognized tribe. This very precise definition thereby eliminates individuals who are members of officially terminated tribes or those who cannot provide legal proof of their heritage. Approximately one-half of the Indian population lives off-reservation and is not assisted by the BIA.[17] While most federal agencies continue to use the term American Indian, "Native American" has grown in popularity, reflecting recent trends toward cultural nationalism.[18] Both terms will be used in this report.

This report is equally concerned about the educational status of the four principal disadvantaged minority groups—blacks, Chicanos, Puerto Ricans, and Native Americans. Unfortunately, comparable data are not available for each of these groups. Presentation of data about the status of one group to the apparent exclusion of others should not be construed as denoting a greater emphasis or interest in a particular group, but rather reflects the serious lack of comparable information about other minorities.

How Many Minorities?

The distribution of the principal racial and ethnic groups in the U.S. population is shown in Table 2. In 1970 minority persons represented 16.9 per-

[15] U.S. Bureau of the Census, *Persons of Spanish Origin, op. cit.*
[16] *Ibid.*
[17] Officials at the BIA based this estimate on the U.S. Bureau of the Census, 1970 Census of Population, Subject Reports, Final Report PC(2)–1F, *American Indians* (Washington, D.C.: U.S. Government Printing Office, 1973), and information on the number of American Indians eligible for assistance from the BIA.
[18] Another source of error may derive from data collection efforts in which "Native American" is used, especially when the self-identification technique is used. Some persons may interpret the term to mean native-born Americans, confusing citizenship status with the ethnic definition, thus resulting in an overestimate of persons of American Indian heritage.

TABLE 2 Population Distribution, by Race and Ethnic Identity, All Ages and 20–24-Year Age-Cohort, 1970–1990

Racial/Ethnic Identity	All Ages, 1970	Persons 20–24 Years				
		1970	1975	1980	1985	1990
All persons	203,210,158 (100.0%)	16,099,500 (100.0%)	19,193,879 (100.0%)	20,853,607 (100.0%)	20,048,902 (100.0%)	17,115,336 (100.0%)
White	168,824,712 (83.08%)	13,295,411 (82.58%)	15,545,250 (80.99%)	16,615,939 (79.68%)	15,776,048 (78.69%)	13,281,412 (77.60%)
Total minority	34,385,446 (16.91%)	2,804,089 (17.42%)	3,648,629 (19.01%)	4,237,668 (20.32%)	4,272,854 (21.32%)	3,833,924 (22.40%)
Black	22,539,362 (11.09%)	1,752,961 (10.89%)	2,427,628 (12.65%)	2,817,392 (13.51%)	2,756,070 (13.75%)	2,409,546 (14.08%)
Spanish-surnamed [a]	9,294,509 (4.57%)	817,248 (5.07%)	977,353 (5.09%)	1,153,918 (5.53%)	1,243,417 (6.20%)	1,164,924 (6.81%)
Puerto Rican	1,464,359 (0.72%)	143,550 (0.89%)	145,318 (0.76%)	182,181 (0.87%)	209,138 (1.04%)	214,788 (1.25%)
Chicano	4,643,298 (2.28%)	404,379 (2.51%)	528,742 (2.75%)	624,367 (2.99%)	659,478 (3.29%)	612,192 (3.58%)
Other Spanish	3,186,852 (1.57%)	269,319 (1.67%)	303,293 (1.58%)	347,370 (1.67%)	374,801 (1.87%)	337,944 (1.98%)
Oriental [b]	1,791,003 (0.88%)	168,538 (1.05%)	160,708 (0.84%)	168,283 (0.81%)	171,913 (0.86%)	168,013 (0.98%)
American Indian	760,572 (0.37%)	65,342 (0.41%)	82,940 (0.43%)	98,075 (0.47%)	101,454 (0.51%)	91,441 (0.53%)

[a] An estimated 2.0–2.5 percent of persons classified as Spanish-surnamed are also included in one of the other racial minority categories, resulting in a slight overcount of total minority persons, representing about 0.1 percent of the total U.S. population (minority and nonminority).
[b] Includes persons of Chinese, Japanese, Korean, Filipino, Hawaiian, Polynesian, and other Asian origins and other races.

SOURCE: U.S. Bureau of the Census, 1970 Census of Population: vol. I, *Characteristics of the Population*, part 1, "United States Summary," section 2 (Washington, D.C.: U.S. Government Printing Office, 1973), pp. 593–595, and Subject Reports, Final Report PC(2)–1C, *Persons of Spanish Origin* (Washington, D.C.: U.S. Government Printing Office, 1973), p. 8

cent of the total population, with black and Spanish-surnamed persons comprising the largest proportions. If, however, specific age-cohorts are examined, the population distribution shifts. Minorities represented 17.4 percent of all persons 20–24 years of age. The higher birth rates of Chicanos, blacks, Puerto Ricans, and American Indians are reflected by their higher proportion in the younger cohorts relative to nonminority persons. By the year 1990, minority persons will account for 22.4 percent of the 20–24-year age-cohort, an increase of 5 percentage points over their proportion in 1970. While the number of nonminority persons in this age-group will decline slightly from 1970 to 1990, the number of blacks will increase 38 percent, and for Spanish-surnamed persons the increase will be 43 percent during the same period.

Accordingly, projections of sharp declines for the total college-age population during the 1980's should not overlook the rather different situation for the minority populations. The number of minority persons in the younger cohorts will continue to rise after the nonminority population has begun to fall, and the eventual declines in the minority cohort aged 20–24 will be much smaller, if any.[19]

The figures presented in Table 2 include both citizens and noncitizens residing in this country and thus pose some problems in their use as a standard for assessing the participation of minorities relative to non-minorities in graduate education. Ideally, figures on population distribution by citizenship status and age-cohort for each of the minority groups would allow the most accurate determination of relative participation rates in graduate education. Unfortunately, a variety of factors intervene that complicate such analyses. Varying immigration patterns present an obvious difficulty in projecting population distribution. Many Puerto Ricans, for example, move frequently between Puerto Rico and the U.S. mainland. For a long period of time, there was substantial immigration to the United States, although there are indications that this trend has stabilized or even reversed in the past few years. In 1970, almost four out of five Puerto Ricans residing in this country were born in Puerto Rico, while only one out of seven persons under the age of five was born in Puerto Rico.[20] Apart

---

[19] In general, persons of racial and ethnic identity are more likely to be missed during census counts. In particular, babies and preschool children are undercounted more often than school-age children. The U.S. Bureau of the Census estimated that 10 percent of black children aged 0–4 years were undercounted in 1970, while only 2 percent of nonminority white children were not counted. The projection for the 20–24 age-cohort in 1990 may understate minority persons since these people were under 5 years of age in 1970. A similar conjecture may be made for Puerto Ricans, Chicanos, and Native Americans, since migration patterns, illegal entry, and low income status may encourage or result in an undercount of young children.

[20] U.S. Bureau of the Census, *Persons of Spanish Origin, op. cit.,* p. 46.

from substantial variations in patterns of legal immigration, there is a large influx of illegal immigrants, especially in the southwestern states. Estimates vary as to the numbers of illegal aliens residing in the United States, but clearly these people and their children (who may or may not be U.S. citizens) are poorly educated.

In sum, information on the population representation of minority groups is imperfect. It is apparent, nonetheless, that minority persons comprise a substantial share of the U.S. population and their proportion is growing.

Significance of Citizenship Status in Assessing Minority Representation

The primary subjects of this report are minority persons who are U.S. citizens, with emphasis on native-born U.S. citizens. Careful specification of citizenship status in analyzing educational achievement is important for a number of reasons. First, immigrants to the United States have diverse educational backgrounds. For example, persons born in Puerto Rico are, in general, more poorly educated than those born in this country of Puerto Rican parents. Cubans have a higher educational attainment than other minority groups of Spanish origin. Second, there is the practical difficulty of distinguishing individuals who have immigrated to the United States at an early age and for various reasons may or may not have had an opportunity to obtain a good education from those persons who were educated abroad and then moved to this country. Foreign nationals who enter the United States to study, either under an immigrant or temporary visa, have not been exposed to the socioeconomic, educational, or cultural factors that affect educational attainment for most minorities residing in the United States.[21]

Equal educational opportunity should be a reality for all citizens and permanent residents of the United States; however, it is important to determine whether immigrant (and naturalized) persons are participating fully at all levels of higher education while being careful to avoid attributing the educational achievements (or the lack thereof) of recent immigrant individuals to the long-term resident population. Inclusion of noncitizens in figures reporting enrollments and degrees obtained in higher education may obscure the educational status of U.S. minorities who, in general, are educationally disadvantaged. For example, Asians earned almost 8 percent of all Ph.D.'s awarded by U.S. universities in 1973–74, but native-born Asians received only 0.6 percent of the doctorates conferred

---

[21] Moreover, foreign-born minorities exhibit different characteristics in graduate school than do native minorities in terms of fields of study, time to degree, sex differentials, and financial support patterns.

40

TABLE 3   Doctorates Awarded, by Race and Ethnic Identity, and Citizenship Status, 1973–74 [a]

| | | | | Non-U.S. Citizen | |
Racial/Ethnic Identity	Total	U.S. Native	U.S. Naturalized	Permanent Visa	Tempo- rary Visa
Black	1,010	833	13	42	122
	(100.0%)	(82.5%)	(1.3%)	(4.2%)	(12.2%)
American Indian	124	124	—	—	—
	(100.0%)	(100.0%)	—	—	—
Chicano, Mexican American, Spanish American	214	93	42	17	62
	(100.0%)	(43.5%)	(19.6%)	(7.9%)	(28.9%)
Puerto Rican	60	59	1	—	—
	(100.0%)	(98.3%)	(1.7%)	—	—
Oriental	2,204	142	151	858	1,053
	(100.0%)	(6.4%)	(6.9%)	(38.9%)	(47.8%)
Total Minority	3,612	1,251	207	917	1,237
	(100.0%)	(34.6%)	(5.7%)	(25.4%)	(34.2%)
White	25,552	22,693	749	651	1,459
	(100.0%)	(88.8%)	(2.9%)	(2.5%)	(5.7%)
Total	29,241	24,000	960	1,571	2,710
	(100.0%)	(82.1%)	(3.3%)	(5.4%)	(9.3%)

[a] Represents 89 percent sample of 33,000 doctorates awarded in 1973–1974. Nonrespondents include persons who did not indicate their racial or ethnic identity or who used an out-of-date questionnaire lacking the racial/ethnic question.

SOURCE: Special analysis by NBGE of data from National Research Council, National Academy of Sciences, Doctorate Records File, June 1975.

on native-born citizens, a substantial difference.[22] The former figure appears to indicate that Asians are "overrepresented" in doctoral study, while the latter does not.

With the exception of individuals classified as Chicano, Mexican American, or Spanish American, naturalized citizens represent only a small fraction of doctorates awarded to minority persons. Examination of the birthplace of naturalized citizens in the Spanish category reveals that very few are of Mexican heritage; rather, Cubans and South Americans comprise nearly all persons identified as naturalized or noncitizens in this category. Moreover, very few have graduated from high schools in the United States.[23]

From Table 3 it is observed that noncitizens accounted for 15 percent

[22] Special analysis by NBGE of data from National Research Council, National Academy of Sciences, Doctorate Records File, June 1975.
[23] *Ibid.*, October 1974.

41

of all doctorates awarded in the United States in 1973–74. However, noncitizens comprised 87 percent of all doctorates awarded to Oriental persons; 37 percent earned by Chicano, Mexican-American, and Spanish-American individuals; and one-sixth awarded to blacks in this country.

Further analysis of these data shows that minorities, noncitizens and U.S. citizens, received 12 percent of all doctorates awarded in 1973–1974; however, the U.S. native-born minority persons earned only 5.2 percent of total doctorates awarded to all U.S. natives. Noncitizen Orientals represented more than one-half of all minority doctorates. The effect of citizenship status becomes more pronounced if minority participation is examined by field of study. Minorities represented 10 percent of all doctorates awarded in the physical sciences if all citizenship categories are included, but only 3.1 percent of the doctorates awarded to native-born U.S. citizens.[24]

While providing opportunities for graduate study (and perhaps encouraging future permanent employment in this country) for foreign citizens is a worthwhile national goal, it should not be confused with equal educational opportunity for U.S. citizens.

ENROLLMENTS AND DEGREE ATTAINMENT

Assessment of minority participation in graduate education requires articulation of the desired objective and standards by which to evaluate progress toward that objective. We believe the appropriate long-range goal should be participation of minority persons in graduate education proportionate to their representation in the total population. We recog-- nize, however, that cultural patterns specific to certain minority groups may influence the feasibility of attaining this goal. Therefore, while we strongly affirm the desirability of its aim and utility in assessment of progress, we must also inject a note of tentativeness in stating this goal.

Throughout this report, data contrasting minority participation with that of nonminorities are presented. Such comparisons aid in interpretation of the data. We do not, however, intend to suggest that every deviation from white norms of participation should be considered undesirable. Precise arithmetic parity with the nonminority population, according to fine-grained parameters such as discipline specialties or subsets of institutions, is both impractical and unnecessary. Rather, common sense must prevail in distinguishing differences that are reasonable or a matter of preference from those that are unjust.

In the following section we will examine minority student enrollment

[24] Special analysis by NBGE of data from National Research Council, National Academy of Sciences, Doctorate Records File, May 1975.

42

trends relative to those of nonminority students, report degree attainment when such data exist, and describe other patterns of participation, such as distribution among fields and schools. The underlying reasons for the observed trends and patterns are many and complex, and we will comment only briefly on them.

The year 1970 represents both a time when significant changes in graduate minority enrollments were realized and when systematic data collection activities to document the status of minorities were initiated. The importance of having reliable information on minority participation overshadowed the recent social (and often legal) proscriptions against classifying students by racial or ethnic identity. Access was the first concern. To respond to the question, How many minorities are enrolled in graduate school?, we may review four relatively recent data sources. The Office for Civil Rights (OCR) of the Department of Health, Education, and Welfare undertakes a biennial census of minority enrollments in institutions of higher education.[25] Institutions that receive federal financial assistance are required to provide this information. Hamilton surveyed the 302 member institutions of the Council of Graduate Schools in the United States, approximately 40 percent of which were able to estimate enrollment figures for minority students for fall 1971.[26] The National Association of State Universities and Land Grant Colleges (NASULGC) conducts a biennial survey of minority enrollments in graduate and professional schools at its member state and land grant universities, the latest available being fall 1972.[27] The most recent survey was undertaken by the Higher Education Panel of the American Council on Education, which requested information on minority graduate enrollments in 228 doctoral-granting institutions.[28] The data reported in Table 4 show the levels of participation for the four major ethnic and racial groups.

While the data presented in individual surveys are not fully comparable, given variations in institutional coverage, identification techniques, and student status (full-time and part-time), they indicate that minority participation has increased since 1970, especially with respect to black enrollments. In 1972 and 1973 the proportion of black students was roughly

[25] U.S. Department of Health, Education, and Welfare, Office for Civil Rights, *Racial and Ethnic Enrollment Data from Institutions of Higher Education, Fall 1970 and Fall 1972* (Washington, D.C.: U.S. Government Printing Office, 1972 and 1975).

[26] I. Bruce Hamilton, *Graduate School Programs for Minority/Disadvantaged Students* (Princeton, N.J.: Educational Testing Service, 1973).

[27] Adapted from data provided by the National Association of State Universities and Land Grant Colleges (NASULGC), Biennial Survey of Minority Enrollments, 1972, unpublished.

[28] Elaine H. El-Khawas and Joan L. Kinzer, *Enrollment of Minority Graduate Students at Ph.D. Granting Institutions,* Higher Education Panel Reports, No. 19 (Washington, D.C.: American Council on Education, August 1974).

TABLE 4 Enrollment for Master's and Doctorate Degrees, by Racial and Ethnic Identity

Racial/Ethnic Identity	OCR (1970), Full-time [a]	OCR (1972), Full-time [b]	Hamilton (1971), Full- and Part-time [c]	NASULGC (1972), Full- and Part-time [d]	ACE (1973), Full- and Part-time [e]
Total	392,362 (100.0%)	406,093 (100.0%)	286,755 (100.0%)	495,478 (100.0%)	372,964 (100.0%)
White	362,329 (92.3%)	368,812 (90.8%)	271,356 (94.6%)	456,003 (92.0%)	346,472 (92.8%)
Total minority	30,033 (7.7%)	37,281 (9.1%)	15,399 (5.4%)	39,475 (8.0%)	26,492 (7.2%)
American Indian	1,290 (0.3%)	1,664 (0.4%)	708 (0.3%)	1,610 (0.3%)	1,181 (0.3%)
Black	16,334 (4.2%)	21,371 (5.2%)	9,376 (3.3%)	24,257 (4.9%)	16,241 (4.4%)
Asian	7,579 (1.9%)	8,343 (2.0%)	2,420 (0.8%)	6,558 (1.3%)	5,076 (1.4%)
Spanish-surnamed	4,830 (1.2%)	5,903 (1.4%)	2,895 (1.0%)	5,536 (1.1%)	3,994 (1.1%)
Other	—	—	—	1,514 (0.3%)	—

[a] U.S. Department of Health, Education, and Welfare, Office for Civil Rights, *Racial and Ethnic Enrollment Data from Institutions of Higher Education, Fall 1970* (Washington, D.C.: U.S. Goverment Printing Office, 1972).
[b] U.S. Department of Health, Education, and Welfare, Office for Civil Rights, *Racial and Ethnic Enrollment Data from Institutions of Higher Education, Fall 1972* (Washington, D.C.: U.S. Government Printing Office, 1975).
[c] I. Bruce Hamilton, *Graduate School Programs for Minority/Disadvantaged Students* (Princeton, N.J.: Educational Testing Service, 1973).
[d] National Association of State Universities and Land Grant Colleges, figures derived from fall 1972 survey of minority enrollment. Enrollments for first professional degrees are included.
[e] Elaine H. El-Khawas and Joan L. Kinzer, *Enrollment of Minority Graduate Students at Ph.D. Granting Institutions*, Higher Education Panel Reports, No. 19 (Washington, D.C.: American Council on Education, August 1974).

4–5 percent, and total minority enrollments comprised about 6–9 percent of all graduate enrollments.

Table 5 contrasts recent graduate enrollments and doctorates awarded to native-born citizens with the distribution of racial and ethnic groups in the U.S. population. The underrepresentation of minority group persons is clear. The number of black and Spanish-surnamed persons must be doubled or quadrupled (depending on figures used to estimate enrollments) in order to attain parity with their distribution in the U.S. population. Persons of Oriental heritage appear to be well represented in graduate

44

TABLE 5 Percentage Distribution of Estimated Graduate Enrollments, Doctorates Awarded, and U.S. Population, by Race and Ethnic Identity

Racial/Ethnic Identity	Estimated Graduate Enrollments (%)	Doctorates Awarded to Native-born U.S. Citizens, 1973–74 (%)	Distribution in U.S. Population, 1970 (%)
Total	100.0	100.0	100.0
White	90.8–94.6	94.5	83.1
Total minority	5.4–9.1	5.5	16.9
Black	3.3–5.2	3.5	11.1
American Indian	0.3–0.4	0.5	0.4
Oriental	0.8–2.0	0.6	0.9
Spanish-surnamed	1.0–1.4	0.9	4.6
Mexican American, Chicano, Spanish American	—	(0.6)	(3.9)
Puerto Rican	—	(0.3)	(0.7)

SOURCE: See Tables 2, 3, and 4, Chapter 2.

study, although enrollment figures include persons holding permanent visas. Consequently, the situation of native-born U.S. citizens of Asian origin may be less favorable than aggregate figures indicate. Mexican and Puerto Rican Americans appear to have the lowest participation rates relative to other ethnic and minority groups according to the figures presented here.

A NOTE ON NATIVE AMERICAN PARTICIPATION

In comparing enrollment figures of American Indians in colleges and universities with population representation, it appears that Indians *are not* underrepresented in graduate education. How should this be interpreted? First, there seems to be a tendency for college-age persons to identify themselves as American Indian although their Indian heritage may be very distant. In the 1972–73 National Research Council Survey of Earned Doctorates, only 20 individuals identified themselves as American Indian, while an additional 88 persons classified themselves as both American Indian and white, as shown in Table 6. The Bureau of Indian Affairs (BIA) reported that 100 students receiving its assistance earned advanced degrees in 1972–73, a figure that includes master's, doctorate, and first professional degree graduates.[29] The BIA informally estimated that approxi-

[29] U.S. Bureau of Indian Affairs, "Higher Education Scholarship Grants Summary," FY 1965–75. Unpublished.

45

TABLE 6 Doctorates Awarded to Individuals Designated as American Indian Only, and American Indian and White, as Percentage of Total Doctorates, 1972–73 [a]

Racial/Ethnic Identity	No. and Percent of Total Doc- torates Awarded	Distribution in U.S. Population (1970)
American Indian only	20 (0.10%)	
American Indian and white	88 (0.43%)	
Total	108 (0.53%)	0.37%

[a] Represents a 75 percent sample of total doctorates awarded in 1972–73. Nonrespondents included persons who did not indicate their racial or ethnic identity or who used an out-of-date questionnaire lacking the racial/ethnic question.

SOURCE: Special analysis by NBGE of data from National Research Council, National Academy of Sciences, Doctorate Records File, November 1974, and Table 2, Chapter 2.

mately 20 Indians received doctorates in 1973–74, a figure nowhere approaching the 108 reported in the 75 percent sample of the 1972–73 Survey of Earned Doctorates. Hence, a narrower definition of American Indian heritage could substantially deflate many of the figures reported in this chapter.

DISTRIBUTION AMONG DISCIPLINES

Aggregate degree and enrollment statistics on minority representation in graduate education at best are limited in aiding our understanding of the nature and extent of minority involvement in graduate education. In the following section, we will point out significant characteristics in the patterns of minority and nonminority participation.

One of the most stubborn problems that must be addressed is the extremely low level of participation of minorities in certain academic disciplines relative to nonminority students—the physical sciences, mathematics, and engineering. This situation has particular significance in terms of prospective employment opportunities in the coming decade.

Table 7 reports the distribution by field of native-born U.S. citizens earning doctorates in 1973–74, by race and ethnic group.[30] Minorities (excluding Oriental persons) obtained only 2.3 percent of the doctorates

[30] Detailed information on doctorates awarded by race and ethnic identity, sex, field of study, and citizenship status is provided in Appendix A, Tables A–1 to A–4.

46

TABLE 7 Doctorates Awarded Showing Distribution by Race and Ethnic Group <u>Within</u> Fields of Study, 1973–74 (U.S. Native-born Citizens)[a]

Field	U.S. Native-Born Citizens						
	Total	Black	Spanish American[b]	Puerto Rican	American Indian	Oriental	White
Physical sciences and mathematics	3,272 (100.0%)	46 (1.4%)	11 (0.3%)	5 (0.2%)	15 (0.5%)	24 (0.7%)	3,171 (96.9%)
Engineering	1,555 (100.0%)	16 (1.0%)	4 (0.3%)	7 (0.5%)	7 (0.5%)	18 (1.1%)	1,503 (96.7%)
Life sciences	3,337 (100.0%)	69 (2.1%)	16 (0.5%)	6 (0.2%)	15 (0.4%)	33 (1.0%)	3,198 (95.8%)
Social sciences	4,713 (100.0%)	104 (2.2%)	20 (0.4%)	12 (0.3%)	18 (0.4%)	22 (0.5%)	4,537 (96.3%)
Arts and humanities	3,950 (100.0%)	74 (1.9%)	21 (0.5%)	17 (0.4%)	17 (0.4%)	13 (0.3%)	3,808 (96.4%)
Professional fields	1,038 (100.0%)	31 (3.0%)	5 (0.5%)	1 (0.1%)	8 (0.8%)	4 (0.4%)	989 (95.3%)
Education	6,109 (100.0%)	493 (8.1%)	72 (1.2%)	11 (0.2%)	44 (0.7%)	28 (0.5%)	5,461 (89.4%)
Other or unspecified fields	26 (100.0%)	—	—	—	—	—	26 (100.0%)
Total	24,000 (100.0%)	833 (3.5%)	149 (0.6%)	59 (0.2%)	124 (0.5%)	142 (0.6%)	22,693 (94.6%)

[a] Represents an 89 percent sample of total doctorates awarded in 1973–74; see Table 3, Chapter 2, for an explanation of survey coverage.

[b] Includes Chicano, Mexican American, and Spanish American.

SOURCE: Special analysis by NBGE of data from National Research Council, National Academy of Sciences, Doctorate Records File, May 1975.

granted in the physical science and engineering fields. In the social sciences the situation was somewhat brighter, with blacks, Chicanos, Puerto Ricans, and Native Americans receiving 3 percent of the total. In education this percentage rises to 10 percent of all doctorates. These data provide emphatic support for two conclusions. First, minority group persons are underrepresented in all fields of study. Their overall numbers must be increased roughly fourfold to achieve population parity. Second, there are striking differences in participation *among* disciplines. While a 700 percent increase in the number of minority doctorates in the physical sciences is needed to reach parity with nonminority participation, a 60 percent increment would be adequate in education.

These differences in participation among the various disciplines have often led to broad generalizations about overrepresentation and concentration in fields such as education, but such conclusions warrant further discussion. Tables 7 and 8 show that while 59.2 percent of the blacks who earned doctorates received their degrees in education, blacks represented only 8.1 percent of all U.S. native-born students awarded a doctorate in education in 1973–74, about two-thirds the proportion that would be expected relative to their representation in the United States population. Similarly, while 48.3 percent of the Chicanos received a doctorate in education, they accounted for only 1.2 percent of all doctorates awarded in education that year. The field distribution problem should be viewed as one of varying degrees of underrepresentation among disciplines: There are not too many minority doctorates in education; rather, there are more relative to their presence in other disciplines.

Several possible explanations exist for the relative concentration of blacks and Chicanos in education. First, minorities may be "tracked" in high school and to some extent in college, directed away from the "hard" disciplines, such as mathematics and physics, into "soft" fields, such as the social sciences and education. Thus, the pool of minority baccalaureates with the appropriate academic preparation needed to pursue advanced work in the natural sciences is limited, for a decision to study a natural science in graduate school must generally be made prior to undergraduate school in order to gain the requisite mathematics skills and basic courses in physics and chemistry. A related factor is the lower intellectual self-confidence of minority students as they enter college relative to that of nonminority students;[31] consequently they may avoid disciplines perceived to be especially rigorous.

Second, in the case of black students, elementary and secondary teach-

[31] See Alan E. Bayer, *The Black College Freshman: Characteristics and Recent Trends,* American Council on Education Research Reports, No. 7 (Washington, D.C.: American Council on Education, 1972).

48

TABLE 8 Doctorates Awarded Showing Distribution Among Fields of Study, by Race and Ethnic Group, 1973–74 (U.S. Native-born Citizens)ᵃ

Field	U.S. Native-Born Citizens					
	Black	Chicano, Mexican American, Spanish American	Puerto Rican	American Indian	Oriental	White
Physical sciences and mathematics	46 (5.5%)	11 (7.4%)	5 (8.5%)	15 (12.1%)	24 (16.9%)	3,171 (14.0%)
Engineering	16 (1.9%)	4 (2.7%)	7 (11.9%)	7 (5.6%)	18 (12.7%)	1,503 (6.6%)
Life sciences	69 (8.3%)	16 (10.7%)	6 (10.2%)	15 (12.1%)	33 (23.2%)	3,198 (14.1%)
Social sciences	104 (12.5%)	20 (13.4%)	12 (20.3%)	18 (14.5%)	22 (15.5%)	4,537 (20.0%)
Arts and humanities	74 (8.9%)	21 (14.1%)	17 (28.8%)	17 (13.7%)	13 (9.2%)	3,808 (16.8%)
Other professional fields	31 (3.7%)	5 (3.3%)	1 (1.7%)	8 (6.5%)	4 (2.8%)	989 (4.4%)
Education	493 (59.2%)	72 (48.3%)	11 (18.6%)	44 (35.5%)	28 (19.7%)	5,461 (24.1%)
Unspecified fields	— (0.0%)	— (0.0%)	— (0.0%)	— (0.0%)	— (0.0%)	26 (0.1%)
Total	833 (100.0%)	149 (100.0%)	59 (100.0%)	124 (100.0%)	142 (100.0%)	22,693 (100.0%)

ᵃ Represents an 89 percent sample of total doctorates awarded in 1973–74; see Table 3 for an explanation of survey coverage.

SOURCE: Special analysis by NBGE of data from National Research Council, National Academy of Sciences, Doctorate Records File, May 1975.

49

ing historically has been one of the few professional employment opportunities available to educated blacks.[32] The black colleges emphasized teacher training, and this tradition continues to some extent today. For example, in 1970–71, education accounted for 69 percent of the master's degrees granted by the black graduate schools.[33] It follows that whereas role models for the teaching profession are visible to blacks, there is only a handful of black Ph.D. physicists, mathematicians, and other natural scientists. Lack of peer identification and information on career opportunities are related deterrents to entering scientific study. In sum, it should not be surprising that few blacks have enrolled in the natural sciences relative to their participation in education at the graduate level.

Some signs indicating change in recent years do exist. The proportion of black students in education at the undergraduate level has declined. Whereas, in 1965–66, 45 percent of the bachelor's degrees awarded by black colleges were in the field of education, by 1970–71, this figure had dropped to 35 percent. During this same period the comparable national figures for all students declined from 23 to 21 percent.[34] These data show that although a greater proportion of black students than of white students major in education in college, the disparity is rapidly diminishing. The nationwide contraction of employment opportunities in teaching, concomitant with the expansion of opportunities for blacks in other fields, has served to encourage this shift from education. The trend has continued. In 1973–74, 27 percent of the blacks who received a bachelor's degree from all colleges and universities were in education, while the corresponding figure for all students (white and nonwhite) dropped only slightly, to 19 percent.[35]

For other minority groups, such as Mexican Americans and American Indians, education continues to be a popular field of study given the strong concern about the need for more minority teachers and education.[36]

---

[32] See, for example, Gunnar Myrdal, *An American Dilemma, The Negro Problem and Modern Democracy,* Volume I (New York: Pantheon Books, 1944), reprint of 20th anniversary edition published by Harper and Row, 1975, pp. 304–332, and Frank Bowles and Frank A. DeCosta, *Between Two Worlds* (New York: McGraw-Hill, 1971), pp. 41, 42.

[33] Elias Blake, Jr., Linda J. Lambert, and Joseph L. Martin, *Degrees Granted and Enrollment Trends in Historically Black Colleges: An Eight-Year Study* (Washington, D.C.: Institute for Services to Education, 1974), p. 44.

[34] *Ibid.,* p. 38.

[35] American Council on Education, Higher Education Panel, preliminary figures, 1975.

[36] U.S. Commission on Civil Rights, *A Better Chance to Learn: Bilingual-Bicultural Education,* Clearinghouse Publication 51 (Washington, D.C.: U.S. Government Printing Office, May 1975), p. 142.

Recent court decisions such as *Lau* v. *Nichols,* which ruled "that school systems have an affirmative obligation to provide students who are unable to speak and understand English a meaningful opportunity to participate in their school's instructional program" and state legislation requiring bilingual–bicultural education have increased the demand for minority educators.[37] While national trends indicate an overall decrease in the need for persons trained in the field of education, the special circumstances of certain minority groups may run counter to these trends.

A related phenomenon is documented in Table 9, which shows that a significantly greater percentage of blacks awarded doctorates from 1972 to 1974 shifted into education from other disciplines in which they received their baccalaureate degrees. The retention rate in all noneducation fields is lower for black students, with education being the prime recipient of the flow from other disciplines.

For example, only 44 percent of the black doctorates who received bachelor's degrees in the physical sciences continued in those fields for doctoral work, while one-third changed to education. In comparison, 68 percent of white doctorates with undergraduate degrees in the physical sciences earned a doctorate in the same field and only 8 percent shifted to education. The net effect of these disciplinary shifts by blacks is important. Thus, while 34 percent of the black doctorates received a baccalaureate in education, almost 60 percent earned a doctorate in education. For white students this pattern of discipline changes is also evident, but less pronounced.

These data suggest two concerns. The field distribution problem must be addressed during the high school and early undergraduate years to motivate students and ensure adequate academic preparation for advanced work in certain fields such as the natural sciences and engineering. Nonetheless, students with appropriate undergraduate preparation for advanced study in the natural science disciplines have shifted out of these fields at successive levels of higher education. Therefore, efforts to encourage a wider distribution of black students among disciplines may also be effectively directed to alleviating the causes of these shifts during undergraduate and graduate study.

[37] For a discussion of this issue, see Henry J. Casso, "Higher Education and the Mexican American," in *Economic and Educational Perspectives of the Mexican American* (New York: The Weatherhead Foundation, forthcoming); U.S. Commission on Civil Rights, *Teachers and Students.* Mexican American Education Study. Report V. (Washington, D.C.: U.S. Government Printing Office, March 1973); and U.S. Commission on Civil Rights, *The Southwest Indian Report* (Washington, D.C.: U.S. Government Printing Office, May 1973).

TABLE 9 Doctorates Conferred to U.S. Native-born Blacks and Whites, by Doctorate and Baccalaureate Fields, 1972–74 [a]

Field of Baccalaureate	Field of Doctorate							
	Physical Sciences	Engineering	Life Sciences	Social Sciences	Arts and Humanities	Professional Fields	Education	Total
Blacks								
Physical sciences	**73** **(43.5%)**	10 (6.0%)	17 (10.1%)	4 (2.4%)	3 (1.8%)	4 (2.4%)	57 (33.9%)	168 (100.0%)
Engineering	2 (5.7%)	**23** **(65.7%)**	— (0.0%)	4 (11.4%)	— (0.0%)	4 (11.4%)	2 (5.7%)	35 (100.0%)
Life sciences	2 (1.1%)	— (0.0%)	**94** **(51.9%)**	5 (2.8%)	3 (1.7%)	— (0.0%)	77 (42.5%)	181 (100.0%)
Social sciences	— (0.0%)	— (0.0%)	1 (0.4%)	**106** **(43.1%)**	7 (2.8%)	13 (5.3%)	119 (48.4%)	246 (100.0%)
Arts and humanities	1 (0.4%)	— (0.0%)	— (0.0%)	11 (4.9%)	**91** **(40.8%)**	10 (4.5%)	110 (49.3%)	223 (100.0%)
Professional fields	— (0.0%)	— (0.0%)	4 (5.1%)	8 (10.3%)	8 (10.3%)	**10** **(12.8%)**	48 (61.5%)	78 (100.0%)
Education	— (0.0%)	— (0.0%)	4 (0.8%)	25 (5.3%)	12 (2.5%)	7 (1.5%)	**426** **(89.9%)**	474 (100.0%)
Total	78 (5.5%)	33 (2.3%)	120 (8.5%)	163 (11.6%)	124 (8.8%)	48 (3.4%)	839 (59.7%)	**1,405** **(100.0%)**

Whites

Physical sciences	**5,462** (68.3%)	349 (4.4%)	936 (11.7%)	361 (4.5%)	155 (1.9%)	107 (1.3%)	624 (7.8%)	7,994 (100.0%)
Engineering	300 (8.8%)	**2,556** (74.9%)	103 (3.0%)	124 (3.6%)	38 (1.1%)	189 (5.5%)	104 (3.0%)	3,414 (100.0%)
Life sciences	119 (2.2%)	19 (0.4%)	**4,332** (80.3%)	237 (4.4%)	48 (0.9%)	57 (1.1%)	580 (10.8%)	5,392 (100.0%)
Social sciences	26 (0.3%)	13 (0.2%)	156 (2.0%)	**5,588** (70.5%)	338 (4.3%)	276 (3.5%)	1,532 (19.3%)	7,929 (100.0%)
Arts and humanities	57 (0.6%)	12 (0.1%)	87 (0.9%)	1,059 (11.0%)	**6,066** (63.0%)	367 (3.8%)	1,987 (20.6%)	9,635 (100.0%)
Professional fields	94 (3.7%)	55 (2.2%)	196 (7.7%)	476 (18.6%)	231 (9.0%)	**788** (30.9%)	714 (28.0%)	2,554 (100.0%)
Education	89 (1.6%)	4 (0.1%)	178 (3.2%)	311 (5.6%)	341 (6.2%)	104 (1.9%)	**4,479** (81.3%)	5,506 (100.0%)
Total	6,147 (14.5%)	3,008 (7.1%)	5,988 (14.1%)	8,156 (19.2%)	7,217 (17.0%)	1,888 (4.5%)	10,020 (23.6%)	**42,424** (100.0%)

a Data for the year 1972–73 represent a 75 percent sample of total doctorates awarded in 1972–73; see Table 6 for an explanation of survey coverage. Data for 1973–74 represent an 89 percent sample of total doctorates awarded that year; see Table 3 for an explanation of survey coverage.

NOTE: The table reads as follows: Of 168 black students who received a baccalaureate in the physical sciences and who received a doctorate in 1972–73 or 1973–74, 73 (or 43.5 percent) earned their doctorate in the physical sciences, 10 (or 6.0 percent) earned their doctorate in engineering, etc.

SOURCE: Special analysis by NBGE of data from National Research Council, National Academy of Sciences, Doctorate Records File, November 1974 and May 1975.

53

TABLE 10 Median Age at Doctorate and Time to Degree, by Race and Ethnic Identity, 1973–74 (U.S. Native-Born Citizens Only)

Racial/Ethnic Identity	Median Age at Doctorate	Median Number of Years			
		Baccalaureate to Doctorate	Baccalaureate to Graduate School Entry	Graduate School Entry to Doctorate	Registered Time in Graduate School
Total doctorates, all fields					
White	31.2	8.4	1.1	7.6	5.9
Black	36.7	12.4	1.4	9.9	5.9
Chicano, Mexican American, Spanish American	33.6	9.7	1.2	8.4	5.8
Puerto Rican	31.4	9.3	1.2	8.9	7.0
American Indian	33.0	8.9	1.2	7.8	5.7
Oriental	30.3	7.8	1.1	7.3	5.9
Noneducation majors only					
White	30.3	7.6	1.1	7.1	5.8
Black	33.5	10.2	1.2	8.7	6.0
Chicano, Mexican American, Spanish American	31.6	8.2	1.2	7.6	5.8
Puerto Rican	30.9	8.9	1.1	8.5	7.0
American Indian	31.1	8.2	1.1	7.4	5.7
Oriental	29.7	7.1	1.1	6.9	5.8

SOURCE: Special analysis by NBGE of data from National Research Council, National Academy of Sciences, Doctorate Records File, June 1975.

MEASURES OF TIME TO DEGREE IN DOCTORAL STUDY

Patterns of attendance in doctoral study vary among racial and ethnic groups. Typically, black, Chicano, and American Indian students are older than white students upon completion of doctoral work. The data in Table 10 show that minority students delay entry to graduate study slightly and require from 1 to 2 years longer to earn a doctorate than do white students. The time actually registered in graduate school, however, is similar for all groups of students (with the exception of Puerto Ricans). The net effect of delayed entry to graduate school and longer time to degree is a lengthening of the median time from date of bachelor's degree to Ph.D., 4 years longer for blacks and about 1 year more for other minority groups relative to white students. Several factors that contribute to this situation may be suggested. First, there are variations among disciplines in the period of time normally required to earn a Ph.D. For example, doctoral recipients in education are generally older than those in other fields, whereas chemistry Ph.D.'s move rapidly through doctoral study. Excluding the field of education from the measures of time to degree (since 60 percent of black Ph.D.'s major in education) reported in Table 10, disparities among various racial and ethnic groups are reduced, but do not disappear. In examining the data for noneducation majors, it is apparent that the prime difference occurs in the time required to complete a doctorate once enrolled in graduate study. Since the registered time is similar for all students, this implies that minority students, especially blacks, either drop out of graduate school for a period of time during the course of their studies or attend on a part-time basis.

The financial situation of students may be a major determinant of attendance patterns, since a student may feel obliged to interrupt studies or to combine education and work. This circumstance may be further complicated by the fact that as a student grows older and assumes family and other responsibilities, that student's financial needs also increase.

A third possibility suggested by some observers is that minority students may first seek a master's degree and, after attaining greater intellectual self-confidence and a wider knowledge of academic and professional opportunities, may later decide to pursue a terminal degree.

DISTRIBUTION AMONG GRADUATE SCHOOLS

Which schools have been successful in enrollment of minority students (or alternatively, which schools have minorities chosen to attend or been able to attend) and which schools have awarded a significant proportion of advanced degrees to minority students? Since the quality of graduate

TABLE 11   Percentage of Graduate Students Enrolled in Public and Private Ph.D.-Granting Institutions, by Race and Ethnic Identity, Fall 1973

Racial/Ethnic Identity	Enrolled in Public Institutions (%)	Enrolled in Private Institutions (%)
All students	76	24
White	76	24
Minority students	78	22
Black American	78	22
Spanish-surnamed American	78	22
American Indian	86	14
Asian American	78	22

SOURCE: Elaine H. El-Khawas and Joan L. Kinzer, *Enrollment of Minority Graduate Students at Ph.D. Granting Institutions,* Higher Education Panel Reports, No. 19 (Washington, D.C.: American Council on Education, August 1974).

programs varies among institutions, as well as the program offerings and emphases, the choice of institution a student attends is extremely important. Are minorities attending the same kinds of schools as nonminorities?

To answer this question, the distribution of minority students between public and private institutions, using figures reported in the American Council on Education survey of minority enrollments of Ph.D.-granting institutions, was examined. Table 11 presents the percentage distributions. No significant differences in enrollment in public and private institutions were observed. Only American Indian enrollments appear to differ from those of all students.[38]

It is well understood that the quality rankings of Ph.D. programs and faculty influence the type of employment opportunities available to doctorate recipients. The most prestigious graduate universities in the country emphasize scholarly research in their training of Ph.D. students, with the general expectation that the next generation of faculty in that set of institutions will be drawn from their students. Other doctoral-granting institutions have followed the research Ph.D. model, but their graduates have been less successful in entering academic careers in the major research universities.[39] Still other graduate schools have focused on training for nonacademic careers or teaching in undergraduate institutions.

At present, if a student hopes to embark upon a research and teaching career in a major research university, the chances of doing so are

[38] Given the small number of American Indian students reported in the survey, the difference is not significant.
[39] Even more so in the current discouraging academic market.

56

TABLE 12   Doctorates Awarded by AAU Institutions as a Percentage of
Total Doctorates, by Race and Ethnic Identity, 1972–73 (U.S. Native-born Citizens)

Racial/Ethnic Identity	Doctorates Awarded (%)
White	53
Total minority	44
Black American	46
Mexican American, Chicano, Spanish American	33
Puerto Rican American	47
American Indian	46
Oriental	43

SOURCE: Special analysis by the NBGE of data from National Research Council, National Academy of Sciences, Doctorate Records File, November 1974.

enhanced if that student has obtained a Ph.D. from one of the top-ranked graduate schools.[40] For this reason it is useful to compare the proportions of minority and nonminority persons who received doctorates from institutions that are members of the Association of American Universities (AAU), widely regarded as including the majority of major research universities of acknowledged excellence in this country.[41] Table 12 shows the percentage of doctorates awarded by race and ethnic group by AAU institutions. The data show that a smaller proportion of native-born minorities earned doctorates from AAU universities relative to whites.[42] Chicanos, in particular, are less likely to have attended an AAU institution for their doctoral study.[43]

A relatively small number of institutions produce the majority of doctorates granted in this country. The data in Table 13, which show the percentile distribution of institutions by number of degrees, indicate that this general pattern is more pronounced with respect to black Ph.D. recipients. In 1973–74, over one-half of the doctorates earned by blacks

[40] Several prestigious research institutions indicated in the NBGE affirmative action survey (see Chapter 4) that their new faculty were drawn almost exclusively from other AAU member universities or departments highly ranked in the American Council on Education rating of graduate programs.
[41] Two Canadian universities are members of the AAU.
[42] The relation between choice of discipline and different emphases in fields of study offered by AAU and non-AAU institutions may be one determinant of attendance patterns.
[43] If attendance at AAU and non-AAU institutions is examined with respect to citizenship status, we find that noncitizens are more likely to attend AAU schools. While 54 percent of the minorities (all citizenship groups) received doctorates from these schools, 63 percent of the whites did so. Special analysis by National Board on Graduate Education of data from National Research Council, National Academy of Sciences, Doctorate Records File, November 1974.

TABLE 13 Distribution of Institutions by Cumulative Percentage of Doctorates Awarded, by Race, 1973–74 [a]

Total Black Doctorates (%)	No. of Institutions	Total White Doctorates (%)	No. of Institutions
25	7	25	13
50	24	50	36
75	57	75	75
100	269	100	269

[a] Includes U.S. citizens and noncitizens holding permanent visas.

SOURCE: Special analysis by NBGE of data from National Research Council, National Academy of Sciences, Doctorate Records File, June 1975.

were awarded by only 24 of the 269 institutions that granted one or more Ph.D.'s that year.

From Table 14 we see that 110 graduate schools did not award a doctoral degree to a single black person in 1973–74. Well over two-thirds of the Ph.D.-granting institutions did not report any Hispanic persons or American Indians among their degree recipients. A handful of large public universities, particularly those located in the midwestern states, have produced the largest number of minority doctorates. These data suggest the potential for a broadening of efforts to increase minority participation. If those schools that granted no doctorate degrees to minority individuals were to make a modest commitment to encourage and assist only one or two minority persons to earn a Ph.D. degree each year, the collective impact would represent a substantial gain.

TABLE 14 Distribution of Institutions by Number of Doctorates Awarded, by Race and Ethnic Identity, 1973–74

Racial/Ethnic Identity	Distribution of Institutions by No. of Doctorates Awarded				
	0	1–2	3–5	6–9	10 or More
White	1	18	29	23	195
Black	110	61	51	22	15
Chicano, Mexican American, Spanish American	190	56	17	5	1
Puerto Rican	228	37	4	0	0
American Indian	190	69	7	3	0
Oriental	104	59	42	27	37

SOURCE: Special analysis by NBGE of data from National Research Council, National Academy of Sciences, Doctorate Records File, June 1975.

TABLE 15 Enrollments in Graduate Study by Race and Ethnic Identity, Including Blacks Enrolled in Black Graduate Schools

Racial/Ethnic Identity	OCR (1970), Full-time	OCR (1972), Full-time	NASULGC (1972), Full- and Part-time [a]
Total students	392,362 (100.0%)	406,093 (100.0%)	495,478 (100.0%)
White	362,329 (92.3%)	368,812 (90.8%)	456,003 (92.0%)
Total minority	30,033 (7.7%)	37,281 (9.1%)	39,475 (8.0%)
Black (in nonminority schools)	13,019 (3.3%)	17,388 (4.3%)	19,190 (3.9%)
Black (in black graduate schools)	3,315 (0.8%)	3,983 (1.0%)	5,067 (1.0%)
Other minority	13,699 (3.5%)	15,910 (3.9%)	15,218 (3.1%)

[a] Includes enrollments in graduate and professional schools.
SOURCE: See Table 4, Chapter 2.

THE CONTRIBUTION OF THE BLACK GRADUATE SCHOOLS

Many universities have made substantial efforts to attract minority graduate students and their success has been reflected in part by the increases in national figures reporting minority enrollments. However, a substantial number of black graduate students is currently enrolled in the predominately and historically black graduate schools. Table 15 presents the figures for black enrollments in graduate schools drawn from the two OCR surveys and the NASULGC survey reported previously.

We find that the black graduate schools enroll approximately one-fifth of all black graduate students. At present there are about 30 historically and predominately black graduate schools. Enrollments in the black graduate schools are growing. In fall 1967, total enrollments in the historically black graduate schools were 8,488; by 1973, this figure had climbed to 19,919, an increase of more than 100 percent.[44]

A final point must be mentioned. Many nonminority students attend the black graduate schools; some of these schools have become predominately white. The black graduate schools continue to provide advanced education for a substantial part of the black population, while

[44] Blake, Lambert, and Martin, *op. cit.*, p. 26.

59

attracting a growing number of nonminority and other minority students. A more extensive discussion of enrollment trends is included in the Supplement, "Mission, Status, Problems, and Priorities of Black Graduate Schools," to this volume.

RELATIVE IMPACT OF LAW AND MEDICAL SCHOOL ENROLLMENTS

In recent years law and medical schools have been deluged by student applicants; minority students are no exception to this trend. Concomitant with the general upsurge in student interest are special efforts by these schools to recruit minorities into law and medicine. While acknowledging the real need for more minority doctors and lawyers, graduate schools of arts and sciences often point to the loss of promising graduate students to these professional fields of study. To assess the quantitative impact of growing minority enrollments in law and medicine, relative to the potential pool of graduate students, recent enrollment figures may be examined. (See Tables A-8 and A-9 in Appendix A for data reporting trends in minority student enrollments in law and medicine.) Presently, minorities (including Asians) represent 7 and 10 percent of total enrollments in law and medical schools, respectively; minority participation has risen at a rapid rate in the past few years.[45]

Law study attracts students from a broad spectrum of discipline backgrounds in undergraduate schools. But medical schools compete directly for a much more limited pool of students with undergraduate degrees in the natural science fields, in which blacks, Chicanos, Puerto Ricans, and American Indians are most underrepresented. In 1973–74, about 3,800 minorities (excluding Asians) were enrolled in medical schools; this can be compared with about 3,300 students enrolled in 154 Ph.D. institutions in the natural sciences, which account for about one-half of the master's and doctoral enrollments in the natural science fields in all graduate schools, as shown in Table 16. It is clear that minorities are much better represented in medical education than in the natural science fields in graduate schools. In general, graduate schools have expressed concern about the effect of the overall student trend toward medicine on the potential pool of natural science graduate students; with respect to the avail-

---

[45] However, first-year minority enrollments in medicine declined in fall 1975. The American Bar Association, *Law Schools and Bar Admission Requirements: A Review of Legal Education in the United States—Fall 1974* (Chicago: American Bar Association, 1975), and American Association of Medical Colleges, *Medical School Admission Requirements, 1975–1976* (Washington, D.C.: American Association of Medical Colleges, 1975).

TABLE 16   Enrollments in Medical Schools and in Natural Science Fields
in Ph.D.-Granting Institutions, by Race and Ethnic Identity, 1973–74

Racial/Ethnic Identity	Enrollments in Medical Schools	Enrollments in Natural Science Fields in Ph.D.-Granting Institutions [a]
Total, all students	50,716	106,227
	(100.0%)	(100.0%)
Total minority	3,761	3,257
	(7.4%)	(3.0%)
Black	3,045	2,118
	(6.0%)	(2.0%)
Hispanic	619	892
	(1.2%)	(0.8%)
American Indian	97	247
	(0.2%)	(0.2%)

[a] Represents approximately one-half of the total graduate enrollments in natural science fields, masters and doctoral programs.

SOURCE: Elaine H. El-Khawas and Joan L. Kinzer, *Enrollment of Minority Graduate Students at Ph.D. Granting Institutions,* Higher Education Panel Reports, No. 19 (Washington, D.C.: American Council on Education, August 1974), and Association of American Medical Colleges, Division of Student Studies, Washington, D.C.

ability of qualified minorities for graduate study in the natural sciences, the impact is much more severe.

THE STATUS OF WOMEN MINORITY STUDENTS

Women presently obtain only 20 percent of all doctorates awarded.[46] There has been extensive discussion of the factors contributing to the overall low participation rate for women in doctoral study, but little research has focused specifically on minority women. It has been suggested, however, that additional cultural factors may intervene to restrict participation of minority women in graduate education—cultural attitudes about childbearing and the *machismo* tradition in Latin cultures are examples of concerns that have been cited. From Table 17, it is observed that the proportion of doctorates earned by women does vary according to racial

[46] Special analysis by NBGE of data from National Research Council, National Academy of Sciences, Doctorate Records File, November 1974 and June 1975.

61

TABLE 17 Proportion of Doctorates Awarded to Men and Women, by Citizenship Status, Race and Ethnic Identity, 1972–74 [a]

Racial/Ethnic Identity	Total (%)	U.S. Native (%)	U.S. Natural- ized (%)	Non-U.S. Citizens (%) Perma- nent Visa	Non-U.S. Citizens (%) Tempo- rary Visa
Black					
Men	75	71	67	92	92
Women	25	29	33	8	8
Chicano, Mexican American, Spanish American					
Men	85	83	73	84	96
Women	15	17	27	16	4
Puerto Rican					
Men	74	74	—	—	—
Women	26	26	—	—	—
American Indian					
Men	79	79	—	—	—
Women	21	21	—	—	—
Oriental					
Men	87	79	78	88	89
Women	13	21	22	12	11
White					
Men	80	80	70	79	89
Women	20	20	30	21	89

[a] Represents a 75 percent sample for 1972–73 and an 89 percent sample for 1973–74 of total doctorates awarded for the 2 years. See Tables 3 and 6 for an explanation of survey coverage.

SOURCE: Special analysis by the NBGE of data from National Research Council, National Academy of Sciences, Doctorate Records File, November 1974 and June 1975.

and ethnic identity and citizenship status. From 1972 to 1974, native-born black and Puerto Rican women received a larger proportion of all doctorates awarded to blacks and Puerto Ricans relative to women of other ethnic and racial groups, where as the proportion of other Spanish American women was slightly lower.[47]

Variations among minority groups in doctoral attainment for men relative to women are modest, and, overall, the figures are quite similar to those for nonminority persons. The most notable difference is the higher

[47] All women (minority and nonminority) are substantially less represented among noncitizens who earn doctorates. This is consistent with the fact that many noncitizens enter the natural science fields, in which few women have chosen to study.

62

TABLE 18 Proportion of Bachelor's Degrees Awarded to Men and Women, by Race and Ethnic Identity, 1973–74

Racial/Ethnic Identity	Bachelor's Degrees Awarded (%)	
	Men	Women
Total, all students	55	45
Nonminority	56	44
Black	43	57
Spanish American	56	44
Asian American	55	45
American Indian	63	37

SOURCE: American Council on Education, Higher Education Panel, preliminary figures, 1975.

proportion of females among black doctorates, reflecting perhaps the historical role of women in the black community. Examination of data on the proportions of men and women awarded bachelor's degrees reveals a somewhat different pattern, as shown in Table 18. While men received 55 percent of the baccalaureates awarded to all students, for blacks the situation was reversed. Black women received a majority (57 percent) of total bachelor's degrees earned by blacks. Surprisingly, women of Spanish American background earned the same proportion of degrees relative to men as did nonminority women. This implies that the commonly assumed impact of male dominance in Latin cultures has not been predominant in influencing educational attainment at this level. On the basis of these figures, it cannot be demonstrated that the *relative* availability of women in the pool of Hispanic persons eligible for graduate study is a constraint on the feasibility of increasing the numbers of Hispanic women in doctoral work.

Perhaps most significant is the fact that differences in the male/female ratios converge and show less variation at the doctoral level than in undergraduate education. This suggests that the social, economic, and cultural factors common to all women exert the greatest influence on educational attainment at the doctoral level rather than cultural elements specific to individual ethnic or racial groups.

The number of minority women earning advanced degrees has risen. Joseph L. McCarthy and Dael Wolfle estimated from their survey of 46 AAU universities that minority women (including Asians) earned 24 percent of all doctorates awarded to minorities from 1969 to 1972 in those schools, but this figure increased to 31 percent during the succeeding 3-year period.[48] Data reported in the National Research Council's *Sum-*

---

[48] Joseph L. McCarthy and Dael Wolfle, "Doctorates Granted to Women and Minority Group Members," *Science,* 189 (12 September 1975), p. 857.

mary Report: Doctorate Recipients from United States Universities indicated that while minority women (U.S. citizens) accounted for 23.5 percent of total doctorates awarded to minorities in 1972–73, their proportion rose to 27 percent the following year.[49] Despite these gains, the absolute number of minority women earning doctoral degrees remains low. In 1973–74, black, Hispanic, and American Indian women represented only 1.4 percent of all doctorates granted that year.[50]

PROSPECTS FOR FUTURE PARTICIPATION

The now famous "benign neglect" phrase has stimulated various individuals and groups to devote considerable time and energy to monitoring the progress of minority groups in various sectors of society.[51] The optimism born of the tensions of the 1960's has been replaced by the realism of the 1970's. The rapid growth of minority participation has leveled off; many fear that newly won gains are tenuous and may easily be lost.[52] Recent evidence pertinent to assessment of minority progress may be cited.

Throughout the 1960's there has been a steady convergence in the proportions of white and black high school graduates enrolling in college. Figures reported by the U.S. Bureau of the Census, shown in Table 19, indicate little difference in college entry rates for black and white 1974 high school graduates. The primary features of this trend have been the decrease in college enrollment by whites (falling 10 percentage points from a peak of 57 percent in 1968), accompanied by a rise in black entrants. Although the data for blacks appear promising, the unexplainably large year-to-year fluctuations in the black participation rates must be considered in interpretation of these figures.[53]

Moreover, findings drawn from a longitudinal study of a national sample of 18,000 high school seniors are inconsistent with those based on the census data reported above for blacks. Table 20 indicates that, while 47 percent of white high school graduates enrolled in college in fall 1972,

[49] National Research Council, Commission on Human Resources, *Summary Report: Doctorate Recipients from United States Universities* (Washington, D.C., National Academy of Sciences, May 1974 and June 1975).

[50] U.S. citizens only. Special analysis by NBGE of data from National Research Council, National Academy of Sciences, Doctorate Records File, June 1975.

[51] Robert B. Hill, "Benign Neglect Revisited: The Illusion of Black Progress" (Paper read at Annual Conference of the National Urban League, July 24, 1973, Washington, D.C.).

[52] Paul Delaney, "Blacks Say Drive to Spur College Enrollment Ends," *The New York Times,* 26 March 1975.

[53] The small number of black persons surveyed introduces the possibility of large errors stemming from sampling variability.

TABLE 19 Percentage of High School Graduates Attending College in October following Graduation, 1964–74

Year	White (%)	Black (%) [a]
1974	47	48
1973	48	33
1972	49	44
1971	54	42
1970	52	44
1969	55	37
1968	57	46
1967	53	42
1966	52	32
1965	52	43
1964	49	39

[a] For the years 1964 to 1969, the figures for blacks are defined as "Negro and Other Races."
SOURCE: U.S. Bureau of the Census, Current Population Reports, Series P-20: "School Enrollment: October 1970," No. 222, "Social and Economic Characteristics of Students: October 1971 (1972, 1973)," Nos. 241, 260, 272 (Washington, D.C.: U.S. Government Printing Office), and "October 1974," No. 278 (Advance Report), February 1975; U.S. Department of Labor, Bureau of Labor Statistics, "Employment of High School Graduates and Dropouts October 1972," Special Labor Force Report 155, in *Monthly Labor Review*, June 1973; and unpublished figures from U.S. Bureau of the Census, 1975.

only 38 percent of black graduates did so. Although the figure reported for whites entering college is similar to that estimated by the Bureau of the Census, substantial inconsistencies exist between the two surveys for black participation. According to the longitudinal study, there were significant differences in 1972 between college enrollment rates for black and white high school graduates, whereas the census data show a more modest disparity.

A further consideration is that many more black youth fail to complete high school than do white students. In 1973, 28 percent of blacks between

TABLE 20 Proportion of 1972 High School Graduates Enrolled in College, October 1972 and October 1973, by Race

Race	Proportion Enrolled in College (%)	
	October 1972	October 1973
Black	38.2	33.8
White	46.7	41.5

SOURCE: Preliminary unpublished figures made available by the National Center for Educational Statistics, from "National Longitudinal Study of the High School Class of 1972."

65

	Enrolled in College (thousands)	
Year	Black	White
1974	814	7,781
1973	684	7,324
1972	727	7,458
1971	680	7,269
1970	522	6,759
1969	492	6,827
1968	434	6,255
1967	370	5,905

SOURCE: U.S. Bureau of the Census, Current Population Reports, Series P-20: "School Enrollment: October 1970," No. 222, "Social and Economic Characteristics of Students: October 1971 (1972, 1973)," Nos. 241, 260, 272 (Washington, D.C.: U.S. Government Printing Office); and "October 1974," No. 278 (Advance Report), February 1975.

the ages of 18 and 21 had dropped out of high school, compared with 14 percent of the whites.[54]

Annual figures on total college enrollments for blacks reported by the U.S. Bureau of the Census have been the subject of considerable controversy and warrant brief comment. The data presented in Table 21 show that, after experiencing a decline the preceding year, black enrollments in college jumped 20 percent in fall 1974, while the corresponding figures for whites rose only 6 percent. However, some observers have disputed the accuracy of these figures, given the large sampling variability in the figures resulting from the small size of the sample of black persons on which the estimates were based.[55] While these data definitely do indicate a general trend of increased black enrollments in recent years, they cannot be used to pinpoint annual enrollment levels.

Other, less optimistic evidence exists. Figures reported in Table 22 indicate the continuation of marked disparities in college attendance according to race and ethnic identity. Although college participation by whites has declined slightly since 1970, enrollment proportions for blacks have been fairly stable, while those for persons of Spanish origin have risen. Nonetheless, college attendance rates for blacks and Hispanic people remain only about two-thirds the level observed for white youth.[56]

[54] U.S. Bureau of the Census, Current Population Reports, Series P-20, No. 272, "Social and Economic Characteristics of Students: October 1973" (Washington, D.C.: U.S. Government Printing Office, 1974), Table 1.

[55] The standard error of the difference from 1973 to 1974 in black enrollments in college is about 60,000.

[56] If the ratio of college students to all high school graduates between the ages of 18 to 21 is calculated, the gap between minority and nonminority persons is narrowed.

TABLE 22 Proportion of Persons 18–21 Years of Age Enrolled in College, by Race and Ethnic Identity

	Proportion Enrolled in College (%)		
Year	Black	White	Spanish
1974	22	32	23
1973	19	33	20
1972	22	35	16
1971	24	36	N/A
1970	21	36	N/A

SOURCE: U.S. Bureau of the Census, Current Population Reports, Series P-20: "School Enrollment: October 1970," No. 222, "Social and Economic Characteristics of Students: October 1971 (1972, 1973)," Nos. 241, 260, 272 (Washington, D.C.: U.S. Government Printing Office), and No. 278 (Advance Report), February 1975.

Following several years of increases, it was reported that the number of black students as a percentage of full-time college freshmen declined in fall 1973 and again in 1974. The figures reported in Table 23 show that the year 1972 appeared to represent a peak in terms of black participation, when blacks comprised 8.7 percent of entering freshmen enrollments; 2 years later, this figure had fallen to 7.4 percent. However, in 1975 the proportion of blacks among entering college freshmen jumped to 9 percent. Interestingly, the largest gain occurred in the university sector, where traditionally blacks have been least likely to enroll; in 1974, blacks comprised 3.4 percent of entering university freshmen but accounted for 5.4 percent the following year.[57]

In sum, there is a general consensus that steady gains in college enrollment of minority students were registered throughout the 1960's until 1972. There is sharp disagreement, however, about the status of minority participation in the past few years. Existing data are erratic and contradictory, and, moreover, the experiences related by individual institutions with respect to minority enrollment since that time have been varied.

Figures for degrees conferred are an important measure of achievement in undergraduate education and serve as a proxy for the pool of potential graduate students. Unfortunately, reliable data on the number of bachelor's degrees earned by minorities have not been available. In the past, estimates for blacks earning baccalaureates have been derived by summing degrees awarded by the traditionally black colleges with various guesses as to the number attained by black students in predominately

[57] Alexander W. Astin, Margo R. King, John M. Light, and Gerald T. Richardson, *The American Freshman: National Norms for Fall 1974* (Los Angeles: Cooperative Institutional Research Program, 1975), p. 41.

TABLE 23   Black Freshmen as a Percentage of Total Freshmen Enrollments in Colleges and Universities, 1966–74 [a]

Year	Black Freshmen as a Percentage of all Freshmen
1975	9.0
1974	7.4
1973	7.8
1972	8.7
1971	6.3
1970	6.2 [b]
1969	6.0
1968	5.8
1967	4.3
1966	5.0

[a] First-time, full-time freshmen.
[b] Original published figure was incorrect; a revised figure was obtained from the Cooperative Institutional Research Program, January 1975.

SOURCE: American Council on Education Research Reports, *National Norms for Entering College Freshmen, Fall 1966–Fall 1972* (Washington, D.C.: American Council on Education), and *The American Freshman: National Norms for Fall 1973, Fall 1974 and Fall 1975* (Los Angeles: Cooperative Institutional Research Program).

white colleges and universities.[58] The number of bachelor's degrees conferred by black colleges rose sharply from 16,000 in 1967 to 25,000 in 1972, but black enrollments in white colleges and universities have shown an even greater expansion.[59] Since over three-fifths of all full-time undergraduate black students attended nonminority 4-year institutions in 1972,[60] it has been thought that a majority of the baccalaureates awarded to blacks would be conferred by these schools. Some observers, however, have questioned the productivity of nonminority colleges in terms of black graduates, lending further uncertainty to estimates of total bachelor's degrees awarded to black students.

In order to obtain more reliable information about baccalaureate attainment, the National Board on Graduate Education together with the Institute for the Study of Educational Policy requested the American

[58] Egerton estimated that 79.5 percent of bachelor's degrees received by blacks in 1969 were awarded by traditionally black institutions, while the Task Force on a Commission on Higher Education for Blacks estimated that in 1970 78 percent of black-earned baccalaureates would come from the black institutions. "Task Force Report on Higher Education for Blacks" (Washington, D.C.: Institute for Services to Education, 1973, unpublished).
[59] Blake, Lambert, and Martin, *op. cit.*, p. 37.
[60] U.S. Department of Health, Education, and Welfare, Office for Civil Rights, *Racial and Ethnic Enrollment Data from Institutions of Higher Education, Fall 1972* (Washington, D.C.: U.S. Government Printing Office, 1975).

TABLE 24 Distribution of Bachelor's Degrees Awarded, Graduate Enrollments in Ph.D.-Granting Institutions, and U.S. Population, by Race and Ethnic Identity

Racial/Ethnic Identity	Bachelor's Degrees, 1973–74 (%)	Graduate Enrollments, Fall 1973 (%) [a]	U.S. Population, 1970 (%)
All Persons	100.0	100.0	100.0
Nonminority	92.3	92.8	83.0
Total minority	7.7[b]	7.2[b]	16.9
Black	5.3	4.4	11.1
Spanish-surnamed	1.2	1.0	4.5
Asian	1.0	1.4	0.9
American Indian	0.3	0.3	0.4

[a] In Ph.D.-granting institutions.
[b] Figures do not add to subtotal because of rounding errors.

SOURCE: American Council on Education, Higher Education Panel, preliminary figures, 1975, and Table 4 in this chapter.

Council on Education to undertake a survey of baccalaureate degrees awarded in 1973–74, by race and ethnic identity. Data were obtained from a stratified sample of all institutions in the United States that confer a bachelor's degree.[61] (Preliminary survey findings are reported in Appendix A, Table A-7.)

The distribution of baccalaureates awarded is contrasted with the racial and ethnic composition of the U.S. population in Table 24. Minorities earned 7.7 percent of all bachelor's degrees conferred in 1973–74. Spanish-surnamed persons appear to have the lowest participation rate relative to their distribution in the population, receiving only 1.2 percent of total bachelor's degrees, while blacks earned about half the number of degrees that would be expected on the basis of population representation.

The figures for blacks are lower than had been previously estimated. Slightly less than one-half of all baccalaureates earned by blacks were conferred by the predominately black colleges, although these schools enroll far fewer than one-half of black students in 4-year institutions. This fact raises serious questions about the effectiveness of nonblack institutions in assisting black students to successfully complete their under-graduate education.[62]

[61] All data reported from this survey represent preliminary estimates; final figures will be published shortly in a forthcoming report of the Higher Education Panel of the American Council on Education.
[62] A number of possibilities are suggested. Black students may experience higher attrition rates relative to white students attending the same (nonminority) institutions, or black students may be enrolling in those institutions where attrition is typically

While much of the preceding evidence suggests a stabilization of minority enrollment at the undergraduate level, it does not shed light on whether this general trend may be extended to minority achievement in graduate education. Separate predictions must be made with respect to future participation at the graduate level.

The availability of minority persons with baccalaureates eligible for consideration for admission to graduate school is a key indicator. These data permit determination of whether graduate schools have succeeded in enrolling minority students in reasonable proportions relative to their availability in the pool of college graduates. As shown in Table 24, black and Spanish-surnamed graduate enrollment proportions appear to be lower than baccalaureate attainment, while Asian participation in advanced study is higher. The differences are not striking, but do suggest that, at least in terms of aggregate numbers, more blacks and Spanish-surnamed persons may be eligible to continue to graduate school than actually enroll.

Sharp increases in doctoral attainment by minorities in the past few years have been reported. Joseph McCarthy and Dael Wolfle found that the number of Ph.D.'s awarded to minorities by institutions that are members of the Association of American Universities had increased 78 percent from the 3-year period 1969–72 to the period 1972–75.[63] Whereas minorities (including persons of Asian origin) had accounted for 3.3 percent of all doctorates in the earlier period, 3 years later minority men and women received 5.8 percent of doctorates.

Comprehensive data showing trends in doctoral attainment are available from the annual Survey of Earned Doctorates, which began including racial and ethnic information in 1972–73. Minority persons (including Orientals) received 11.2 percent of all doctorates in 1972–73; the comparable figure for 1973–74 was 12.6 percent. From Table 25 it is evident that about one-half of this percentage growth resulted from greater Oriental participation and one-half by an increase in black doctorates. Hispanic persons earning doctorates showed only slight growth, while the figures for American Indians remained unchanged.

Further examination of degrees awarded by citizenship status shown in Table 26 indicates that the expansion in black doctorates occurred among native-born persons while the rise in the proportion of Orientals earning

---

greater for all students than in other schools. Alternatively, black students who attend predominately black colleges may be more likely to complete their undergraduate work than are all students (minority and nonminority) in other colleges and universities.

[63] See Appendix A, Table A-5, for detailed figures on doctorates awarded by field for 1969–72 and 1972–75. Fields of study experiencing the highest growth in minority participation were the social sciences, education, and the arts and humanities. The actual numbers, however, remained low.

TABLE 25 Distribution of Doctorates Awarded, by Race and Ethnic Identity, 1972–73 and 1973–74 (U.S. Citizens and Noncitizens)

Racial/Ethnic Identity	Doctorates Awarded	
	1972–73 (%)	1973–74 (%)
Total, all persons	100.0	100.0
White	88.8	87.4
Total minority (including Oriental)	11.2	12.6
Oriental	6.9	7.5
Minority subtotal	4.3	5.1
Black	2.9	3.5
Chicano, Mexican American, Spanish American	0.9	1.0
Puerto Rican	0.1	0.2
American Indian	0.4	0.4

SOURCE: Special analysis by NBGE of data from National Research Council, National Academy of Sciences, Doctorate Records File, December 1974 and June 1975.

doctorates was due to noncitizens with temporary visas. The total number of doctorates earned by persons holding temporary visas grew substantially, lending greater significance to the percentage increase of Oriental noncitizen doctorates.

The distribution of minority doctorates among fields of study did not change appreciably. About 60 percent of black Ph.D.'s earned their degrees in education in both years. The proportion of blacks in the natural science fields rose slightly, although the absolute change was negligible since the overall number of persons in many natural science fields had declined in recent years. The social science fields showed a slight growth in the proportion of blacks earning Ph.D.'s. (See Appendix A, Tables A-1–A-4 and A-10–A-13, for detailed information on doctorates awarded, by race and ethnic identity, sex, citizenship status, and field of study for the years 1972–73 and 1973–74.)

Assessment of trends in doctorate attainment in the near future may be made by comparison of the percentage of doctorates conferred to minority persons in 1973–74 with enrollments in Ph.D.-granting institutions, as presented in Table 27. If current enrollment proportions exceed degrees attained, then prospects for future participation should be favorable, under the assumption that increases in persons entering graduate school should precede expansion in award of doctorates.[64] This expectation is supported only in part by the data. The relative proportions of minority student

[64] Subject, however, to two conditions: First, minority students must be enrolled in doctoral study in contrast to master's programs in proportions similar to those of all students, and second, attrition rates must be similar to those for all students.

71

TABLE 26 Distribution of Doctorates Awarded, by Citizenship Status, Race and Ethnic Identity, 1972–73 and 1973–74 [a]

| Racial/Ethnic Identity | U.S. Citizens (%) | | | | Non-U.S. Citizens (%) | | | |
| | Native-born | | Naturalized | | Permanent Visa | | Temporary Visa | |
	1972–73	1973–74	1972–73	1973–74	1972–73	1973–74	1972–73	1973–74
Black	2.8	3.5	0.9	1.4	2.9	2.7	5.0	4.5
Chicano, Mexican American, Spanish American	0.5	0.6	4.9	4.8	1.2	1.3	3.0	2.8
Puerto Rican	0.2	0.2	0.1	0.1	—	—	—	—
American Indian	0.5	0.5	—	—	—	—	—	—
Oriental	0.6	0.6	15.1	15.8	54.1	54.6	33.7	38.9
Total minority	4.6	5.4	21.0	22.1	58.2	58.6	41.7	46.2
White	95.5	94.6	78.9	78.0	41.8	41.4	58.2	53.8
Total, all persons (Sample N)	100.0 (20,662)	100.0 (24,000)	100.0 (850)	100.0 (960)	100.0 (1,437)	100.0 (1,571)	100.0 (2,047)	100.0 (2,710)

[a] Represents a 75 percent sample for 1972–73 and an 89 percent sample for 1973–74 of total doctorates awarded. See Tables 3 and 6, Chapter 2, for an explanation of survey coverage.

SOURCE: Special analysis by NBGE of data from National Research Council, National Academy of Sciences, Doctorate Records File, December 1974 and June 1975.

72

TABLE 27 Graduate Enrollments in Ph.D.-Granting Institutions, Fall 1973, and Doctorates Awarded, 1973–74, by Race and Ethnic Identity

Racial/Ethnic Identity	Graduate Enrollments in Ph.D. Institutions, Fall 1973 (%) [a]	Doctorates Awarded, 1973–74 (%) [a]
All persons	100.0	100.0
White	92.9	90.8
Total Minority	7.1 [b]	9.1
Black	4.4	3.3
Spanish-surnamed	1.1	1.0
American Indian	0.3	0.5
Asian	1.4	4.3

[a] Includes U.S. citizens and persons holding permanent visas.
[b] Figures do not add to subtotal because of rounding errors.

SOURCE: Appendix A, Tables A-1, A-2, A-3, and A-6.

enrollment and degree attainment are similar. All minority persons comprise 7 percent of enrollments and 9 percent of Ph.D.'s conferred. Black enrollment proportions are higher than degree attainment, while the figures for Spanish-surnamed and American Indian persons show no significant difference. Asian participation follows a different pattern. Asians comprise only 1 percent of total graduate enrollments but receive over 4 percent of doctorates. Their apparent "overrepresentation" in doctoral attainment may stem from a choice of doctoral in preference to master's study or greater persistence in degree attainment. From the data presented, some expansion of black Ph.D.'s in the next few years might be predicted, but no increase could be forecast for Spanish-surnamed or American Indian Ph.D.'s.

As indicated previously, minority Ph.D.'s are typically older than non-minority recipients. This fact has caused some observers to speculate that the very recent expansion of minority enrollments in graduate education may reflect, in part, a one-time phenomenon. The opening up of opportunities for minorities in higher education in the last decade may have encouraged many older persons to return to school for advanced study. Certainly, various federal and private financial aid programs in the late 1960's and early 1970's focused on assisting black college faculty to upgrade their academic credentials. Hence, once the initial inflow of students from this source has been accommodated, then a rather different rate of participation may emerge. Following this line of reasoning, recent trends in doctoral attainment may be inappropriate predictors of the long-run outlook.

In response to indications of a leveling off of minority enrollments in

73

several graduate schools, the National Board on Graduate Education examined first-year graduate minority enrollments to determine if there is a slowdown or decline similar to that suggested for black students at the undergraduate level.[65] A short letter was sent to 66 graduate deans requesting information about first-year minority enrollments (excluding Asians) in master's and doctoral programs for fall 1973 and 1974. Institutions were also asked to indicate changes in the number and academic qualifications of minority applicants. Finally, the graduate deans were encouraged to comment briefly on reasons for any changes observed in application and enrollment trends.

The sample of institutions surveyed was not intended to be representative of all graduate schools, although geographic location and the mix of public and private institutions were considered. All but a few offered doctoral work, and most of the graduate schools known to have major programs to promote minority participation at the graduate level were included in the survey.

Fifty-eight (88 percent) of the institutions surveyed responded to this inquiry, only three of which were unable to provide any information. Fifteen institutions reported data in a form different from that requested, i.e., for total minority enrollments, for a different time period (1972–74), or for only a single year. Most of these schools did, however, offer their impressions of recent enrollment trends despite data inadequacies. Thirty-three graduate schools provided the data as requested.

Overall, the responding institutions reported a slight decline in first-year minority enrollments in graduate study. About one-third of the graduate schools noted enrollment increases, while one-third recorded a decline. While the limitations of the data necessarily preclude extrapolation to a national trend, substantial shifts in the distribution of minority students among schools were observed and merit discussion. Two significant patterns emerged. Graduate schools showing the greatest enrollment increases were located in the southern and border states; most stated that they had recently initiated special efforts to recruit more minority students and to inform students of the opportunities for graduate study at those schools. Other institutions enrolling more minorities had also recently expanded their recruitment or financial support programs. By and large, schools reporting enrollment increases were able to point to specific reasons for that growth. However, several schools with already existing large-scale programs to attract minority students experienced enrollment declines despite those efforts. Most of these schools were uncertain as to the cause of these declines. Some perceived a stabilization of minority enrollments

[65] Lincoln E. Moses, "Report to the Faculty Senate, Spring Quarter, 1975" (Stanford, Calif.: Stanford University, unpublished).

74

nationwide. Several stressed that lack of financial assistance curtailed minority participation, while others commented that opportunities for professional study drew many potential students from graduate school. *Every* institution that had reduced special activities benefiting minority students reported enrollment declines. The availability of qualified minority students did not seem to be a factor in the enrollment declines, since about one-half of the institutions surveyed believed that the qualifications of their minority applicants had improved, while only one university indicated an opposite experience. Whether the effect of observed distributional shifts among schools has resulted in a net increase or a net decrease in minority access nationwide requires further analysis.

In sum, the findings of this survey call into question the validity of the "benign neglect" hypothesis. For whatever reasons, the process has not been set into motion wherein increased minority participation in graduate education can be taken for granted. Increases in minority enrollments are no longer the rule at all institutions.

The U.S. Commission on Civil Rights asked if "the Nation's conscience was now catching up with its laws." [66] A similar question may be asked with respect to minority participation in graduate education. Or is the revolution in minority access to graduate study diminishing, as I. Bruce Hamilton suggests? [67] The evidence presented thus far on this point is equivocal. It remains to a more subjective interpretation of the prospects for future participation, presented in subsequent chapters of this volume, to address this question.

[66] U.S. Commission on Civil Rights, *Twenty Years After Brown: The Shadows of the Past* (Washington, D.C.: U.S. Commission on Civil Rights, June 1974), p. 106.
[67] I. Bruce Hamilton, "Irresistible Force Meets Immovable Object: A Study of American Graduate Schools' Response to the Black Revolution" (Ph.D. dissertation, Stanford University, 1974).

3 Barriers to Participation

To many, attainment of a bachelor's degree signifies that, at last, socio-economic and cultural disparities among persons of various income and racial and ethnic backgrounds are removed. Presumably, for those persons holding bachelor's degrees negative effects of family background, low socioeconomic status, and inadequate educational resources have been overcome and should no longer cause some individuals to be disadvantaged relative to the majority of society. Minority men and women with bachelor's degrees should be able to obtain good-paying jobs and clearly are not candidates for unemployment or welfare.[1] The "culture of poverty" so often attributed to low-income minority persons has been dispelled, and, while an individual with a baccalaureate may not enjoy the advantages of inherited wealth or high social status, that individual certainly will not be disadvantaged. In essence, the graduate has obtained all the basic credentials necessary to succeed in this society according to his or her motivation and individual abilities.

But the situation may assume a somewhat different character if viewed in terms of capacity to pursue graduate education. Are, in fact, all students more or less equal with respect to capability to attend graduate school—apart from motivation and intellectual potential?

[1] The Bureau of Labor Statistics recently projected a growing gap between the availability of jobs requiring college-level education and the number of college graduates through 1985. As a result, many persons will be forced to accept employment below the skill level for which they were trained. See U.S. Department of Labor, Bureau of Labor Statistics, *Occupational Manpower and Training Needs, Revised 1974* (Washington, D.C.: U.S. Government Printing Office, 1975).

It is recognized that individual circumstances may prevent some who desire to attend graduate school from doing so. Financial status, personal obligations, poor undergraduate preparation, and influence of family background may in individual cases prevent talented students from pursuing graduate study. All students, minority and nonminority, share the possibility of these handicaps, but for minority students these barriers intrude more often and more intensely.

We have classified barriers affecting minority participation into four broad groups—financial, educational, psychosocial, and cultural. They are not mutually exclusive; to the contrary, their impacts on minority students are increased by virtue of their interrelation.

FINANCIAL BARRIERS

Some argue that it is inappropriate to regard any person with a bachelor's degree as financially disadvantaged with respect to graduate school attendance. Parental income is not relevant, and the student should be able and willing to borrow in order to finance further education if a stipend or some other form of financial aid is unavailable. While there is movement toward an entitlement concept in undergraduate student finance, no similar sentiment is expressed for graduate education. We believe, however, that attainment of a bachelor's degree does not automatically erase all financial inequalities with respect to capability to pursue graduate education. Inadequate financial resources are not a circumstance limited to minority students alone, but many more minority students come from low-income families relative to nonminority students. Moreover, combined with other factors that act to deter minorities from attending graduate school, financial barriers may have a greater impact on minority participation than for majority students.

We will first review the financial status of minority families and then examine patterns of undergraduate finance for minority *vis-à-vis* nonminority students. Findings from a variety of surveys and analyses are presented in the following section. None of the individual analyses is comprehensive nor entirely satisfactory; for this reason, the findings of several have been presented. Taken together, they provide a consistent and convincing description of differences between the financial situation of minority and nonminority students.

Family financial circumstance clearly influences the amount of money that parents will be able to contribute toward the costs of the student's college education. In 1969 the median family income of minority families was substantially lower than that of white families despite significant gains

TABLE 28   Median Family Income, by Race and Ethnic Identity, 1969

Racial/Ethnic Identity	Median Family Income ($)	Ratio to White Income
All persons	9,590	
White	9,961	1.00
Black	6,067	0.61
Mexican American	6,962	0.70
Puerto Rican	6,165	0.62
American Indian	5,832	0.59

SOURCE: All persons, white, black: U.S. Bureau of the Census, 1970 Census of Population, Vol. I, *Characteristics of the Population*, Section 1, Table 94; Mexican American, Puerto Rican: U.S. Bureau of the Census, *Subject Reports*, Final Report PC(2)-1C, "Persons of Spanish Origin," Table 10; American Indian: U.S. Bureau of the Census, *Subject Reports*, Final Report PC(2)-1F, "American Indians," Table 10.

TABLE 29   Percentage Changes in Median Family Income, by Race

Race	1965–69	1969–73
Black	32.1	−0.2
White	16.2	6.1

SOURCE: U.S. Bureau of the Census, Current Population Reports, Special Studies, Series P-23, No. 48, "The Social and Economic Status of the Black Population in the United States, 1973" (Washington, D.C.: U.S. Government Printing Office, 1974), Table 8.

during the 1960's.[2] Figures given in Table 28 show that black, Puerto Rican, and American Indian incomes were less than two-thirds that of nonminority families, while Mexican American families earned about 70 percent as much as nonminority families.[3]

According to figures presented by the Bureau of the Census, both the absolute and relative disparities between black and white family incomes have widened in recent years. The data presented in Table 29 show that throughout the 1960's the income levels of black families increased more

[2] One exception is the Asian origin population. The median family income for Chinese families was $10,610 in 1969, while for the Japanese population the median family income was $12,515. U.S. Bureau of the Census, Subject Reports, "Japanese, Chinese, and Filipinos in the United States," Final Report PC(2)-1G, 1973.

[3] The influence of disparities in income levels between minority and nonminority families on ability to finance college attendance is compounded by differences in family size. The median number of children under 18 years in white families is 2.3, while the corresponding figures for black and Spanish-heritage families are 2.8 and 2.7. U.S. Bureau of the Census, 1970 Census of Population. Vol. 1, *Characteristics of the Population,* Part 1, "U.S. Summary," Section 2 (Washington, D.C.: U.S. Government Printing Office, 1973), Table 266.

TABLE 30   Parental Income of High School Seniors, by Race, 1972

Gross Family Income ($)	Black (%)	White (%)
<3,000	25.1	3.0
3– 5,999	25.0	8.6
6– 8,999	24.5	20.2
9–11,999	14.3	23.2
12–14,999	5.5	18.1
>15,000	5.7	26.9

SOURCE: U.S. Department of Health, Education, and Welfare, Office of Education, National Longitudinal Studies of the High School Class of 1972, *Tabular Summary of Student Questionnaire Data*, Vol. II (Washington, D.C.: U.S. Government Printing Office, 1974), p. 445.

TABLE 31   Distribution of Estimated Parental Income of Entering Freshmen, Fall 1971

Estimated Parental Income ($)	Black (%)	White (%)
<4,000	24.5	4.0
4– 5,999	19.4	5.9
6– 7,999	15.9	9.4
8– 9,999	11.8	12.6
10–12,999	10.4	18.7
12.5–14,999	6.9	14.7
>15,000	11.0	25.0

SOURCE: Alan E. Bayer, *The Black College Freshman: Characteristics and Recent Trends*, American Council on Education Research Reports, No. 7 (Washington, D.C.: American Council on Education, 1972), p. 39.

rapidly than those of white families, thus narrowing the gap. From 1969 to 1973, however, median black family income fell 0.2 percent, while white family income increased 6.1 percent. By 1974, the ratio of black to white family income had declined to 0.58.[4]

Examination of the family income levels of high school seniors in 1972 reveals different distributions according to racial identity as shown in Table 30. Over one-half of black high school students reported parental incomes under $6,000, compared with 12 percent of white students. While only 6 percent of black students had family incomes above $15,000, more than one-fourth of white students did.

Comparison of the estimated family incomes of entering freshmen (Table 31) with the parental income of high school seniors by race reveals

[4] U.S. Bureau of the Census, Current Population Reports, Special Studies, Series P-23, No. 54, "The Social and Economic Status of the Black Population in the United States, 1974" (Washington, D.C.: U. S. Government Printing Office, 1975), Table 9.

TABLE 32 Planned Sources of Support for College Education, High School Seniors, 1972

Source of Support	Black (%)	White (%)
Parents	66.8	80.4
Savings or summer earnings	76.9	85.2
Earnings while taking courses	55.9	54.2
Other relatives (not parents)	21.5	7.2
College work–study program	53.0	22.3
NDSL program	30.2	9.9
EOG	37.7	7.6
Federal guaranteed student loan	24.9	10.4
Other loan	39.7	25.2
Private scholarship or grant	25.0	21.7
Social security benefits	16.5	7.8
Other	36.7	21.3

SOURCE: U.S. Department of Health, Education, and Welfare, Office of Education, National Longitudinal Study of the High School Class of 1972, *Tabular Summary of Student Questionnaire Data*, Vol. II (Washington, D.C.: U.S. Government Printing Office, 1974), p. 445.

that the distribution of family income for black freshmen is markedly higher than that of black high school seniors. The distribution of family income for white freshmen, however, remains similar to that of white high school seniors. This suggests that financial factors have contributed to differential college entry rates.

Minorities plan to meet their college expenses in different ways than do nonminority students, as illustrated in Table 32. Minority high school seniors planning to continue to college expected to receive parental support less frequently than nonminorities, while they planned to utilize Educational Opportunity Grants (EOG), work–study programs, and loans more often than did white students.

The magnitude of differences in anticipated parental contributions toward the costs of a student's college education is shown in Table 33. The disparities are sizeable; the median expected contribution from black parents is $161, far less than that for white students, $1,145. For Chicanos, the expected contribution is also low, while students from Puerto Rican and Native American families indicated that their parents would contribute only slightly more. About 70 percent of black, Mexican-American, and Puerto Rican students estimated that parents would contribute less than $625 per year toward the costs of their education, while only one-third of white students estimated a similar figure.[5]

[5] College Entrance Examination Board, *College-Bound Seniors, 1974–75* (New York: College Entrance Examination Board, 1975), p. 32.

80

TABLE 33 Expected Parental Contribution Toward Education, High School Seniors, by Race and Ethnic Group, 1974–75

Contribution ($)	American Indian (%)	Black (%)	Mexican American (%)	Puerto Rican (%)	White (%)
< 625	59	77	74	69	33
625–1,199	14	9	11	11	19
1,200–1,799	7	4	5	5	12
1,800–2,399	6	3	3	4	10
2,400–2,999	3	2	1	2	5
3,000–3,599	1	1	1	1	2
> 3,600	10	5	4	9	21
Median contribution	$ 419	$161	$194	$ 258	$1,145
Mean contribution	$1,314	$672	$667	$1,057	$2,523
No. of respondents	2,096	56,730	10,368	4,753	597,704

SOURCE: College Entrance Examination Board, *College-Bound Seniors, 1974–75* (New York: College Entrance Examination Board, 1975), p. 32.

Table 34 indicates that in 1971 black freshmen relied on loans, scholarships, and grants more than did nonblack students in financing college. Not surprisingly, nonblack freshmen indicated parental aid as the most frequent source of financial assistance almost twice as often as did blacks.

More recent data reveal large differences in the proportions of entering college freshmen that were assisted by federal aid programs. Table 35 compares federal sources of support for all full-time freshmen enrolled in fall 1975 with the subset of students in the predominantly black colleges. These data reveal that a higher percentage of freshmen in black colleges relative to freshmen in all institutions received support from each of the

TABLE 34 Major Sources of Support for Black and Nonblack Freshmen [a]

Source of Support	Black (%)	Nonblack (%)
Part-time or summer work	22.6	29.4
Savings from full-time employment	10.2	9.4
Parental or family aid or gifts	31.8	56.0
Scholarships and grants	40.1	18.0
Loans—NDEA/government insured/college	28.3	13.9
Other loans	11.6	5.9

[a] Percentage figures do not add to 100 percent because respondents indicated multiple sources of support.

SOURCE: Alan E. Bayer, *The Black College Freshman: Characteristics and Recent Trends*, American Council on Education Research Reports, No. 7 (Washington, D.C.: American Council on Education, 1972).

TABLE 35   Percentage of Entering Freshmen Receiving Assistance from Federal Student Aid Programs, All Institutions and Predominantly Black Colleges, Fall 1975

	Percentage of Students Receiving Aid	
Assistance Programs	All Institutions	Predominantly Black Colleges
Basic Educational Opportunity Grant	27	76
Supplemental Educational Opportunity Grant	6	24
College Work–Study	12	37
Guaranteed Student Loan	9	11
National Direct Student Loan	10	25

SOURCE: Alexander W. Astin, Margo R. King, and Gerald T. Richardson, *The American Freshman: National Norms for Fall 1975* (Los Angeles: Cooperative Institutional Research Program, 1975), pp. 49, 50.

five federal aid programs cited.[6] The most striking disparity is in Basic Educational Opportunity Grant (BEOG) awards; over three-fourths of black college students obtained BEOG support, compared with one-fourth of all students.

The extensive participation of black college students in these federal programs is corroborated by figures reported in Table 36, which identify recipients according to minority and nonminority status. Minority students received almost one-half of all BEOG and SEOG (Supplementary Educational Opportunity Grant) awards in 1974–75, roughly four times the total enrollment proportion of minorities in colleges. Overall, minority students comprised about one-third of the total number of students assisted through these federal student aid programs. Since eligibility is determined on the basis of financial need, it is evident that the federal commitment to alleviating financial barriers to undergraduate study has benefited the minority population.

Nonetheless, the extent to which federal and other student assistance programs have compensated for disparities in financial circumstance that affect college access remains unclear. The BEOG program did not award the maximum authorized grant of $1,400 until 1975–76 and is limited to

[6] The Basic Educational Opportunity Grant (BEOG) program provides direct grants to full-time and part-time students, awarded on the basis of financial need. Supplemental Educational Opportunity Grant (SEOG) funds are alloted to institutions that, in turn, select aid recipients with "exceptional" financial need. Both the BEOG and SEOG programs are limited to undergraduate students. The College Work–Study (CWS) program provides federal funds to pay 80 percent of the salaries of students. Through the National Direct Student Loan (NDSL) program students may receive low-interest loans from participating institutions. Under the Guaranteed Student Loan (GSL) program, loans are made directly by lending institutions and guaranteed by the federal government.

82

TABLE 36 Percentage of Minority and Nonminority Students Receiving Aid under U.S. Office of Education Assistance Programs, 1974–75

Assistance Programs	No. of Recipients	Percentage of Recipients	
		Minority	Nonminority
Basic Educational Opportunity Grant	543,000	48	52
Supplemental Educational Opportunity Grant	350,000	48	52
College Work–Study	575,000	33	67
Guaranteed Student Loan	669,000	18	82
National Direct Student Loan	749,000	29	71
Total, all programs [a]	1,584,000	34	66

[a] Unduplicated count. Excludes Guaranteed Student Loan Program and includes persons receiving aid under State Scholarship Incentive Grant program.

SOURCE: Frank J. Atelsek and Irene L. Gomberg, *Student Assistance: Participants and Programs, 1974–75*, Higher Education Panel Reports, No. 27 (Washington, D.C.: American Council on Education, 1975), Table 4.

students who entered postsecondary education after April 1973. In 1974–75, the average award to students attending public 2-year institutions was $580, while the average amount for students in private 4-year colleges and universities was $660.[7] These figures may be compared with estimated college costs for 1975 reported by the College Entrance Examination Board, ranging from $2,100 for public 2-year institutions (commuter budget) to $4,400 for private 4-year institutions (resident budget).

The preceding discussion has detailed differences in minority and nonminority family incomes and has suggested that minorities place greater reliance on scholarships, work–study programs, and loans in financing their undergraduate education in contrast to nonminority students, who receive more parental assistance. It has also sketched the importance of federal aid programs to undergraduate minority students. These facts have implications for the minority student's decision whether to continue to graduate school. A number of considerations influence any student's decision to seek an advanced degree. The student's perception of the likely financial and nonpecuniary rewards, stemming from career possibilities available with an advanced degree, must be weighed against the opportunity costs (income that might have been earned while in school), as well as the direct costs of graduate school attendance.

All students face a similar decision, but for many minority students the

[7] Frank J. Atelsek and Irene L. Gomberg, *Student Assistance: Participants and Programs, 1974–75*, Higher Education Panel Reports, no. 27 (Washington, D.C.: American Council on Education, 1975), Table 11.

situation is more difficult. Minorities holding a baccalaureate, in general, have an opportunity to earn an income well above that of their families. Financial security is a more important reason for attending undergraduate school for minority than for nonminority students. Consider then the situation of the minority student who must decide whether to try to attend graduate school. Typically, the student has received less financial support from parents and borrowed more than nonminority college students. Concern about financing has been more characteristic of the minority student. One graduate dean described many potential minority graduate students as "worn out" from efforts to pay for their undergraduate education. Graduate students are ineligible for aid through the BEOG and SEOG programs. The prospect of borrowing additional sums to continue to graduate school is not inviting. Moreover, there are risks. After spending several years in graduate school (perhaps incurring additional debt but certainly not enjoying an extravagant life-style), the student may fail to attain a degree. Even if the student does earn a degree, that student must then face an uncertain job market. Thus, a potential graduate student must decide whether to settle for a baccalaureate degree and seek immediate employment or opt for graduate study with all its attendant risks—academic and financial. For many minority students, the risks may be judged unacceptable, and the financial rewards associated with attainment of an advanced degree may be perceived as inadequate to justify the costs of graduate study.

The role of loans in college student finance has recently come under increasing scrutiny. One issue involves determination of how much debt a student should be expected or allowed to assume in order to finance higher education. At the graduate level two developments are pertinent. First, there has been a sharp drop in fellowship support in recent years, offset primarily by a marked increase in self-support among full-time students in science and engineering. Accordingly, it seems likely that loans will play a larger role in student finance in the future. On the other hand, concern about the high default rate in some sectors of postsecondary education has caused some to consider limiting a student's reliance on loans.[8]

Another factor significant at the graduate level is that individual indebtedness from undergraduate education may be sufficiently high to discourage potential graduate students from undertaking advanced study in the absence of nonloan financial support. Some graduate school administrators have suggested that minority students have assumed a higher debt

---

[8] See David W. Breneman and Shari Collins, "The Special Problems of Graduate Student Loan Finance," unpublished draft prepared for the College Entrance Examination Board, 1975; and Cheryl M. Fields, "Student Groups Seek Limit on Loans," *The Chronicle of Higher Education,* 1 December 1975, p. 9.

burden than nonminority students, thus placing them at a relative disadvantage in financing graduate work. From a survey of nearly 8,000 students who had enrolled in graduate study, Elaine H. El-Khawas and Ann S. Bisconti found that 60 percent of white students who had enrolled for advanced study had not borrowed any money for undergraduate education, while only 35 percent of black students reported no indebtedness.[9] Unfortunately, systematic study of this subject is lacking. Analysis of cumulative debt by race and ethnic group, income level, and cost of institution attended is required for informed consideration of this question.

A second broad consideration in comparing financial need at the graduate level for minority and nonminority students is quite straightforward—how to do it?

Assessment of financial need at the graduate level is conceptually and operationally difficult. Students from both high-income and low-income families may consider themselves to be financially independent of their parents, and, consequently, income differentials among students become negligible, since few have assets or are employed. Most graduate schools do not consider need in the award of financial support, although some do require financial statements from parents for calculation of student need. (Recent trends, however, point to a contrary position wherein extension of the 18-year-old age of majority may undermine the assumption of parental responsibility for support of undergraduate students.)

Apart from determination of the legal obligation of parents in assisting graduate students, another, more elusive consideration arises. There is a fuzzy line between the student who requests financial aid because he or she chooses not to ask for parental assistance in financing graduate study and the student whose family simply does not have the resources to contribute to the student's education. Moreover, while a student may not receive direct financial aid from family, he or she may have been given an automobile, be covered by family medical insurance, receive room and board during vacations, or have general backup financial security in the event of an emergency. These are not uncommon patterns of secondary (although important) assistance for many graduate students, but for the minority student from a low-income family, these "intangibles" may not be available, and, in fact, the student may feel an obligation to contribute to the family's support.

Unfortunately, information on the financial status of all graduate students is deficient and almost nonexistent for minority graduate students. On the basis of limited evidence, some differences may be shown. Table 37

[9] Elaine H. El-Khawas and Ann S. Bisconti, *Five and Ten Years After College Entry,* Vol. 9, No. 1 (Washington, D.C.: American Council on Education, 1974), Table 145.

TABLE 37 Important Sources of Financial Support for Graduate or Professional Study

Source of Support	Arts and Humanities (%)	Natural Sciences (%)	Social Sciences (%)	Law (%)	Medicine (%)	All Fields (%)
Parental or family aid	46	38	47	71	76	49
Spouse's employment	18	23	21	28	23	21
Scholarship or fellowship from school	37	46	43	33	46	36
Other scholarship or fellowship	14	19	21	13	24	16
Loan from school	24	21	30	44	46	25
Loan from other source	17	15	20	31	38	20
Research assistantship	13	41	28	4	13	18
Teaching assistantship	32	47	33	5	8	24
Other university employment	23	20	26	16	17	20
Employment outside university	39	32	40	53	32	38
Personal savings	43	46	47	62	19	47

SOURCE: Leonard L. Baird, *The Graduates: A Report on the Characteristics and Plans of College Seniors* (Princeton, N.J.: Educational Testing Service, 1973), p. 74.

86

TABLE 38 Minimum Level of Financial Support Required to Attend Graduate School, Black and Spanish-speaking Persons, 1973–74

Minimum Support Required	Percent of Students Indicating Support Required	
	Black	Spanish-speaking
No support	3	5
Loan only	5	7
Tuition payment	22	26
Living expenses	2	4
Tuition and living expenses	68	58

SOURCE: Data provided by the Educational Testing Service and Institute for the Study of Educational Policy, January 1975.

indicates the planned sources of support for seniors anticipating graduate study based on a survey of the characteristics and plans of college seniors. From the data presented, it is evident that nearly one-half of all students expected some family assistance. However, analogous to the situation at the undergraduate level, minority students typically will be less able to draw on family resources as a source of support than nonminority students.

From data shown in Table 38, we find that 68 percent of black graduate school aspirants and 58 percent of Spanish-speaking aspirants indicated that they would need financial assistance to cover both tuition and living expenses in order to be able to attend graduate school. While interpretation of these data is necessarily limited because of lack of comparable figures for nonminority persons, they do suggest that minority students perceive finances to be a major consideration in deciding whether to pursue graduate study.

At the graduate level, other considerations are introduced in award of financial aid that relate to the educational implications of various support mechanisms. These are discussed in Chapter 5.

EDUCATIONAL BARRIERS

Award of a bachelor's degree clearly does not certify equality of educational outcome. Colleges and programs within colleges differ as to curricular emphases, degree requirements, and standards for evaluating achievement. Student performance varies within institutions. The academic qualifications of a potential graduate student are a function of the undergraduate school attended, the type and quality of programs pursued within individual institutions, and the performance of students within

87

individual programs. Recognition that the academic preparation of all baccalaureate holders is not equal has special implications for minority participation in graduate education. Graduate schools seek well-qualified, competitive students; "open admissions" philosophies are not accepted. It is important to clarify the factors affecting the educational preparation of minority students to assist graduate schools in identifying promising minority students and to understand the strengths and weaknesses of their educational backgrounds.

The distribution of minorities among undergraduate schools differs from that of nonminority students. Minority students are more likely to enroll in 2-year colleges but less likely to attend universities and private 4-year colleges than are nonminority students.[10] Alexander W. Astin found that black, Spanish, and American Indian freshmen students were "most highly concentrated in the two-year and the least selective four-year institutions."[11] Judy Roizen reported that in 1970 a larger proportion of black undergraduate students attended the lowest-quality 4-year colleges than did white college students."[12] She suggested, moreover, "that blacks are less likely than whites from comparable homes to attend college. Further, able blacks are more likely than whites of comparable ability to attend lower-quality institutions."[13] Uneven distribution among different types of public institutions poses another concern. For example, in 1970–71, blacks, Chicanos, and American Indians represented 7.4 percent of the student body of the University of California and 11.2 percent of the students of the California state colleges and universities, while in 1969 they represented 17.5 percent of community college enrollments.[14]

The high enrollment proportions in 2-year schools have been the subject of extensive debate. Some have suggested that 2-year colleges facilitate

[10] See U.S. Bureau of the Census, Current Population Reports, Special Studies, Series P-23, No. 54, "The Social and Economic Status of the Black Population in the United States, 1974" (Washington, D.C.: U.S. Government Printing Office, July 1975), Table 69; Institute for the Study of Educational Policy, Report No. 1, *Equal Educational Opportunity for Blacks in U.S. Higher Education: An Assessment* (Washington, D.C.: Howard University, 1975), Table 2–22; and Alexander W. Austin, Margo R. King, John M. Light, and Gerald T. Richardson, *The American Freshman: National Norms for Fall 1974* (Los Angeles: Cooperative Institutional Research Program, 1975), p. 41.
[11] Alexander W. Astin, *The Myth of Equal Access in Public Higher Education* (Atlanta: Southern Education Foundation, 1975), p. 5.
[12] Judy Roizen, "Black Students in Higher Education," in *Teachers and Students,* ed. by Martin Trow (New York: McGraw-Hill, 1975), pp. 139–140.
[13] *Ibid.,* p. 153.
[14] Nairobi Research Institute. *Blacks and Public Higher Education in California* (prepared for the Joint Committee on the Master Plan for Higher Education, California Legislature, Sacramento, February 1973).

access and thus serve as a genuine stepping-stone to further undergraduate study. Others contend that 2-year institutions will be an educational "dead end" for many minority students, thereby reducing overall baccalaureate attainment for minority students relative to nonminority students.[15]

For many years the vast majority of black students attended the historically black colleges. In the last decade opportunities for undergraduate study in predominately white colleges and universities have increased for all minority persons, although in 1973–74 almost half of black students earned their baccalaureates from the black colleges.[16] These schools are in a transitional phase. From an externally imposed near monopoly on higher education for black students, they are moving to a more open environment in which they have wider access to resources. But now they must also compete for students and faculty with nonminority schools. Their status warrants discussion.

Some claim that the quality of education available in black colleges is not, on average, as high as that offered in nonblack colleges and universities. Inadequate finance and enforced isolation have left a legacy of limited educational resources in many of these institutions. Moreover, the opening of opportunities in white colleges and universities for black students and faculty has drawn many of the best individuals from these colleges. Others disagree with the above assessment. They point to the fact that black colleges and universities have, in the face of overwhelming obstacles, educated most of the outstanding black leaders, scholars, and professionals. Sixty percent of the 1972–73 black doctorates earned their baccalaureates from a black college.[17] Moreover, these institutions have had considerable success with students who enter college with very poor educational backgrounds. This role, in which they have developed special expertise, is one that other institutions have been less willing or ineffective in performing. And finally, supporters emphasize that, as desegregation has occurred, federal and state assistance to these schools has increased; thus, the academic capabilities and resources of these schools have improved significantly.

---

[15] For students who aspire to a bachelor's degree, Astin contends that enrolling in a 2-year institution reduces the chances of earning a baccalaureate by about 12 percent (taking into account differences in individual characteristics such as initial abilities, motivation, career goals, and study habits). Alexander W. Astin, *The Myth of Equal Access in Public Higher Education* (Atlanta: Southern Education Foundation, 1975), pp. 9–10.

[16] Higher Education Panel, American Council on Education, unpublished preliminary figures, 1975.

[17] Special analysis by NBGE of data from National Research Council, National Academy of Sciences, Doctorate Records File, November 1974.

We offer an additional comment: Black colleges, similar to white colleges, provide a diversity of program offerings and intellectual challenge. Some schools prepare large numbers of students who continue to doctoral work at the most prestigious universities in the country; others provide terminal education for their undergraduate students. Freeman Hrabowski compared the academic performance in graduate school of black students who graduated from white colleges with those who received their undergraduate education at the historically black colleges. His findings showed academic achievement in graduate study as measured by grade point average, retention rate, and graduation rate to be similar for both groups of students.[18] It is important to recognize that characterization of these schools according to a simple stereotype is inappropriate, will necessarily be inaccurate, and may be counterproductive.

In addition to differences *among* institutions in the calibre of academic training offered, the quality of undergraduate education also varies *within* individual institutions. Differences in educational preparation may derive in part from "benevolent tracking" at the undergraduate level, directed to minority students for several reasons. Well-meaning faculty and counselors may direct a deserving student into less rigorous courses or make special exceptions rather than see that student fail or perform poorly. While these actions may stem from good intentions, they can also result from inability, indifference, or lack of willingness of faculty and counselors to devote extra time and energy to assist a student struggling with academic difficulties. For whatever reason, this form of "benevolent tracking" is bound to be counterproductive by creating false perceptions on the part of the student about the level of academic achievement normally required and about his or her own performance.

Numerous Educational Opportunity Programs (EOP) have been initiated in colleges and universities throughout the country, designed to assist educationally disadvantaged students in achieving a college education.[19] The goal of these programs is to increase the college completion rates of students, and one obvious way, unfortunately, may be to direct them into less demanding courses of study. The "talent-searched," "upward-bounded" and "EOP'ed" minority students may simply not receive the same kind of educational preparation as does the majority of graduate aspirants.

It is not possible to evaluate the magnitude and effect of "benevolent tracking" in colleges and universities, and generalization must be avoided.

---

[18] Freeman Alphonsa Hrabowski, "A Comparison of Graduate Academic Performance of Black Students who Graduated from Predominantly Black Colleges and from Predominantly White Colleges" (Ph.D. dissertation, University of Illinois at Urbana–Champaign, 1975).
[19] These programs are not limited to minority students, although minority students predominate.

Many EOP programs—perhaps a majority, perhaps almost all—successfully assist educationally disadvantaged students in strengthening their academic weaknesses and thus do prepare students to proceed to graduate school. The New York State Higher Education Opportunity Program reported that 26.5 percent of their graduates entered graduate and professional schools directly after graduation, no mean accomplishment for students designated as a high-risk population at the undergraduate level.[20] This may be compared with a national figure of 35 percent reported by El-Khawas and Bisconti for persons awarded a baccalaureate in 1970 who enrolled in graduate or professional study the following year.[21]

Unfortunately, the presence of large numbers of minority students in EOP-type programs can have a "spillover" effect on other minority students in college.[22] Phillip E. Jones suggests that the deficit model of education employed in EOP programs by definition assigns "qualities of inferiority to the learning experience of black and other minority students." [23] Faculty may simply perceive all minority students, regardless of academic background and performance, to be educationally disadvantaged and therefore overlook and fail to encourage those students with high academic potential to continue to graduate school. This "Pygmalion effect" has been well documented at other levels of education [24] and causes a serious problem in higher education. William M. Boyd found that:

Many black students feel that professors view them as incompetents. For example, a student said a professor "told me I would probably need special help without knowing me or my abilities." The students feel that this injects self-fulfilling prophecy, if not out-right inequality, into the grading process. Grades tend to be lower than performance would dictate.[25]

Another factor may affect the educational preparation of minority students for graduate school. The target population of EOP-type programs that encourage and assist disadvantaged students to enter and complete undergraduate school may not be the same as the potential pool of minor-

[20] State of New York, "Higher Education Opportunity Program, Final Report 1973–74" (unpublished), p. 31.
[21] Elaine H. El-Khawas and Ann S. Bisconti, op. cit., p. 65.
[22] Ronald W. Lopez and Darryl D. Enos, "Chicanos and Public Higher Education in California" (Report prepared for Joint Committee on the Master Plan for Higher Education, California Legislature, Sacramento, December 1972), pp. 31–33.
[23] Phillip E. Jones, "A Descriptive Analysis of the Administrative Structure of Selected Educational Opportunity Programs" (Ph.D. dissertation, University of Iowa, May 1975), p. 81.
[24] See Robert Rosenthal and Lenore Jacobson, "Teacher Expectation and Pupils' Intellectual Development," in Pygmalion in the Classroom (New York: Holt, Rinehart, and Winston, 1968).
[25] William M. Boyd, II, Desegregating America's Colleges: A Nationwide Survey of Black Students, 1972–73 (New York: Praeger Publishers, 1974), p. 11.

ity graduate students. The so-called nondisadvantaged minority student does not need help entering or merely getting through college, but that student might need special assistance in selecting a program of study suitable for later admission to graduate school and in performing at a high level in that curriculum. Sowell argues that current fashions in recruiting and admissions practices have caused capable black students to be bypassed in favor of less-qualified students. While these "middle-class" students may, in fact, need counseling and guidance, such help is not available to them.[26]

Apart from the quality of the educational preparation of minority students there is also the problem of "automatic tracking." For certain fields of study—chemistry, mathematics, engineering, physics—a student must have completed specific prerequisites in high school. Beatrice Bain and Lucy Sells note that 4 years of high school mathematics are required for entrance into the first-year mathematics course at the University of California at Berkeley, which, in turn, is required of those majoring in all natural science and engineering fields.[27] The long time period necessary to obtain the basic academic prerequisites almost precludes advanced study in most science fields if a student does not make a decision to study a scientific discipline in high school. And clearly, if certain prerequisites are not available in a minority student's high school or if that student is "tracked" into noncollege preparatory curricula, then the chances of entering certain fields in college and graduate school are slim.

Minority students exhibit less confidence in their academic abilities than do nonminority students and, moreover, recognize those academic weaknesses, according to Bayer's survey of entering freshmen.[28] Table 39 compares the perceptions of black and nonblack freshmen regarding academic areas in which they may need special assistance. Mathematics appears to be a major concern for both black and nonblack students; however, more than one-half of black freshmen students indicated a need for special help in this area.

The extent to which minority students with educationally disadvantaged backgrounds "catch up" during their undergraduate college careers is unknown. Yet quantitative and basic writing skills are two areas commonly

[26] This issue is discussed at length in Thomas Sowell, *Black Education: Myths and Tragedies* (New York: David McKay Co., 1972).

[27] Beatrice Bain and Lucy Sells, "Preparatory Education for Women and Minorities," in *Developing Opportunities for Minorities in Graduate Education* (Proceedings of the Conference on Minority Graduate Education at the University of California, Berkeley, May 11 and 12, 1973), pp. 36–39.

[28] Alan E. Bayer, *The Black College Freshman: Characteristics and Recent Trends,* American Council on Education Research Reports, No. 7 (Washington, D.C.: American Council on Education, 1972), p. 43.

TABLE 39   Percentage of Black and Nonblack Freshmen Indicating Need for Special Assistance, by Subject Area, Fall 1971

Subject Area	Percentage Needing Special Assistance	
	Black	Nonblack
English	24	16
Reading	14	10
Mathematics	55	35
Social studies	8	4
Science	29	21
Foreign language	33	20

SOURCE: Alan E. Bayer, *The Black College Freshman: Characteristics and Recent Trends,* American Council on Education Research Reports, No. 7 (Washington, D.C.: American Council on Education, 1972).

cited by graduate school personnel in which academic preparation could be improved for minority graduate students. Many graduate institutions have made special efforts to strengthen the competencies of minority students in these specific areas (and often of nonminority students as well).

Assessment of the quality of academic preparation is central to the admissions process. Minority student admissions has been the subject of extensive debate at all levels of higher education, but it is a more sensitive issue in graduate education where ordinarily admissions are highly competitive. Competition based on merit is the norm, and "picking winners" is the legitimate objective of graduate school admissions.[29] Consequently, student applicants are generally evaluated on the basis of undergraduate grade point average, scores on standardized tests, and, to a lesser extent, letters of recommendation, demonstrated academic ability being a key factor. The basic dilemma is how to identify strong academic potential in students with mediocre records of achievement. Many minority students present lower cumulative grade point averages than nonminority students. However, minority students tend to be "late bloomers," experiencing their most significant social adjustment and academic difficulties in the first 2 years of college.[30]

Ethnic and racial minority students typically receive lower scores on

[29] See B. Alden Thresher, "Uses and Abuses of Scholastic and Achievement Tests," in College Entrance Examination Board, *Barriers to Higher Education* (New York: College Entrance Examination Board, 1971).

[30] See Charles V. Willie and Arline S. McCord, *Black Students at White Colleges* (New York, Praeger Publishers, 1972), and James M. Hedegard, "Experiences of Black College Students at Predominantly White Institutions," in *Black Students in White Schools,* ed. by Edgar G. Epps (Worthington, Ohio: Charles A. Jones Publishing Co., 1972), pp. 43–59.

standardized aptitude tests than do nonminorities. Widespread reliance on these tests serves to exclude disproportionate numbers of minority applicants, and use of tests has generated considerable controversy.

Many contend that standardized tests are inherently biased toward middle-class white values and experience and, therefore, are invalid measures of minority student intellectual potential. Most published research on the predictive validity of tests does suggest, however, that test scores are positively correlated with minority student college grades and thus do not appear to be intrinsically biased against minorities. Nonetheless, doubts remain, since most studies have focused only on academic performance in the first year of college, and little is known about longer-term achievement in succeeding years of college. In light of the difficult academic and social adjustments that minority freshmen must make, some claim that first-year grade average is not a fair measure of academic success. Carmen S. Scott addressed this point in a recent study and found that such tests were not useful for predicting long-term college success for blacks, but were more reliable for Chicano and nonminority students.[31]

Even if tests are inherently neutral evaluation instruments, the effects stemming from their use constitutes a barrier to minority participation. Some argue that such tests reflect past educational and socioeconomic background and, therefore, further penalize the minority student who has not had educational advantages comparable to those available to white students. Other critics state that such tests do not assess intellectual potential, but rather predict academic performance in colleges and universities whose norms are those of mainstream American society, which norms are, in turn, integrated in the tests. This point of view does not argue as much for changes in the tests, but rather for changes in institutional philosophies and practices to recognize greater cultural diversity. Still others may agree with the substance of this statement but dissent from the implications expressed above, especially with respect to graduate and professional education. In their view, cultural distinctions are irrelevant to the acquisition of a specialized body of knowledge and skills as demanded by the standards of high-quality professional performance and scholarship.

At the graduate level, standardized aptitude tests are limited predictors at best for attainment of the Ph.D. degree for all students. Warren W. Willingham reported that these aptitude tests are much less reliable predictors for graduate performance than for undergraduate achievement, with the correlation between tests and Ph.D. attainment ranging from 0.18 to 0.26 (validity coefficients). When test scores and undergraduate

---

[31] See Carmen S. Scott, "Predictive Validity of College Admission Tests for Anglo, Black, and Chicano Students at the Junior Year of Studies," (Ph.D. dissertation, 1975).

grade point averages are combined as a single predictor, the figure increases to 0.40.[32]

Apart from questions concerning their differential impact on minorities, there is broad agreement that tests are only modest predictors of graduate school success for all students. Tests and grade point averages have been used as efficient selection criteria in the absence of more definitive criteria.[33] Organizations that administer these tests caution against mechanical interpretation of test scores.

Scores on the GRE [graduate record examination], as on similar standardized tests, cannot completely represent the potential of any candidate, nor can they alone reflect individuals' chances of long-term success in an academic environment. This is particularly true for ethnic minority and economically disadvantaged students, whose educational experience—in and out of school—has generally differed significantly from that of the majority of students. It should be remembered that the GRE provides measures of developed abilities, reflecting the product of educational and social experience over a long period.[34]

Attrition in graduate school is high and influenced by a host of other factors, such as motivation, persistence, and compatibility with departmental expectations and resources, that are not measured by tests.

Graduate schools have, by and large, recognized that standardized tests represent a major obstacle to minority admissions. Hamilton found that one-half of the graduate schools surveyed normally required students to

[32] Warren W. Willingham, "Predicting Success in Graduate Education," *Science* 183 (January 25, 1974):274.

[33] Willingham also expresses pessimism about the feasibility of improving the predictive validity of tests, since the range of talent is considerably narrower at the graduate level and a variety of other factors may affect graduate school success. He concludes that the most productive approach for improving selection procedures lies instead in development of better definitions of success, i.e., specification of the objectives of graduate training programs in relation to career performance. Robyn M. Dawes argues that current admissions procedures prevent empirical evaluation of the correlation between selection variables and student achievement. See Warren Willingham, *op. cit.,* p. 278, and Robyn M. Dawes, "Graduate Admission Variables and Future Success," Science 187 (February 28, 1975):721–723.

[34] Educational Testing Service, GRE *Guide to the Use of the Graduate Record Examinations, 1974–75* (Princeton: Educational Testing Service, 1974), p. 16. ETS further cautions that "Test scores of educationally disadvantaged students should be considered diagnostic as well as selective and should never be used in isolation. The uncritical use of test scores to forecast individual students' performance is inappropriate, especially so with respect to students handicapped in their earlier educational preparation. For the most valid estimate of these students' potential, consideration should be given to multiple criteria, some of which may go beyond traditional academic measures. In addition to GRE scores and undergraduate record, evidence of motivation, drive, and commitment to education should be assessed, as well as indications of leadership qualities and interest and achievement in the chosen field of study."

95

TABLE 40 Median Educational Attainment (Years of School Completed), By Race and Ethnic Identity, 1970

Racial/Ethnic Identity	Years Completed, Age 25 or Older	Years Completed, Ages 25–34
Black	9.8	12.1
White	12.1	12.6
Chicano	8.1	10.1
Puerto Rican	8.7	9.9
Cuban	10.3	12.2
Asian [a]	12.4	14.0
American Indian[b]	9.8	11.7
All Persons	12.1	12.6

[a] Japanese, Chinese, and Filipino only.
[b] The measures obtained are probably artificially high since the Census counts are biased toward Indians residing in urban areas rather than those living on reservations.

SOURCE: U.S. Bureau of the Census, 1970 Subject Reports: PC(2)-1B, PC(2)-1C, PC(2)-1F, PC(2)-5B.

take the GRE test, but one-half of these schools would waive or modify the requirement for minority students. Of those schools that normally specified a minimum acceptable test score, 97 percent would be willing to waive such a minimum for a minority applicant.[35]

The Educational Pyramid

Low participation rates in graduate education should not be surprising given the substantial attrition rates of minority students throughout the educational system. If educational progress is viewed as successive levels of a pyramid, it is clear that minorities cluster at the bottom but are scarce at the apex—the graduate and professional levels. Successful efforts to increase minority participation in graduate education depend on development of an adequate pool of minorities with undergraduate degrees qualified to proceed to graduate school. This, in turn, must be preceded by increases in the proportion of minority students completing high school and thereby qualified to continue to college. Participation rates of minorities in higher education have been previously documented. It is also necessary to examine the success of minority students as they progress from lower to higher levels in the educational pyramid.

In 1970, the median educational attainment of all persons age 25 or older was 12.1 years of school completed. For minority persons, with the exception of Asians, the level of schooling was from 2 to 4 years lower, as

[35] I. Bruce Hamilton, *Graduate School Programs for Minority/Disadvantaged Students* (Princeton, N.J.: Educational Testing Service, 1973), p. 39.

96

shown in Table 40. However, examination of the educational level of persons 25–34 years old reveals that disparities in years of schooling have shrunk, although the educational levels of Chicanos, Puerto Ricans, and American Indians remain well below the national average. On the other hand, the educational achievement of Asian persons in this age-group clearly surpasses that for the population as a whole.

Despite these gains, high school graduation rates continue to show sharp differences according to ethnic and racial identity. Figures presented in Table 41 indicate that in 1973 one out of every seven white persons who were 20 or 21 years old had not completed high school; however, over one-third of black and more than 40 percent of Spanish-origin persons had not graduated from high school.

Retention rates from first grade to college entrance for minority and nonminority students in the five southwestern states are shown in Figure 1. According to these data, 86 percent of Anglo (white) students graduate from high school, compared with 67 percent of black and 60 percent of Chicano children. Moreover, while 49 percent of Anglo students enter college, less than one-third of blacks and fewer than one-fourth of Mexican Americans continue to college.

The sharpest disparities in rates of progress to higher levels of the educational pyramid occur at college entrance. While 57 percent of Anglo high school graduates enroll in college, fewer than one-half of blacks and about one-third Mexican Americans do so. The implications of these figures depart from the customary view that greater productivity at lower levels of education is an absolute precondition for increased minority participation in higher education. While we do not intend to downgrade the importance of strengthening the productivity of elementary and secondary education, it is suggested here that substantial gains in minority participation in higher education can be achieved now by focusing on the already existing pool of minority high school graduates in providing assistance for entrance to and completion of college.

TABLE 41 Percentage of Persons 20 and 21 Years Old That Are High School Graduates, by Race and Ethnic Identity, 1973

Racial/Ethnic Identity	Percentage High School Graduates
White	85
Black	68
Spanish origin	58

SOURCE: U.S. Bureau of the Census, Current Population Reports, Series P-20, No. 272, *Social and Economic Characteristics of Students: October 1973* (Washington, D.C.: U.S. Government Printing Office, 1974), Table 1.

97

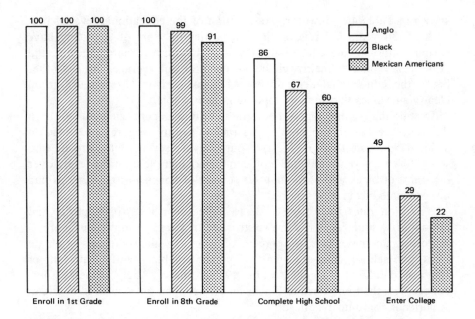

FIGURE 1 Estimated retention rates, first grade to college entry, selected racial/ethnic groups, five southwestern states, 1969. SOURCE: U.S. Commission on Civil Rights, Mexican American Education Study, Report II, The Unfinished Education: Outcomes for Minorities in the Five Southwestern States (Washington, D.C.: U.S. Government Printing Office, October 1971), p. 11.

Although existing data are imperfect, there are indications that attrition is higher for minority students than for the general college student body; accordingly, efforts directed to enrolled undergraduate minority students can be effective in increasing the number of minority students qualified and interested in pursuing advanced study.

A somewhat different, yet key, consideration is the relation between parents' educational level and student achievement. The data in Table 42 compare the educational attainment of the parents of 1972–73 doctorate recipients with that of the general population for black, Hispanic, and white persons. More than one-half of the parents of black and Hispanic Ph.D.'s failed to complete high school, in contrast to only 25 percent of white parents. Overall, the educational levels of black and Hispanic parents are lower than those of whites, although similar proportions of black and white women were college graduates. Hispanic women recorded the lowest college graduation rate.

The parents of doctorate recipients are much better educated than are

98

TABLE 42 Comparison of Educational Levels of Parents of 1972–73 Doctorᵃⁱᵉ Recipients and Total Population, by Race and Ethnic Identity

Racial/Ethnic Identity	Educational Level (%)		
	Less Than 12 Years School	Four Years High School or 1–3 Years College	Four or More Years College
Parents of doctorate recipients (1972–73) [a]			
Black			
Men (N=503)	54	28	17
Women (N=506)	44	37	19
Hispanic [b]			
Men (N=115)	57	22	21
Women (N=118)	60	34	6
White			
Men (N=18,571)	30	38	31
Women (N=18,594)	22	56	22
All persons aged 45–64 years (1970)			
Black			
Men	80	17	3
Women	77	19	4
Hispanic [c]			
Men	75	20	5
Women	77	20	3
White			
Men	52	37	12
Women	48	45	7

[a] U.S. native-born citizens.
[b] Includes persons identified as Chicano, Mexican American, Spanish American, or Puerto Rican.
[c] Includes persons identified as being of Spanish origin or descent.

SOURCE: U.S. Bureau of Census, 1970, *Subject Reports:* PC(2)-1C and PC(2)-1B and 1970 Census of Population, *Characteristics of the Population,* Vol. I, Part 1, United States Summary—Section 1; and special analysis by NBGE of data from National Research Council, National Academy of Sciences, Doctorate Records File, November 1974.

all persons between the ages of 45 and 64 years (the age-group assumed to roughly correspond with the parents of Ph.D. recipients), indicating that Ph.D. recipients typically come from families with above-average educational background. These data suggest that family educational background is a significant influence on student achievement. Doctoral study does not, however, appear to be limited to minority persons from families that might be considered an educational elite, since a majority of black and Hispanic parents did not complete high school.

99

PSYCHOSOCIAL BARRIERS

The cause and effect relation of psychosocial barriers to participation in graduate education eludes systematic measurement. Yet internalized beliefs, motivation, self-confidence, and social perceptions do influence student views of the benefits and expectations of advanced study as well as the quality of the individual student experience.

Minority students aspire to advanced study more frequently than do nonminority students. In 1971, 57 percent of black freshmen planned to earn a graduate or professional degree, while only 42 percent of nonblack freshmen indicated plans for advanced study.[36] In 1971, 59 percent of whites and 68 percent of blacks who had been freshmen in 1966 indicated their intention to obtain an advanced degree at some time.[37]

These figures should not be surprising given the strong ethos in this country concerning the role of education as the means to socioeconomic mobility. According to J. Thomas Parmeter:

Part of the aspiration to go to graduate school for most (black) students is composed of the recognition that they have survived one step and that continuation and more degrees means even greater status and reward.[38]

Or as Samuel Proctor stated:

Education is the corridor through which America's minorities move from rejection, deprivation, and isolation to acceptance, economic sufficiency, and inclusion.[39]

Yet despite high levels of aspiration, minorities have not entered graduate education to the extent that these figures might predict. While 80 percent of black college seniors indicated plans to continue to advanced study, Parmeter reported that only 20 percent planned to attend graduate or professional school in the fall immediately after college graduation.

Influence of family and friends is important. The effect of parents' education on the educational attainment of children has been demonstrated.[40] While general educational aspirations of minorities are very high, minori-

---

[36] Alan E. Bayer, *op. cit.,* p. 41.

[37] Elaine El-Khawas and Ann S. Bisconti, *op. cit.,* Table 13.

[38] J. Thomas Parmeter, "Impact of the Thirteen College Curriculum Program on Graduating Seniors: Motivational and Attitudinal Facts" (Washington, D.C.: Institute for Services to Education, 1974, unpublished).

[39] Samuel Proctor, "Racial Pressures on Urban Institutions," in *The Campus and the Racial Crisis,* ed. by Daniel C. Nichols and Olive Mills (Washington, D.C.: American Council on Education, 1970), p. 43.

[40] National Commission on the Financing of Postsecondary Education, *Financing Postsecondary Education in the United States* (Washington, D.C.: U.S. Government Printing Office, December 1973), pp. 402, 405, 406.

ties may not receive the thoughtful advice and guidance necessary to make those aspirations a reality. Knowledge about the specific educational requirements for high-level career positions and of available opportunities for graduate study is essential, and lack of first-hand information from family and friends hinders a student in making decisions about education. The absence of persons with advanced degrees to serve as appropriate role models for the aspiring student weakens the link between wishful thinking and the practical knowledge needed to formulate a meaningful objective and to take the necessary actions to achieve it.

The importance of appropriate role models for minority youth also underscores the need to increase the ethnic and racial diversity of college and university faculty. Moreover, the presence of minority faculty and staff serves to reassure the potential student that an institution is indeed receptive to the presence of minority students.

For enrolled minority students, aspects of the graduate school environment may present problems. While minority students may express general satisfaction with the quality of the intellectual experience in graduate school, for some the personal experience may be less satisfactory. This is a source of deep concern since student–faculty and informal student relations within a department may exert a strong influence on an individual's academic success. Faculty can provide encouragement, important feedback on student performance, and information about research and employment opportunities. Good peer relations offer informal learning opportunities and social support in dealing with academic and personal difficulties.

Many minorities encounter problems in adjusting to graduate school. These may stem, in part, from the fact that many have come from small undergraduate and ethnically homogeneous institutions.[41] A common complaint is that minority students interact less frequently with faculty and fellow students, especially in social or other informal situations. It is not surprising then that minority students often express feelings of isolation. In a survey of 550 minority graduate students at a leading research university, Birt L. Duncan found that one-half of minority students desired major changes in the way they were treated by their department (while only 10 percent of white students indicated similar sentiments).[42] According to Duncan, minority students believed that faculty regarded them in a condescending manner and that their experience in graduate school had diminished their intellectual confidence and self-esteem. Moreover, two-thirds of minority students reported that they often observed discrimination against minority students, although only 4 percent of white students and

[41] Preliminary data from The Ford Foundation's midpoint evaluation of their minority Ph.D. fellowship program.
[42] Birt L. Duncan, "Minority Students: No Longer Separate But Still Not Equal," in *Scholar in the Making,* ed. by Joseph Katz *et al.* (forthcoming).

faculty perceived less favorable treatment of minorities.[43] Another study of minority graduate students at a major private university reported that over four-fifths of the students were satisfied with the institution's intellectual climate; however, almost one-half found the university's sensitivity to ethnic concerns to be unsatisfactory, while slightly more than 20 percent considered it satisfactory.[44]

Another concern is that in an atmosphere where there are few minority students or faculty, there may be a tendency to regard a minority student as the spokesman for a particular racial or ethnic group. One black graduate student complained that students and faculty:

kept coming up to me, as though I was a famous person, to inquire as to what the black community thinks? . . . to have to spend half of one's time in a graduate seminar just letting people know you're not Paul Robeson, W. E. B. DuBois, and Malcolm X all rolled into one takes a lot of time, and it wears one out, intellectually as well as physically.[45]

Another form of this type of perception may cause minority students to:

believe that they are 'used' by departments for information about, or access to, minority community members without sufficient involvement in or influence on the nature and direction of the research.[46]

This situation may also cause the minority student to become involved in various nonacademic activities directly related to his or her minority status as, for example, the minority representative on departmental or university committees or *de facto* counselor for younger minority students. Such demands may become excessive and detract from time and energy needed for academic studies.[47]

The issues characterizing a broad spectrum of minority concerns can be summed up as a feeling of "second-class" citizenship.[48]

Many minority students think that the advising they receive is quite inadequate. Where student interest relates to minority concerns, advice is seen as condescending.

[43] *Ibid.*

[44] Stanford University, *The Minority Report: A Review of Minority Student Concerns in the Graduate and Professional Schools* (Stanford, Calif.: Stanford University, September 1974), pp. 6, 7.

[45] John H. Bracey, Jr., "The Graduate School Experience: A Black Student Viewpoint," *The Graduate Journal* VIII (1971): 448.

[46] Stanford University, *op. cit.*, p. 3.

[47] This circumstance is especially serious with respect to young minority faculty. See William Moore, Jr., and Lonnie H. Wagstaff, *Black Educators in White Colleges* (San Francisco: Jossey-Bass, 1974).

[48] Rudolph O. de la Garza, "A Chicano View of Graduate Education: Where We Are and Where We Should Be," in *Proceedings of the Fourteenth Annual Meeting, Council of Graduate Schools in the United States,* Phoenix, Arizona, December 4–6, 1974, pp. 77–83.

Others believe that their faculty assume them to be less prepared and qualified, before knowing what their actual capabilities are. Faculty approach them on the assumption that they are less qualified, often despite objective criteria which demonstrate preparation as adequate as the non-minority students.[49]

Whether or not these perceptions are entirely accurate should not be the central issue; the fact is, they do exist for many students. And their existence cannot but fail to affect the educational experience of those students.

CULTURAL BARRIERS

Minority group cultures are not cognates of the majority white culture in this society. In recent years cultural pluralism has become more visible, and the concept of the "melting pot" has been increasingly questioned.[50] The term "culturally disadvantaged" is often heard in reference to minority group participation in education. It implies a cultural deficit; if certain things are done to compensate for the lacks in the minority culture in order to "make over" minority persons in the image of mainstream American culture, then everything will be set right.[51] The educational problems of many minority persons will largely vanish.

Strong objections to this view have been voiced. Designation of "cultural disadvantage" may be based on *difference* but, nonetheless, implies *inferiority*. Being "disadvantaged" refers to those cultural and environmental deficiencies that would be detrimental to an individual's performance in education regardless of ethnic or racial status. Low socioeconomic status, family environment, and limited exposure to cultural and intellectual resources could properly be considered indications of a disadvantaged situation. While these may be associated with minority group status for various reasons, they should not be construed as arising from that group's culture *per se*.

Some cultural differences clearly do cause minorities in certain circumstances to be at a disadvantage relative to majority persons. Language is obvious. The child who does not understand English is severely handicapped in school. It has been suggested that the Mexican-American culture

[49] Stanford University, *op. cit.*, p. 4.

[50] At the undergraduate level, numerous colleges specifically focused on the special concerns and problems of individual minority groups have been established. See Laurence Hall, *New Colleges for New Students* (San Francisco: Jossey-Bass, 1974), pp. 102–176, for description of several new institutions directed to encouraging cultural and racial diversity in higher education.

[51] See Thomas P. Carter, *Mexican Americans in School: A History of Educational Neglect* (New York: College Entrance Examination Board, 1970), pp. 36–38.

TABLE 43   Age at First Marriage, By Race and Ethnic Identity, 1970

Group	Persons 14–79 Years Old	
	Men	Women
White	23.5	20.8
Black	23.1	20.2
Spanish origin	23.3	20.4

SOURCE: U.S. Bureau of Census, 1970 Census of Population, Subject Reports, Final Report PC(2)-1C, "Persons of Spanish Origin" (Washington, D.C.: U.S. Government Printing Office, 1973), Tables 1 and 8.

places a higher value on interpersonal relations and is more susceptible to fatalistic views of life than is the Anglo-white culture, wherein individualism and career success are dominant values. Similarly, Indian children have been characterized as not valuing autonomy and individual success in the same way as do the majority of Americans. While certain cultural differences are real, it is important to avoid stereotypes, and, unfortunately, stereotypes have often led teachers and employers to respond to minority persons in ways that assume inferiority. In graduate education some of the most obvious barriers deriving from cultural differences presumably have dropped away—language difficulties, for example.

The influence of cultural patterns of early marriage on the educational attainment of women warrants examination, since household and childcare responsibilities may bar further education. The situation of Spanish women, in particular, has been of special concern in view of the *machismo* tradition in Latin culture. Interestingly, the figures shown in Table 43 do not indicate large differences in age at first marriage among the white, black, and Spanish-origin populations. Although women from every ethnic and racial background typically marry at an earlier age than do men, the experience of Spanish women resembles that of nonminority women. Moreover, the educational level of Spanish-origin women is very similar to that of Spanish men.[52] In fact, the ratio of women to men in baccalaureate attainment is about equal for both Spanish American and nonminority persons.[53]

There is yet another dimension to the relation between cultural distinc-

[52] In 1970, the median number of years of school completed by males of Spanish origin 14 years or over was 10.1, while the corresponding figure for women was 9.9. U.S. Bureau of the Census, Census of the Population: 1970, Vol. I, *Characteristics of the Population,* Part 1, "United States Summary," Section 2 (Washington, D.C.: U.S. Government Printing Office, 1973), Table 199.

[53] See Table 16.

tions and educational attainment. Some minority persons feel they must, in essence, relinquish their cultural identity if they wish to succeed in American society in terms of education, employment, and so on, or choose to remain close to their cultural heritage and community and thus not attain the socioeconomic and educational status of majority Americans.[54] Integrating or maintaining ethnic identity in one's education and employment presents a problem for some minority students, especally Chicanos and Native Americans. One graduate student of Mexican-American heritage described his dilemma:

> The change came gradually but early. When I was beginning grade school, I noted to myself the fact that the classroom environment was so different in its styles and assumptions from my own family environment that survival would essentially entail a choice between both worlds. When I became a student, I was literally "remade." Neither I nor my teachers considered anything I had known before as relevant. I had to forget most of what my culture had provided, because to remember it was a disadvantage.[55]

The legitimacy of approaching one's intellectual study and professional goals from an ethnic perspective is also a source of disagreement. The vocal debate about "black studies" and nationalistic programs, their intellectual foundation, and the modes used to implement such programs have perhaps obscured more thoughtful discussion of broadening discipline coverages and approaches. The logic of a "black physics" is unrealistic, but sociological methods and theories applied to certain problems affecting the black population or the literary contributions of American Indian writers deserve consideration.

For the minority student who enters graduate school to acquire professional expertise that may be applied to resolution of problems in his or her ethnic community, conflicts can emerge.[56] The expectations of this student, often grounded in a strong ethnic consciousness, may differ from the academic and professional concerns of faculty in graduate departments.

[54] See Barre Tolkien, "Worldview, the University Establishment, and Cultural Annihilation" (Paper presented at University of Washington, 1974), and U.S. Congress, Senate, *Toward Equal Educational Opportunity: The Report of the Select Committee on Equal Educational Opportunity* (Washington, D.C.: U.S. Government Printing Office, December 31, 1972), pp. 284–285.

[55] Richard Rodriguez, "On Becoming a Chicano," *Saturday Review,* 8 February 1975, pp. 46–47.

[56] See Henry J. Casso, "Higher Education and the Mexican American," in *Economic and Educational Perspectives of the Mexican American* (New York: The Weatherhead Foundation, forthcoming), and Jack Forbes, "The Needs and Problems of Native American Students," in *Developing Opportunities for Minorities in Graduate Education* (Proceedings of the Conference on Minority Graduate Education, University of California, Berkeley, May 11 and 12, 1973).

The research interests of the students may lie outside the realm of traditional faculty definitions of what constitutes scholarly inquiry.[57]

The central problem in graduate student research focuses on the question: Do minority students have the flexibility and encouragement to research what they want to research? . . . the answer varies from department to department, depending on departmental views of what constitutes legitimate research, whether there are minority faculty teaching in the department and whether there is encouragement to seek funds to support such research.

Many students believe that their true research efforts are curtailed by departmental restraints and by lack of encouragement and support from faculty; further, many students feel that research on minority communities is regarded by definition as second-rate research.[58]

[57] Part of this incompatibility may perhaps be avoided by providing better information to an applicant concerning the resources and expectations for research in specific departments, thus enabling a student to select a department that will be supportive of his research interests. See the discussion of this subject in Chapter 5.

[58] Stanford University, *op. cit.*, p. 3.

4 Present Context of Graduate Education and Impact on Minority Participation

Clearly the present is not regarded as the best of all possible worlds for higher education, especially when contrasted with the expansionary decade of the sixties. For black, Hispanic, and Native American persons who made great strides toward the goal of full participation in all aspects of American society during the last 20 years, the path toward equality is now beset with a new array of forces affecting society in general and higher education in particular. These have special meaning to minority groups. We cannot speak of minority group concerns as if they can be dealt with in a vacuum. In today's climate of slowed growth and diminished resources, there is energetic competition on the part of institutions and individuals for moneys and employment opportunities. The current educational aspirations of minorities might have been more easily satisfied 10 years ago, when enrollments were expanding, federal aid to higher education generous, and the labor market for all college-educated personnel vigorous. To restate what is almost a truism—new groups and new programs can more easily enter and claim a share of an expanding, prosperous system than one that is fixed and assailed by competing demands. An understanding of the present context of higher education as it influences minority group participation in graduate education is essential to consideration of constructive action.

Myriad financial difficulties have dominated the higher education headlines for the last few years. Institutions have experienced declines in federal funds received; graduate student support has fallen from a high of 51,446 federal fellowship and traineeship awards in 1968 to 18,472 in

1974.[1] Federal expenditures for research in colleges and universities have levelled off, and a number of special support programs such as the National Science Foundation Science Development Program have been terminated. State appropriations for higher education have also stabilized in terms of constant-dollar per-student expenditures at the university level, concomitant with drops in foundation and private gifts impelled by the discouraging economic outlook in this country. While revenue growth has slowed, higher education, a labor-intensive activity with productivity difficulties, has experienced severe cost pressures.[2]

What, then, does this mean in terms of effects on minority group participation? First, there is simply less student aid money available for all students, not just minority students who on an average require more financial support to attend graduate school. In the 1960's, when student support was plentiful, it was easier to allocate resources to support minority students. Now minority students are aspiring to graduate study in larger numbers than ever before but must compete for limited aid funds. Moreover, recruitment activities and supportive services impose additional costs on institutions that are already financially pressed. Simply put, choice among priorities is more difficult today because there is a fixed pool of financial resources and increasing financial demands upon institutions.

The women's movement in this country, which emerged as a powerful force following the civil rights movement of the early 1960's, has deflected attention from the situation of blacks, Chicanos, Puerto Ricans, and American Indians. While women's and minority groups are seeking similar broad objectives and together have bolstered public concern about civil rights issues, nonetheless they are also frequently forced to compete for student aid, faculty positions, and other employment opportunities, as well as public visibility and support. Often the individual needs and concerns of the two groups have been naively merged. Distinctions must be drawn. Women are not a numerical minority and do not suffer the same kinds of "disadvantage" as do minority groups, for women do graduate from high school at the same rates as men, receive better grades than men throughout high school and college, and score well on standardized tests.[3]

[1] Figures exclude graduate students supported by National Institutes of Health/ Alcohol, Drug Abuse, and Mental Health Administration (NIH/ADAMHA). The majority of students supported in FY 1974 are terminal master's degree candidates in professional programs. See Federal Interagency Committee on Education, *Report on Federal Predoctoral Student Support,* Part 1 (Washington D.C.: U.S. Government Printing Office, 1970), and *Report on Federal Predoctoral Student Support* (forthcoming).

[2] For discussion of this issue, see National Board on Graduate Education, *Federal Policy Alternatives Toward Graduate Education* (Washington, D.C.: National Academy of Sciences, January 1974).

[3] See Carnegie Commission on Higher Education, *Opportunities for Women in Higher Education* (New York: McGraw-Hill, 1973), pp. 35–79.

A major challenge for women is to destroy the typical image of the "women's role" that inhibits aspirations and confidence in intellectual and leadership abilities, as well as society's expectations of their performance. While minority groups, too, must remove societal stereotypes about abilities and performance, they must also face a host of socioeconomic barriers and prejudice. The women's movement must seek ways to release and encourage developed potential; minorities must strive to develop the potential of individuals as well as ensure opportunities to utilize their capabilities. It is not surprising, then, that because of their numerical strength and the availability of heretofore underutilized talents and skills, women have been able to marshal a greater wealth of creative and financial resources in support of their movement. Disadvantaged minority groups with smaller numerical constituencies possess less power in absolute terms; moreover, their efforts are diffused over a broader range of issues pertaining to advancement to equality. It is unfortunate, perhaps, that the civil rights movement embraces two important causes that often are placed in the position of having to compete with each other for resources, employment opportunities, and public concern.

There are developments favorable to minority concerns in higher education. The surge of interest in nontraditional programs that offer education at new times and new places to meet the needs of a broader spectrum of students, innovative modes of learning, and creative curricula and discipline content can encourage participation. Since many minority students must continue to work while in school or desire to enter programs "relevant" to their interests, nontraditional education offers real opportunities. Moreover, it has been reported that students and institutions show the greatest interest in development of these new forms of education at the graduate level.[4] Professionally oriented master's programs for persons wishing to upgrade or renew their occupational skills are at the forefront of these trends. At least one graduate institution has established a number of graduate degree programs directed to the needs and interests of minority groups.

While admissions to many graduate schools remains highly competitive, many emerging institutions, which initiated programs in the 1960's and have not attained a "critical mass," are seeking students to maintain or expand their enrollments. This will be more significant as forecast declines in undergraduate enrollments, projected to begin in the early 1980's, diminish the pool of potential graduate students. Thus, faced with a situation of excess capacity, schools may seek to broaden their recruitment efforts and provide programs to attract a wider spectrum of students.

[4] David P. Gardner and Joseph Zelan, "A Strategy for Change in Higher Education: The Extended University of the University of California" (Paper prepared for Conference on Future Structures of Postsecondary Education, OECD, Paris, France, June 26–29, 1973).

The several developments cited above will clearly influence the progress of minority participation, although the complexity of and uncertainties associated with these trends preclude precise analysis of their effects. There are, however, three issues with the potential to exert a more direct impact. First, the overall decline in the labor market for persons holding advanced degrees has led many to question the wisdom of increasing access to graduate study. The second issue stems from the implications of affirmative action regulations for higher education employment, and the third pertains to the legality of activities designed to assist minority students. These are discussed in the following sections.

THE LABOR MARKET FOR ADVANCED-DEGREE HOLDERS

Reductions in federal support for graduate students have been justified in large part by the belief that the availability of highly educated persons is generally adequate to meet national manpower needs. Moreover, projected declines in the number of openings for new faculty in colleges and universities are a source of serious concern. In light of these developments the obvious question arises: Why encourage large numbers of students to pursue doctoral study in the face of employment prospects that are pessimistic in the academic sector and ambiguous, at best, in the nonacademic market?

In an earlier report, NBGE expressed "unease with simplistic references to a Ph.D. 'glut' " and associated policies that fail to recognize the limitations of manpower forecasting. Of special significance is the probability "that shortages within certain disciplines may coexist with surpluses in others." [5] Graduates in fields that are oriented toward academic employment will encounter a difficult job market, while the outlook for disciplines that emphasize professional applications or possess the flexibility for nonacademic alternatives will be more favorable. Newly emerging manpower requirements—expertise in energy R&D, for example—will also affect the character of the employment situation for highly educated persons. Interestingly, few minority persons have enrolled in disciplines such as the arts and humanities, which are among those with the most depressed job market. [6] On the other hand, only a small number of minority students have entered professionally oriented fields such as economics and engineering, which have broad employment potential.

Many perceive the concentration of black and Mexican-American students in education to be problematic in light of a general decline in demand

[5] National Board on Graduate Education, *Doctorate Manpower Forecasts and Policy* (Washington, D.C.: National Academy of Sciences, November 1973), pp. 9, 15.
[6] Hispanic students enrolled in Romance languages and area studies are an exception to this general pattern.

for graduates in that field. Evaluation of this contention leads to yet another question: Will the labor market experience of minority persons earning advanced degrees differ from that of nonminorities, and, if so, why? Two possibilities are suggested.

First, a demand for highly educated minority persons may be generated by institutions and agencies that serve minority communities. With respect to the field of education, greater involvement of the minority population in shaping and administering elementary and secondary education requires more qualified professionals. The disproportionately low representation of minority administrators and teachers in school systems with high minority enrollments has been the subject of frequent criticism.[7] Another stimulus to the need for minority educators comes from bilingual–bicultural programs mandated by the federal government and individual states. At the college level, minority faculty wishing to update their credentials will constitute a major source of doctoral students in the education disciplines.

Apart from education, there are several fields in which a substantial share of employment opportunities may derive from minority-related manpower needs. Professional training in law and medicine is a clear-cut illustration. In addition, other disciplines, such as economics, psychology, and the health sciences, may have applications specific to minority concerns. For example, the National Institute of Mental Health has declared that the training of more minority researchers and other professionals is integral to its capability to provide appropriate mental health services to minority communities.

A second factor that may distinguish the labor market experience of minority doctorates from that of nonminorities is the impact of affirmative action regulations. One of the most controversial issues is whether minority persons now enjoy an advantage in obtaining employment. In a 1970 survey of 785 black Ph.D.'s, Kent G. Mommsen reported that they had received an average of three to four offers of other positions or inquiries about availability in the previous year and that a median raise of $6,000 would be required in order for the respondents to consider changing positions.[8] Mommsen concluded that during a time believed to

---

[7] See U.S. Commission on Civil Rights, *Toward Quality Education for Mexican Americans,* Mexican American Education Study, Report VI (Washington, D.C.: U.S. Government Printing Office, February 1974); Thomas P. Carter, *Mexican Americans in School: A History of Educational Neglect* (New York: College Entrance Examination Board, 1970); Special Subcommittee on Indian Education, *Indian Education: A National Tragedy—A National Challenge,* Report of the Committee on Labor and Public Welfare, U.S. Senate (Washington, D.C.: U.S. Government Printing Office, 1969).

[8] See Kent G. Mommsen, "Black Ph.D.'s in the Academic Marketplace," *Journal of Higher Education* XLV, No. 4 (April 1974), pp. 253–266.

have a general "oversupply" of doctorates, the demand for minority Ph.D.'s was high. Lester claimed that compliance pressures from the federal government have created a special market for black faculty wherein they receive salary offers higher than those made to white Ph.D.'s with equivalent or better qualifications.[9] According to Sowell, the antidiscrimination laws of the 1960's have created a financial premium for qualified black academics, although salary differentials between minority and nonminority groups are small.[10] Others, however, dispute the claim that affirmative action and the low supply of minority Ph.D.'s have operated to confer an absolute employment advantage for qualified minorities. Marcus Alexis contends that salary differentials are inadequate indices of the actual employment status of faculty; rather, teaching load, institutional prestige, and research and library facilities are the major considerations.[11] William Moore and Lonnie H. Wagstaff stated that "the demand of white institutions for black scholars is more myth than reality." [12] They also expressed concern that minority scholars will be prevented from devoting time comparable to that given by white academics to advancement of their professional careers, especially in research. Their minority status can impose excessive responsibilities for committee work and other activities dealing with minority students, as well as requests to serve as a liaison to the black community. Moreover, Moore and Wagstaff questioned the sincerity of employers that may hire minorities for positions that do not offer genuine career opportunities.

Clearly, colleges and universities have expressed deep concern about the size of the pool of minority Ph.D.'s available for employment as faculty, and this concern has been the explicit stimulus in some institutions for implementation of efforts to increase minority participation in doctoral study. At the same time, however, colleges and universities have been adamant about their intention to select the individual whom they believe to be best qualified for a particular position, irrespective of race or ethnic identity. While affirmative action may result in informing a broader range of potential candidates of the availability of openings and in bringing more minority applicants to the attention of institutions, this is very different from saying that a minority person will be given a preference in an employ-

---

[9] Richard A. Lester, *Antibias Regulations of Universities* (New York: McGraw-Hill, 1974), p. 47.

[10] See Thomas Sowell, *Affirmative Action Reconsidered: Was It Necessary in Academia?* (Washington, D.C.: American Enterprise Institute for Public Policy Research, December 1975).

[11] See Marcus Alexis, "The Case for Affirmative Action in Higher Education" (Testimony submitted to U.S. Department of Labor, Hearings on Executive Order No. 11246, October 8, 1975).

[12] William Moore, Jr., and Lonnie H. Wagstaff, *Black Educators in White Colleges* (San Francisco: Jossey-Bass, 1974), p. 41.

ment decision. Current evidence of an affirmative action-induced demand is not persuasive insofar as being used as the sole rationale for encouraging minority students to pursue doctoral study despite a generally pessimistic academic market.

Our response to the question posed initially, Is it sensible to encourage minority students to enter advanced study in light of uncertain employment prospects?, is "yes," with certain caveats. Careful counseling to inform potential students of realistic career opportunities is essential—for all students, not just minorities. Moreover, we believe that some employment openings for minority students with training in certain disciplines, primarily those with a professional orientation, may arise from the manpower needs of the minority community. The field of education is one example. Third, affirmative-action efforts will definitely benefit minority persons in expanding their representation in the pool of applicants considered for employment; however, we are uncertain about the effect of ethnic and racial identity on selection of the individual to be hired at the doctoral level.[13] We are also concerned about a working environment that may disadvantage the minority scholar in academic achievement (such as excessive nonacademic responsibilities). A final consideration to be emphasized is that even geometric increases in hiring minority persons with advanced degrees as faculty or in business and industry will effect only small changes in the racial composition of the total work force in the near future.

IMPLICATIONS OF AFFIRMATIVE ACTION IN HIGHER EDUCATION

Few minority men and women hold academic positions in colleges and universities. Alan E. Bayer reported that in 1972–73 only 0.9 percent of university faculty were black and even smaller proportions were Mexican Americans, Puerto Ricans, or American Indians.[14] The 1975 Ladd–Lipset survey of U.S. faculty members indicated that blacks represented about 2 percent of the faculty of major research universities and that "that proportion has remained basically the same over the last decade."[15] Moreover, according to Ladd and Lipset, "blacks are no more heavily represented in the young faculty groups than in the older, and they

[13] Ethnic and racial status probably *will* influence decisions concerning faculty appointments in ethnic studies or administrative and support personnel to work directly with minority students.

[14] A higher proportion of faculty in 4-year institutions was reported, but these figures include the predominately black colleges. Alan E. Bayer, *Teaching Faculty in Academe: 1972–73*, Research Reports, Vol. 8, No. 2 (Washington, D.C.: American Council on Education, August 1973), p. 31.

[15] Everett C. Ladd, Jr. and Seymour M. Lipset, "Professors' Religious and Ethnic Backgrounds," *Chronicle of Higher Education*, No. 2 (September 22, 1975):2.

remain clustered at the less prestigious schools." [16] These figures reflect the paucity of highly educated minorities that arose from limited educational opportunities and of indifference and reluctance of colleges and universities to employ minorities in the past. Today, however, there is general recognition of the importance of expanding career opportunities for minority persons in higher education institutions. A variety of social, moral, and educational tenets sustains this objective. There is a national need for minority faculty and a derivative need for minority persons with doctoral degrees.

Need, however, is not synonymous with demand. On the one hand, the leveling off and projected declines in higher education enrollments have created a situation wherein there will be few openings for new faculty. Traditionally, about one-half of new Ph.D.'s have accepted academic appointments each year. Currently, however, an imbalance between the number of doctorates awarded relative to available positions in colleges and universities exists in many fields. On the other hand, the lack of minority representation on faculties is a fundamental concern, stimulated in part by federal civil rights efforts. Two major federal thrusts have generated a need (but not necessarily employment demand) to expand the pool of minority Ph.D.'s.

One stimulus arises from a suit brought against the Department of Health, Education, and Welfare alleging failure to fulfill its enforcement responsibilities under Title VI of the Civil Rights Act of 1964, which forbids racial discrimination in institutions receiving federal assistance. In *Adams* v. *Richardson* it was charged that several states continued to maintain segregated systems of higher education in violation of Title VI. As a consequence of this action, in 1973 ten southern and border states were ordered by the Court of Appeals for the District of Columbia to submit comprehensive plans for desegregation of their systems of higher education. Desegregation of faculties in both the traditionally black and traditionally white public higher education institutions was one component. Whatever the specific procedures used to achieve compliance under the state desegregation plans, the expansion of qualified black faculty (presumably with Ph.D.'s) is essential. Exchange of faculty between historically black and historically white colleges is encouraged as one means of promoting desegregation; however, the effect of faculty transfers should not be to integrate faculties in certain institutions at the expense of diminishing the quality or size of faculties in other (primarily black) institutions. At present, the small number of black advanced-degree holders precludes meaningful integration of college faculties in these states.

The second development affecting the outlook for academic employment

16 *Ibid.*

114

of minorities stems from affirmative action responsibilities specified by the Office for Civil Rights (OCR) of the Department of Health, Education, and Welfare to implement Executive Order 11246.[17] An institution subject to the provisions of the executive order must agree to:

not discriminate against any employee or applicant for employment because of race, color, religion, sex, or national origin. The contractor will take affirmative action to ensure that applicants are employed, and that employees are treated during employment, without regard to their race, color, religion, sex, or national origin.[18]

A key provision of the *Higher Education Guidelines* developed by OCR requires the institution to:

determine whether women and minorities are "under-utilized" in its employee work force, and, if that is the case, to develop as a part of its affirmative action program specific goals and timetables designed to overcome that underutilization. Underutilization is defined in the regulations as "having fewer women or minorities in a particular job than would reasonably be expected by their availability." [19]

Considerable debate and confusion have surrounded development of goals and timetables that are required by regulations implementing the executive order.[20] Lacking accurate data, utilization analysis has been on extremely shaky grounds. It has been made more difficult by ambiguities in the methodology and fundamental debates about its conceptual basis. Consideration of goals and timetables in this section centers on two important questions: first, what is the relation between employment targets and the current pool of minority doctorates? Second, what are the implications of

[17] Amended by Executive Order 11375. Obligations under the Executive order apply to higher education institutions that hold federal contracts, approximately 1,000 colleges and universities.

[18] Executive Order 11246, as amended.

[19] U.S. Department of Health, Education, and Welfare, Office of the Secretary, Office for Civil Rights, *Higher Education Guidelines* (Washington, D.C.: USDHEW, October 1972), p. 3.

[20] Controversy has characterized civil rights enforcement efforts in higher education since their inception. Colleges and universities have expressed fears about potentially harmful federal intrusion into areas of traditional faculty autonomy. Universities also point to compliance requirements that they believe to be arbitrary, inconsistent, and excessive—as well as costly. The enforcement agencies, in turn, question higher education's sincerity and commitment in identifying and changing institutional practices that may be sources of bias against women and minorities. Civil rights groups charge both universities and the federal enforcement agencies with failure in carrying out their responsibilities to ensure equal opportunity. The general public is confused by a combination of misinterpretation, rhetoric, accusation, and personal opinion. It is beyond the intent and scope of this discussion to attempt to assess the performance of the various organizations, agencies, and institutions involved in affirmative-action concerns.

these plans for the responsibilities of institutions and government in the production of minority Ph.D.'s?

In order to obtain the information required to respond to these questions, NBGE surveyed the 46 U.S. member institutions of the Association of American Universities (AAU), generally regarded as comprising the leading research universities in this country. (See Appendix B for survey instrument.) In the survey, institutions were asked to specify their affirmative-action employment targets for minority faculty in tenure-track positions for a 3-year period. Separate figures for individual minority groups were requested, but an institution was permitted to define the particular discipline, school, college, or other unit for which data were available. Institutions were also asked to indicate whether noncitizens were included in their figures and to describe the methods used to calculate their projected hiring targets. Forty-three out of 46 institutions responded to the survey, although several were unable to provide data because they did not have a current affirmative-action plan. Only 29 institutions had numerical goals, although others did have institutional plans that did not specify employment targets.

A not unexpected, yet significant, survey finding was the diversity of responses—in attitudes, perceptions, methodologies, and goals—to affirmative-action requirements.[21] The particular approach used by an institution in undertaking utilization analysis and setting goals and timetables strongly influences the resulting affirmative-action employment targets. For this reason, it is useful to describe the concepts and methods adopted by institutions before discussing the numerical results of the survey.

There is basic disagreement among institutions and others as to the meaning of goals. A committee of the American Association of University Professors interpreted federal requirements for establishment of goals to mean that:

What is asked for . . . is not a "quota" of women or blacks, but simply a forecast of what a department or college would expect to occur given the *non*discriminatory use of proper appointment standards and recruitment practices—with the expectation that where the forecast turns out to be wide of the mark as to what

---

[21] Inconsistencies and ambiguities in guidance provided to institutions by federal enforcement agencies have been the major cause of this confusion. Recently, however, both the Department of Health, Education, and Welfare and the Department of Labor have taken steps to remedy the situation. In August 1975, OCR published a "Format for Development of an Affirmative Action Plan by Institutions of Higher Education," intended to provide detailed clarification for application of affirmative action requirements. The Department of Labor held informal fact-finding hearings in fall 1975 to review implementation of the executive order and in January 1976 announced a five-point program to help expand employment opportunities for minorities and women in higher education.

116

actually happens, the institution will at once make proper inquiry as to why that was so.[22]

The Office for Civil Rights clarified its position:

Goals are good faith estimates of the expected numerical results which will flow from specific affirmative actions taken by a college or university to eliminate and/or counteract factors in the university's employment process which have contributed to underutilization of minorities and women. . . . They are not rigid and inflexible quotas which must be met. Nor should a university strive to achieve goals as ends in themselves.[23]

Although no sanctions are applied if an institution fails to achieve its goals, a few universities, nonetheless, perceived affirmative-action employment targets as synonymous with quotas and thus antithetical to their beliefs. One private institution declared:

We believe . . . that the setting of numerical goals cannot be differentiated from the establishment of quotas for recruitment, which is antithetical to the basic philosophy of the law itself and to the basic policy which any university which seeks excellence must follow: the recruitment of faculty on the basis of their individual ability.

One profound objection to the principle of goals and timetables involves the presumption of a deficiency in the employment of minorities if the individual institutional employment proportions do not match some specified national figures for the availability of qualified minorities. Since the actual numbers of minority persons included in the required analyses are very small, it is impossible to demonstrate statistically the significance of differences between numbers actually employed and numbers that should be employed. Instead, it may be that disparities are due simply to chance rather than reflecting a systematic pattern of underemployment of minorities. In testimony presented to the Department of Labor, William Bowen emphasized that:

Even if it were possible, somehow or other, to obtain perfect availability data a failure to satisfy the kind of exact proportional representation test invoked here need *not* imply that there has been discrimination or that there is "underutilization" in any normative sense. . . . Simply because of the presence of random factors, we should expect that sometimes there will be relatively more members of a particular group employed than could be suggested even by perfect availability data and sometimes relatively fewer members. And the smaller the hiring unit in

[22] American Association of University Professors, "Affirmative Action in Higher Education: A Report by the Council on Discrimination," *AAUP Bulletin,* Summer 1973, p. 178.
[23] Department of Health, Education, and Welfare, Office for Civil Rights, "Memorandum to College and University Presidents," December 1974, p. 4.

question and the smaller the minority group, the greater the importance of random factors.[24]

Bowen contends that attainment of perfect utilization is unrealistic and, moreover, may cause an excessive preoccupation with numbers rather than "good-faith" efforts to ensure equality of employment opportunity. There is no easy answer to this conceptual dilemma. While it is feasible to perform statistically meaningful utilization analysis on a national or, in some instances, an institutional basis, hiring decisions are usually determined at the level of an individual department or other relatively small unit.

One point, however, on which institutions appear to be unanimous is that affirmative action as implemented by these universities should not mean the lowering of standards for faculty qualifications in order to eliminate discrimination against minorities. The American Association of University Professors Committee declared that:

> the further improvement of quality in higher education and the elimination of discrimination due to race or sex are not at odds with each other, but at one. What is sought in the idea of affirmative action is essentially the revision of standards and practices to assure that institutions are in fact drawing from the largest marketplace of human resources in staffing their faculties, and a critical review of appointment and advancement criteria to insure that they do not inadvertently foreclose consideration of the best qualified persons by untested presuppositions which operate to exclude women and minorities.[25]

In a "Memorandum" issued in December 1974, Peter Holmes, Director of OCR, reiterated that:

> Colleges and universities are entitled to select the most qualified candidate, without regard to race, sex, or ethnicity, for any position. The college or university, not the federal government, is to say what constitutes qualification for any particular position.[26]

Several institutions explicitly declared that "reverse discrimination" is not permitted and that they always strive to select the most highly qualified person regardless of race, sex, or national origin.

There are also differing interpretations of the methodology to be used in calculation of goals and timetables. Opinions are mixed as to who should be classified as minorities for purposes of affirmative action;

---

[24] William G. Bowen, "Affirmative Action: Purposes, Concepts, Methodologies" (Unpublished testimony presented before the Department of Labor, Fact Finding Hearings on Executive Order 11246, as amended, September 30, 1975), p. 9.

[25] American Association of University Professors, *op. cit.*, p. 178.

[26] Department of Health, Education, and Welfare, Office for Civil Rights, "Memorandum to College and University Presidents," December 1974, p. 2.

institutions differed in enumeration of the affected classes. The *Higher Education Guidelines,* formulated by the OCR, state that:

the *affirmative action* requirements of determining underutilization, setting goals and timetables . . . were designed to further employment opportunity for women and minorities. Minorities are defined by the Department of Labor as Negroes, Spanish-surnamed, American Indians, and Orientals.[27]

In responding to the NBGE survey, several institutions did not include one or more of the principal minority groups, either because current estimates indicated that a particular group was not underutilized (Asians) or because a specific group was not represented in the institution's geographic region.

Institutions that provided numerical targets also differed in their opinions as to whether data should be reported for individual ethnic and racial categories. Most combined all groups into one category. Many did so because of the absence of availability data or because they considered formulation of goals for the smaller minority groups to be unworkable. A large public university did not separate minority faculty by race because it feared negative consequences. The university stated that it:

does not separate ethnic and racial minorities into specific categories. It is felt that that might have an adverse effect on the purpose of affirmative action by creating a situation where one race must compete with another for a designated slot, rather than using goals as a means of encouraging affirmative action.

An obvious problem, however, in combining minority data into a single group for the purposes of utilization analyses is that the situation of the individual minority groups may be obscured. Differences in availability or in hiring practices for a specific group cannot be detected from aggregated data since disparities in the size of the various minority groups— blacks *vis-à-vis* Native Americans, for example—frustrate accurate interpretation. According to a recent clarification by OCR:

A single goal for minorities for each job is acceptable, unless through the university's evaluation it is determined that one minority is underutilized in a substantially disparate manner to other minority groups in which case separate goals and timetables for such minority groups may be required individually.[28]

Similar ambiguities exist with respect to consideration of citizenship status. Determination of citizenship categories to be included—U.S. citizens or both U.S. citizens and noncitizens—depended on institutional percep-

[27] U.S. Department of Health, Education and Welfare, Office of the Secretary, Office for Civil Rights, *Higher Education Guidelines* (Washington, D.C.: USDHEW, October 1972), p. 2.
[28] Department of Health, Education, and Welfare, Office for Civil Rights, "Format for Development of an Affirmative Action Plan by Institutions of Higher Education," *Federal Register,* 40, No. 165 (August 25, 1975):37066.

tions of the purposes of affirmative action goals. While a few universities focused on native-born U.S. citizens, another university declared that:

For the purposes of meeting affirmative action goals, a minority person's citizenship is not a factor—the individual is still counted as being a black, a Spanish-surnamed, or an Oriental.

Respondents not only differed in their perceptions of what the regulations require, but they also held opposing views on what those requirements should be. One institution noted that:

all of our minority figures reflect the fact that they are American citizens. We feel that the inclusion of foreign faculty members in our affirmative action figures obscures the problem of the American minority person.

Slightly more than one-half of the institutions formulated numerical targets limited to U.S. citizens, while the others did not distinguish between U.S. citizen and noncitizen minorities.

As discussed earlier in this report, we believe that specification of citizenship status and delineation of the individual minority groups are necessary in order to portray accurately the circumstance of U.S. minorities. For example, in 1973–74 Orientals obtained over 60 percent of total doctorates awarded to minority persons in this country, and 87 percent of the Orientals were noncitizens; thus, the exclusion or inclusion of Asians or noncitizens in calculation of availability data has an enormous effect on the resulting figures.[29]

Divergent views also exist on the appropriate discipline or organizational unit within institutions for utilization analysis. The OCR *Guidelines* explicitly require some disaggregation in order to avoid a situation wherein the efforts of a few departments might overshadow inactivity of others. While some universities designated individual departments as the units for analyses, others stated that the small number of faculty in many departments or a projected low rate of faculty turnover precluded establishment of departmental goals.

The small size of some minority groups (as a proportion of the total U.S. population), even if they were not underrepresented in the available pool of qualified applicants, makes utilization analysis on a departmental basis impractical. For example, American Indians represent between 0.3 percent and 0.4 percent of the U.S. population. Even assuming that they are fully represented in the pool of available doctorates, a department would have to employ 333–400 faculty members before parity in employment would indicate that a single faculty member should be a Native American. Many schools have developed goals for clusters of departments,

[29] Special analysis by NBGE of data from National Research Council, National Academy of Sciences, *Doctorate Records File*, June 1975.

for schools, or for entire colleges in order to attain meaningful figures. In its study of institutional and federal policies toward affirmative action, the Carnegie Council on Policy Studies in Higher Education concluded that:

Efforts at "fine-tuning" by the federal government can lead to ludicrous results and be quite counterproductive. The smaller the unit controlled (for example, the department of classics) and the smaller the disadvantaged group (for example, Native Americans), the less likelihood an institution's plan will call for any change.[30]

Institutions also differed in their classification of faculty positions. The NBGE survey specified tenure-track academic faculty for which a doctorate degree is normally required. Positions for which a first-professional or master's degree is appropriate were to be excluded. However, some institutions included academic positions that were not tenure-track, such as instructors. Some observers have expressed concern that minorities may be disproportionately represented in nontenure-track relative to other faculty ranks.[31] While only a few institutions reported ethnic and racial composition by individual faculty ranks in this survey, these universities reported that between 20 and 50 percent of minority faculty held instructor positions. These proportions are above the national norm according to Bayer's data, which showed that instructor positions comprise less than 9 percent of total faculty ranks in universities nationwide.[32]

In a study of affirmative action regulations, Richard Lester contended that goals and timetables should not apply to the hiring of tenured faculty. He claims that the precise discipline specialties and level of scholarship demanded of persons suitable for tenured positions in leading universities preclude meaningful calculation of the pool of qualified candidates.[33]

There is also the practical problem of determining availability at the time an older faculty member was hired. As one institution explained:

Even accurate current availability data cannot be used as a standard for identifying areas of underrepresentation of minorities within departments. The present faculty of a department were hired in past years out of earlier availability pools which differ from those which now exist . . . current availability data cannot be used for the critique of poor hiring practices, nor as a certain basis for establishing future hiring goals.

The Carnegie Council recommended in its report, *Making Affirmative Action Work in Higher Education,* that goals and timetables be limited to entry-level positions, although existing OCR guidelines do not make this

[30] Carnegie Council on Policy Studies in Higher Education, *Making Affirmative Action Work in Higher Education* (San Francisco: Jossey-Bass, 1975), p. 8.
[31] Also in part-time positions. See, for example, Moore and Wagstaff, *op. cit.,* pp. 40–71.
[32] Bayer, *op. cit.,* p. 23.
[33] See Lester, *op. cit.,* pp. 28–29.

distinction. This issue may become effectively moot for institutions that plan to seek persons for nontenured positions only; thus, recent availability data are suitable.[34] Several universities indicated that nearly all hiring will be in the nontenured ranks in order to retain flexibility in faculty composition in future years.

Apart from debate over the conceptual and methodological basis for development of goals and timetables, universities cited two key problems that frustrated efforts to carry out affirmative action requirements: lack of satisfactory availability data and difficulties in predicting future openings for faculty positions.

The absence of accurate, comprehensive data on the number of minority persons with suitable qualifications and, therefore, presumably eligible for employment as higher education faculty has been a major problem. While Bureau of the Census data are appropriately used for nonacademic staff occupational categories, comparable detailed information has not been available for advanced-degree holders. Most institutions queried in our survey requested individual departments to estimate the availability of minorities in their respective disciplines. Information developed by professional associations was frequently suggested as a resource (although most disciplines do not have accurate counts of minority Ph.D.'s). An institution might identify other sources, such as surveys by Fred E. Crossland, James W. Bryant, and others, which, unfortunately, are limited, out-of-date, and rough estimates at best.[35] In its publications, OCR noted a variety of sources for information on the availability of minorities, none of which was comprehensive nor complete.[36] Some institutions appeared to use no availability data at all but chose, rather, to use a rule of thumb in setting targets such as one minority hire per department during a specified time period. Other institutions adjusted department estimates according to the university's employment experience as a whole, while some gathered new data that they believed to be pertinent for the individual institution. Still others set goals based on their own anticipated production of minority Ph.D.'s. *No institution* used comprehensive, accurate availability data, because such data did not exist.

More recently, however, information on the number of doctorates awarded annually by race and ethnic identity has been made available by the National Academy of Sciences, beginning with the year 1972–73. (See Appendix A, Tables A-1–A-4 and A-10–A-13.) The use of these data

[34] Then concern will shift to review of salary and promotion policies.
[35] James W. Bryant, *A Survey of Black American Doctorates,* (New York: The Ford Foundation, 1970), and Fred E. Crossland, "Graduate Education and Black Americans," The Ford Foundation, November 25, 1968, unpublished.
[36] U.S. Department of Health, Education, and Welfare, Office for Civil Rights, *Availability Data: Minorities and Women* (Washington, D.C.: USDHEW, June 1973).

should greatly enhance the accuracy of utilization analysis and facilitate the establishment of realistic employment goals. However, comparable figures for degrees conferred at the master's level and in several professional fields still do not exist. In recognition of this problem, the Department of Labor and Department of Health, Education, and Welfare recently agreed to:

work with public and private agencies to develop improved data on minority and female availability for academic and other professional employment and to make such improved data readily accessible to these institutions.[37]

The second problem cited by institutions is the lack of predictability of faculty openings in the future. The recent stabilization of higher education enrollments and projected declines in the 1980's will preclude expansion of college and university faculties. In a system where the only openings result from deaths, retirements, and a limited amount of faculty mobility, the total number of openings will be relatively small. Complicated by the financial exigencies of many universities and reinforced further by state budget problems and national economic trends, many institutions are caught in budgetary uncertainties and some are facing hiring freezes. Most institutions assumed a "no-growth" model of faculty hiring, which many regarded as essentially speculative, being dependent on faculty resignations, retirements, and deaths.

This circumstance has led many to conclude that specification of ultimate goals that represent some form of ideal parity to be impractical, since an extremely long period of time would be needed to attain such goals. In addressing this point, OCR determined that interim goals could be:

established for three year periods unless special circumstances, such as the expectancy of high turnover and significant availability warrant the establishment of shorter term interim goals.[38]

The preceding discussion has illustrated the wide variation in methods and philosophies adopted by universities in calculation of goals and timetables. In view of the lack of accurate availability data, methodological difficulties and ambiguities in federal directives, these differences are not surprising and, furthermore, are indicators of the confusion that has generally characterized the affirmative-action process.

Moreover, these same problems have also contributed to concern that

[37] U.S. Department of Labor, Office of Information, "5-Point EEO Program for Higher Education Announced by Secretaries of Labor and HEW," Attachment A (news release), January 2, 1976, p. 5.
[38] Department of Health, Education, and Welfare, Office for Civil Rights, "Format for Development of an Affirmative Action plan by Institutions of Higher Education," *Federal Register,* 40, No. 165 (August 25, 1975):37066.

TABLE 44   Estimated Annual Employment Targets for Minority Faculty in AAU Institutions by Minority and Citizenship Status

Estimated Annual Hires/Institution	U.S. Citizens		U.S. Citizens and Noncitizens	
	All Minorities (Including Asians)	All Minorities (Excluding Asians)	All Minorities (Including Asians)	All Minorities (Excluding Asians)
Low estimated annual hires	2.0	1.4	0.4	1.0
High estimated annual hires	36.0	6.3	37.7	20.7
Mean estimated annual hires	14.9	3.3	12.5	8.5
Number of institutions	13	2	10	4
Mean number of current minority faculty/institution	66.5	33.0	85.7	38.3
Ratio: Annual hires/current faculty	0.23	0.10	0.15	0.22

NOTE: Survey responses were not comparable among institutions. Current utilization and projected appointments are inflated because many institutions included positions that normally do not require a doctorate degree. However, these data may also underestimate minority Ph.D. participation, since one institution reported data for minority men only and five institutions did not include figures for professional schools that may have employed some Ph.D. faculty. Overall, the data appear to overestimate goals for minority faculty holding a doctorate degree.

the aggregate of individual institutional employment goals is far larger than the number of minorities qualified to enter such positions. This point was underscored by the Secretary of the Department of Health, Education, and Welfare in testimony presented before the House Subcommittee on Equal Opportunities: "If you add up all the people that institutions have pledged to hire in the country they greatly exceed the available supply." [39]

A question was posed at the outset of this chapter: "What is the relation between the supply of qualified minorities and institutional hiring goals?" A definitive answer to the question is impracticable for the above reasons; however, the numerical results of the NBGE survey of AAU institutions do offer some insights. Projected targets for employment of new minority faculty are shown in Table 44.

[39] Committee on Education and Labor, Subcommittee on Equal Opportunities, U.S. House of Representatives, *Oversight Hearings on Federal Enforcement of Equal Opportunity Laws*, September 23, 24, 30, 1975 (Washington, D.C.: U.S. Government Printing Office, 1975), p. 90.

124

Four categories are specified: (1) all minorities including Asians, U.S. citizens only; (2) all minorities excluding Asians, U.S. citizens only; (3) all minorities including Asians, U.S. citizens and noncitizens; and (4) all minorities excluding Asians, U.S. citizens and noncitizens. Since institutions defined various time periods in their affirmative-action plans, we have converted the hiring goals to an annual basis. The low and high estimates are given, together with the mean value for the number of institutions in each category and ratio of new hires to current faculty.

The numerical range in institutional targets is sizeable, from a low of less than one hire to a high of 38 projected hires per year. The employment goals are larger for institutions that included Asians in their figures, but no significant difference was observed between institutions that included or excluded noncitizens. Over three-fourths of the institutions specified targets that included Asians.[40]

Most universities had rather optimistic goals in light of the numbers of minority faculty currently employed. The ratios of estimated annual employment targets to current minority faculty as shown in Table 44 vary from 0.10 to 0.23, indicating that these institutions plan to double their current number of minority faculty in 4 to 10 years.

According to the NBGE survey, the average institutional projected goal ranges from 12 to 15 new hires per year (including Asians). This may be compared with an annual average of 23 minority doctorates conferred by each AAU institution reported by Joseph McCarthy and Dael Wolfle.[41] Although these figures appear to suggest that the employment targets for AAU institutions are reasonable relative to the numbers conferred by those schools, they exclude the many institutions that employ but do not produce Ph.D.'s as well as nonacademic employers that may seek to hire minority individuals.

There is another more fundamental consideration that bears on the relation between supply and demand. The affirmative-action process as formulated by the Department of Labor is by definition a static concept. Universities must set goals and timetables only insofar as the employment composition of their faculty does not reflect the ethnic and racial composition of the pool of persons qualified for faculty positions. Utilization analysis and the setting of goals and timetables aim only toward establishing an equilibrium. There is no explicit objective that mandates an increase in minority faculty to some absolute level. The static nature of utilization analysis is illustrated in Table 45, which shows the current numbers of black faculty in several departments in one large public university, together

---

[40] Sixteen institutions combined all minorities into a single group; six schools distinguished Asians from other minorities.
[41] See Appendix A, Table A-5.

TABLE 45 Utilization Analysis, Goals, and Timetables for Black Faculty in Selected Departments in One Public Research University

Unit	Total Faculty (Head Count)	Black Faculty (Head Count)	Proportion of Blacks in Unit	Availability	Hires to Parity	Department Goal [a]	Department Timetable [b]
Biological Sciences							
Bacteriology	9	0	0	0.0033	+0.02		
Inst. in biology	1	0	0	0.0000	+0.00		
Botany	15	1	0.0667	0.0000	−1.00		
Medical physics	8	0	0	0.0028	+0.02		
Paleontology	7	0	0	0.0082	+0.05		
Physical education	48	1	0.0208	0.0154	−0.27		
Physiology—anatomy	13	0	0	0.0030	+0.03		
Mus. Vet. Zoo.	3	0	0	0.0109	+0.03		
Biochemistry	16	0	0	0.0028	+0.04		
Molecular biology	12	0	0	0.0034	+0.04		
Zoology	26	0	0	0.0109	+0.28		
Professional schools—social sciences							
Public policy	7	0	0	0.0150	+0.10		
Business administration	52	0	0	0.0096	+0.49		
Criminology	10	0	0	0.0208	+0.20		
Journalism	5	0	0	0.0000	+0.00		
Social welfare	14	0	0	0.0991	+1.38	+1.38	
Education	44	4	0.0909	0.0217	−3.05		10 NT 29 AF
Librarianship	10	0	0	0.0189	+0.18		

Humanities

Art: History	12	0	0.0085	+0.10
Italian	6	0	0.0065	+0.03
Linguistics	11	0	0.0129	+0.14
Near East. Lang.	11	0	0.0160	+0.17
Philosophy	19	0	0.0000	+0.00
Rhetoric	15	0	0.0000	+0.00
Scandinavian	5	0	0.0065	+0.03
Slavic Lang.	9	0	0.0065	+0.05
SSEALL	6	0	0.0065	+0.03
Spanish and Portuguese	12	0	0.0105	+0.12
Classics	16	0	0.0000	+0.00
English	71	0	0.0045	+0.31
French	12	0	0.0087	+0.10
German	17	0	0.0156	+0.26
Oriental Lang.	11	0	0.0065	+0.07
Total	233			

[a] If the number of hires necessary to reach parity was less than one, no goals were established.
[b] Two timetables are established. First, the number of years to attain parity with nontenured faculty is specified; the second figure indicates the time required to attain parity at all faculty ranks.

127

with pertinent availability data, the calculated number of additional hires necessary to attain parity, and the derived goals and timetables.

In the humanities departments, not a single black faculty member was currently employed, and, given the low availability reported, no department formulated goals. Only in one department, social welfare, was a determination of underutilization made. Consequently, that department specified a hiring goal of 1.38 black faculty and a timetable of 10 years in which it was anticipated that parity would be attained at the nontenure level and 29 years for parity at all faculty ranks. In fact, goals and timetables were established for only one out of 75 departments in the university for employment of black faculty and in no departments for Chicanos and Native Americans. Data indicated the number of qualified minorities to be so low that departments were not underutilizing blacks, despite the fact that few departments employed any black faculty.

The foregoing discussion underscores the emerging consensus that implementation of the executive order will not result in substantial expansion in the number of minority persons holding faculty appointments unless the number of minority persons qualified for such positions is first increased.[42] Realization of this goal calls for joint action by universities and the federal government.

Universities are in a unique position relative to other institutions in society. They are directly responsible for producing the pool of qualified persons from which new faculty will be chosen. Universities select those individuals who will be admitted to graduate study and, as a result of the admissions decision, who may ultimately be employed. This special relation between the availability of qualified minorities and the need for minority faculty compels universities to assume the primary role in implementing efforts to increase minority participation in graduate study.

However, the failure of disadvantaged minorities to progress through the education system in adequate numbers is a problem that extends beyond the immediate purview of schools alone. The effects of prejudice and deprivation have left their imprint in all socioeconomic, political, and educational institutions in this country. Only through a broad societal effort can inequities based on race, sex, color, religion, and national origin be abolished, and this requires commitment by the federal government, one of whose fundamental responsibilities is to promote social justice. If the national goal of ensuring equal opportunity at all levels of education,

[42] Lester stated that "There can be no doubt that affirmative action efforts on the supply side are a necessary part of lasting improvement in the utilization of the talents of members of minorities and women as teacher-scholars in universities." Lester, *op. cit.*, p. 59. The Carnegie Council concluded that: "The supply aspects of the equality of opportunity effort are now generally more important than the demand aspects." Carnegie Council, *op. cit.*, p. 7.

128

including graduate study, is to be realized, and if the federally mandated affirmative-action efforts are to result in improvement of the position of minorities as higher education faculty, a federal role is indispensable.

While institutions and the federal government must share this responsibility, determination of their individual roles requires careful consideration. In addressing this point, the Carnegie Council urged that all higher education institutions include within their affirmative-action plans a "supply plan" designed to maximize opportunities for women and minorities in graduate study. Others, however, while clearly supporting the need to increase the number of minorities with graduate training, have warned against placing instructional activities of universities under supervision of federal enforcement agencies.[43] In our view, the close relation between affirmative action in higher education employment and the production of minority Ph.D.'s clearly signals a mutual obligation on the part of government and institutions to address the "supply" problem; however, it should not be construed as subjecting the university's educational process to federal compliance requirements.

LEGAL ISSUES

While most agree on the desirability of increasing minority participation in graduate education, considerable controversy exists about the legality of various programs designed to implement this goal. It is recognized that strict neutrality in the application of traditional criteria for admission and award of financial aid has not in itself brought about large increases in minority enrollment in higher education; rather, a variety of positive efforts has been important in assisting minority students to compensate for past inadequacies in education and socioeconomic circumstance. At the undergraduate level, special efforts that assist minority students are part of the larger national goal of providing equal educational opportunity to all individuals, irrespective of past academic performance or financial situation. Programs have been implemented to serve students designated as disadvantaged (educationally and economically), a large proportion of whom are ethnic and racial minorities.

At the graduate and professional levels, however, admission and finan-

---

[43] See, for example, the letter from Edwin Young, Chancellor, University of Wisconsin, Madison, to John L. Dunlop, Secretary of Labor, Department of Labor, dated September 18, 1975, as cited in testimony presented by Cyrena N. Pondrom before Department of Labor, Fact Finding Hearings on Executive Order No. 11246, as amended, September 30, 1975, and National Association of State Universities and Land Grant Colleges, "The Carnegie Council Does It Again," NASULGC *Circular Letter,* October 31, 1975.

cial aid decisions are determined competitively, based on academic merit. The quasi-entitlement concept predominant at the undergraduate level no longer holds, and broad-scale programs directed to large numbers of educationally and financially disadvantaged persons are considered inappropriate for graduate education.[44] Consequently, the explicit use of race or ethnicity in targeting programmatic efforts appears essential to realization of increased minority participation in graduate education, but such efforts are constrained by questions concerning the legality of incorporating a racial criterion.

The immediate debate centers around issues crystallized in the well-known *DeFunis* v. *Odegaard* case involving "preferential treatment" in admissions. Marco DeFunis claimed that he was denied admission to the University of Washington Law School in 1971, while less-qualified minority students were admitted by virtue of their minority status. The University of Washington asserted its right to "constitutionally take into account, as one element in selecting from among qualified applicants for the study of law, the races of applicants in pursuit of a state policy to mitigate gross under-representation of certain minorities in the law school and in the membership of the bar."[45] In 1973 the Supreme Court of Washington overturned a lower court opinion and ruled in favor of the University of Washington, concluding that consideration of race in the admissions process was justified because it served an overriding state interest—the increased participation of minority persons in the legal profession. The significance of the case was underscored when, upon appeal to the U.S. Supreme Court, over 30 *amicus* briefs were filed, representing more than 70 diverse organizations, such as the AFL–CIO, American Civil Liberties Union, National Urban League, Harvard University, National Association of Manufacturers, American Jewish Committee, and American Indian Law Students, Inc. In April 1974 the Court declared the issues involved in the case to be moot, since DeFunis (who had been admitted under an earlier court order) was about to complete his studies at the University of Washington Law School.

DeFunis argued that his right to equal protection of the laws, as promulgated by the Fourteenth Amendment, had been violated by the University of Washington, which gave "preference solely on the basis of race to certain persons to the exclusion of others in competition for limited spaces available in the law school." The university openly admitted that it had indeed considered racial and ethnic status but had done so in order

[44] See discussion in Chapter 3.
[45] Appellees–Respondents Motion of Dismissal of Appeal or, in the Alternative, Affirmance of the Judgment Below and Statement in Opposition to Certiorari, *DeFunis* v. *Odegaard*, 412 U.S. 312 (1974), p. 3.

to attain a reasonable representation of qualified minority persons in its student body.

The basic precepts of the "equal protection" clause of the Fourteenth Amendment presume the unconstitutionality of racial classifications, although the courts have ruled that, to overcome prior discrimination, race-conscious policies are permitted. The broad questions raised by the *DeFunis* case, and for which there is no clear judicial guidance, are: What is the appropriate constitutional standard by which race-conscious policies in higher education may be judged? What is the justification for use of a racial classification in light of the heavy constitutional burden imposed?

The state supreme court of Washington ruled that "consideration of race as a factor in the admissions policy of a state law school is not a *per se* violation of the equal protection clause of the Fourteenth Amendment," [46] but that the burden of proof was considered to rest with the University of Washington Law School in showing that the racial classification was necessary to accomplish a compelling state interest. The court pointed out several factors that, in its view, did comprise an overriding state interest justifying the university's policy:

In light of the serious underrepresentation of minority groups in the law schools, and considering that minority groups participate on an equal basis in the tax support of the law school . . . providing all law students with a legal education that will adequately prepare them to deal with the societal problems . . . producing a racially balanced student body at the law school . . . the shortage of minority attorneys—and, consequently, minority prosecutors, judges and public officials—constitutes an undeniably compelling state interest. If minorities are to live within the rule of law, they must enjoy equal representation within our legal system.[47]

Marian W. Edelman, in an *amicus* brief submitted to the U.S. Supreme Court supporting the University of Washington's position, did not accept the conventional interpretation that the Fourteenth Amendment requires that all racial classifications that act to stigmatize "insular" and victimized minorities should be considered "suspect." In her view, if a racial classification is designed to remove the heritage of discrimination, it is compatible with the Fourteenth Amendment, which was never intended to frustrate such remedial efforts. The law school was attempting to address the problem of effective exclusion of minorities in the past; its policies were voluntarily adopted and reasonably designed to remedy the heritage of past discrimination.

[A]pproval of remedial racial classification, then, is based on a principle of realism. One might hope that the work of the Fourteenth Amendment could be done simply by forbidding discrimination. But the Court has recognized that, in the real world,

[46] *DeFunis* v. *Odegaard*, 82 Wash. 2d 11, 507 P.2d 1169 (1973).
[47] *Ibid.*

131

the scars of past discrimination have gone too deep; and racially "neutral" remedies for discrimination are too often ineffective.[48]

According to Edelman, " 'It is by now well understood, however, that our society cannot be completely colorblind in the short term if we are to have a colorblind society in the long term.' " [49]

In a brief prepared for Harvard University, Archibald Cox supported the use of racial criteria in the admissions process to promote diversity in the student body in order to enrich the educational experience of all students. Giving favorable weight to minority status is related to reduction of the disadvantages that minorities face in gaining access to higher education and career opportunities and thus satisfies the "compelling state interest" test. An institution should, moreover, have the freedom to select admissions criteria that will further its educational objectives, and this includes giving favorable weight to disadvantaged minorities.

In recent years many institutions of higher education have determined that their objectives should include removing the special obstacles facing disadvantaged minority groups in access to higher education, business and professional opportunities, and professional services—obstacles which are deeply-ingrained consequences of the hostile public and private discrimination pervading the social structure. Giving favorable weight to minority status in selecting qualified students for admission is an important method of reducing these disadvantages.[50]

Alexander M. Bickel and Philip B. Kurland argued a narrow view in opposing preferential treatment and disagreed with the above arguments. They contended that race may be used as a factor for "preference" only where there has been a specific finding of past discrimination and then may be used only to provide a remedy for such discrimination. According to Bickel and Kurland, the University of Washington did not demonstrate that the law school had a past history of racial discrimination, nor was the admissions policy intended to be a remedy for discrimination. Moreover, they stated that:

Generalized historical assertion about conditions somewhere in the United States some time in the past is not the premise of the remedial discrimination cases decided by this Court, nor should it be.[51]

Bickel and Kurland argued that there could be no "compelling state interest" for racial classification except for its use to remove past dis-

[48] Brief for Children's Defense Fund *et al.* as Amicus Curiae, p. 40, *DeFunis* v. *Odegaard,* 416 U.S. 312 (1974).
[49] *Ibid.*
[50] Brief of the President and Fellows of Harvard College as Amicus Curiae, p. 7, *DeFunis* v. *Odegaard,* 416 U.S. 312 (1974).
[51] Brief of the Anti-Defamation League of B'nai B'rith as Amicus Curiae, p. 22, *DeFunis* v. *Odegaard,* 416 U.S. 312 (1974).

crimination.[52] Moreover, even if racial classification had been justified by some other "compelling state interest," they contended that the University of Washington had made very little effort to demonstrate this point in the specific case. Instead, the law school had referred broadly to the "cultural and economic disadvantage" of minorities as one basis for its policies. Bickel and Kurland also pointed out that even "if elimination of cultural deprivation were the compelling principle, however, it was not the guide used for special treatment for admissions to the law school," since all minority students, regardless of economic, cultural, or educational background, were accorded special treatment.[53]

The definition and interpretation of the term "quota" underlies many of the arguments at the heart of the case. Bickel and Kurland construed the University of Washington's admissions policy as representing the use of what they considered to be an illegal quota based on race. In an eloquent statement they declared that:

A racial quota creates a status on the basis of factors that have to be irrelevant to any objectives of a democratic society, the factors of skin color or parental origin. A racial quota derogates the human dignity and individuality of all to whom it is applied. A racial quota is invidious in principle as well as in practice. . . .

The evil of the racial quota lies not in its name but in its effect. A quota by any other name is still a divider of society, a creator of castes, and it is all the worse for its racial base, especially in a society desperately striving for an equality that will make race irrelevant, politically, economically, and socially.[54]

While acknowledging that others make a distinction between "benign" and "invidious" racial classification (the former being allowed; the latter, forbidden), they claim that the use of racial classification by the University of Washington was not "benign" with respect to the excluded student. Moreover, Bickel and Kurland declare that "a racial quota is *always* [emphasis added] stigmatizing and invidious, particularly when it is applied to areas concerned with intellectual competency and capacity." [55] They contend that the intent of a quota should not be at issue, rather, the effect. Cox flatly disagrees:

The policy of the Equal Protection Clause looks to equal treatment of the members of the identifiable groups composing society, not to the elimination or disregard of the special characteristics of their members. In urging that admissions committees need not be blind to the opportunities for increasing diversity among the students

---

[52] About one-third of the states had formal prohibitions against minority enrollment in graduate and professional education. It is possible (and ironic) that racial preference would be required in those schools yet forbidden in other institutions.

[53] *Ibid.*, p. 27.

[54] Brief of the Anti-Defamation League of B'nai B'rith, *op. cit.*, p. 31.

[55] *Ibid.*, p. 24.

133

in a class and thus improving their education *by including students from racial and ethnic minorities,* we do not suggest that race and ethnic origin may always be used as a basis of selection. To use race, color or ethnic origin to exclude members of an insular minority, impose a restrictive quota or enforce segregation is patently unconstitutional.[56]

O'Neil points out that a preferred applicant is not required to accept admission if he perceives such a program as stigmatizing. In his view, abolition of such programs implies "a dangerously gratuitous concern about the welfare of minority groups." [57]

One attribute of the "compelling state interest test" for review of a racial category indicates consideration of the availability of other nonracial alternatives to achieve the overriding public purpose. Bickel and Kurland noted their concurrence with the goal of increased minority representation, but stated that a substantial effort must be made to discover the feasibility of accomplishing these purposes by other, less constitutionally suspect means. They suggested that expansion of law facilities to accommodate less-competitive students, special summer programs, or "open admissions" as possible actions.

Justice William O. Douglas, in a lengthy dissent from the majority opinion in the U.S. Supreme Court's ruling on *DeFunis,* also offered insights into alternative means of selecting students that would not require a racial preference. He noted that the validity of the quantitative measures used in the admissions process had not been challenged in the case at hand, but, in his opinion, "the key to the problem is consideration of each application in a racially neutral way." [58] Separate treatment of minority students as a class would be warranted in some situations in order to "make more certain that racial factors do not militate against an applicant or on his behalf." [59] Justice Douglas referred specifically to use of standardized tests and stated that "My reaction is that the presence of an LSAT test is sufficient warrant for a school to put racial minorities into a separate class in order to better probe their capacities and potentials." [60] Douglas' dissent suggests, in effect, that development of a means of detecting academic promise among *all* disadvantaged applicants is one way to achieve the goal of increased minority participation that would be compatible with constitutional precepts.

O'Neil suggests that the use of standardized tests may be constitutionally

[56] Brief of the President and Fellows of Harvard College, *op. cit.,* p. 26.
[57] Robert M. O'Neil, "Racial Preference and Higher Education: The Larger Context," *Virginia Law Review* 60, No. 6 (October 1974):941.
[58] *DeFunis* v. *Odegaard,* 416 U.S. 312 (1974), (Douglas, J., dissenting).
[59] *Ibid.*
[60] *Ibid.*

vulnerable.[61] The very fact that such tests may serve to exclude disproportionate numbers of minority students (regardless of whether the tests themselves are or are not biased against minorities) can be related to recent court decisions on qualifications for employment. Numerous rulings have stated that criteria for employment that appear to exclude minorities must be validated as predictors of job performance.[62] Extension of this principle to educational institutions could require college and universities to justify their use of admissions criteria that disfavor minorities in relation to academic or even, perhaps, to career performance.

Proponents of preferential treatment argue that although various nonracial alternatives have been proposed as a means of accomplishing the objectives of preferential policies, none is satisfactory. Strict nondiscrimination will not bring about integration and increased minority participation. Elimination of standardized tests is hazardous, since a greater bias may be inserted in selection processes by the use of more subjective criteria, and "open admissions" programs would be economically infeasible at the graduate level. Reliance on improved elementary and secondary education to ultimately solve the problem would require an unacceptably long period of time, especially in view of the fact that little progress in raising performance is currently being observed at these levels. Moreover, such a delay would preclude this and possibly the next generation of disadvantaged minority students from opportunities for advanced study. Finally, use of a "disadvantaged" concept based on socioeconomic and educational background would be a crude and imprecise remedy.

The Supreme Court's decision not to rule on the substance of the *DeFunis* case extends the confusion and uncertainty surrounding these issues, but it also provides time for a constructive rethinking of the current situation. The debate affects efforts to increase minority participation in two broad areas. First, the admissions process at the graduate and professional level has been the focus of the great majority of legal challenges alleging "preferential treatment." [63] This is not surprising, since preferen-

---

[61] See Robert M. O'Neil, *Discriminating Against Discrimination* (Bloomington, Ind.: Indiana University Press, 1975).

[62] The U.S. Commission on Civil Rights criticized the Department of Health, Education, and Welfare for failing to address the responsibility of educational institutions to validate by empirical evidence their selection criteria for employment of faculty, including educational requirements such as the Ph.D. See discussion in U.S. Commission on Civil Rights, *The Federal Civil Rights Enforcement Effort—1974*, Vol. III, *To Ensure Equal Educational Opportunity* (Washington, D.C., January 1975), p. 230.

[63] It should be emphasized that the current discussion concerns "preferential treatment" among qualified students. The decisions involve distinctions about slightly better and slightly less qualified persons, not unqualified applicants.

tial admissions have been more visible than other types of race-conscious policies in higher education. O'Neil comments that:

The impact of preparatory programs and financial aid practices upon non-minority persons is far less clear or direct than the impact of the admissions decision. If a white believes that he would have been admitted had there been no racial preference, his perception of injury is far clearer than that of the student who, once admitted, thinks he might have received a bigger scholarship absent racial preference.[64]

Consequently, majority students are more likely to perceive and assert a bias in the admissions process than in other areas where the decision-making process is more ambiguous and the exclusionary effect of preferential treatment is unclear.[65]

For similar reasons, graduate and professional schools that rely heavily on quantitative measures in evaluation of applicants may be more vulnerable to legal questions if they attempt to give preference to minority students. The University of Washington Law School relied primarily on undergraduate grade point averages and Law School Admission Test (LSAT) scores to calculate, by means of a specific formula, a student's Predicted First-Year Average (PFYA). Students were then ranked according to their PFYA. Minority applications were set aside as a separate group, and more weight was given to other factors in evaluation of those students.

Schools that give greater consideration to subjective factors such as recommendations, past work experience, or statement of purpose would be less susceptible to a *DeFunis*-type challenge. This is not to say that claims of preferential treatment may not be asserted. However, a broader analysis of an applicant's qualifications may serve to assist in discerning those students whose academic potential may be obscured by mediocre records, thus including a greater percentage of minority students than would have occurred through predominant reliance on traditional quantitative criteria.

Ernest Gellhorn and D. Brock Hornby perceive trends in constitutional interpretations toward greater openness in institutional decision making,

[64] Robert M. O'Neil, "Racial Preference and Higher Education: The Larger Context," *Virginia Law Review* 60, No. 6 (October 1974):926.
[65] The link between "preferential admissions" and the exclusion of a nonminority student is difficult to demonstrate. The Washington State Supreme Court commented in its opinion in the *DeFunis* case that "there is no way of knowing that the plaintiff would have been admitted to the law school, even had no minority student been admitted." *DeFunis* v. *Odegaard,* 82 Wash. 2d 11 (1973). In a similar case, *Bakke* v. *Regents of the University of California,* the trial court ruled that the preferential admissions program at the medical school was unconstitutional. The court did not, however, order the plaintiff, a white male, be admitted, since the evidence did not indicate that he would have been accepted in the absence of the special program, given the large number of other qualified applicants.

thereby implying that educational institutions may be required in the future to articulate specific standards and criteria for admissions, to validate admissions criteria, and to inform applicants as to the reasons for the specific decision.[66] If this development is realized, then the issue of "preferential treatment" would become even more sharply posed, and informal, subjective modes of evaluation of students and quasi-preferential treatment would disappear.

The main thrust of such challenges has, moreover, been directed to professional schools in areas such as law and medicine. This may be explained in part by the differences in enrollment pressures between the two sectors. While the number of qualified applicants substantially exceeds the available openings in some professional fields nationwide, only selective graduate schools have applicant pressures of comparable magnitude. Thus, the availability of alternative opportunities for graduate study may serve to discourage such legal challenges.

The second area of concern stemming from the *DeFunis* case is the legality of a broad spectrum of programs that are "targeted" to minority persons—financial aid, summer programs, and supportive services. The main impact has been to create uncertainty and reluctance to implement minority student programs for fear of legal complications. The primary response at the federal level has been to indirectly target assistance to minority students through programs aimed at institutions in which large numbers of minority students enroll or through use of a definition of "disadvantaged," under the assumption that a large proportion of minority students will be included in such a classification. Since the appropriateness of the "disadvantaged" criterion at the graduate level is subject to debate, the net effect has been little federal and state support for increasing minority participation in graduate education, with almost no federal funds specifically available to minorities in predominately white institutions. If such legal uncertainties did not exist, it is possible that a larger share of federal aid would be directed to minority concerns.

These ambiguities also affect institutional and other activities designed to facilitate minority participation. Private foundations have been the object of legal challenge with regard to their programs. In at least one instance, an educational institution was forced to withdraw its cooperation with a privately funded program targeted specifically to undergraduate minority students.[67] Within institutions, legal uncertainties exacerbate internal differences of opinions about the desirability of implementing such

[66] Ernest Gellhorn and D. Brock Hornby, "Constitutional Limitations on Admissions Procedures and Standards," *Virginia Law Review* 60, No. 6 (October 1974):975–1011.
[67] Determination and Conciliation Agreement, Case No. GCEN-305-73, *Palumbo v. Board of Higher Education of the City of New York* et al.

programs.[68] In the absence of a clear legal precedent, such decisions are not simple.

Despite the absence of clear judicial guidance, there are instances, albeit limited, in which Congress and the executive branch have addressed this issue. One federal regulation applicable to programs receiving federal financial assistance through the Department of Health, Education, and Welfare, stemming from Title VI of the Civil Rights Act of 1964, permits consideration of race without a finding of past discrimination. The regulation, which was approved by the President, states that:

Even in the absence of such prior discrimination, a recipient in administering a program may take affirmative action to overcome the effects of conditions which resulted in limiting participation by persons of a particular race, color or national origin.[69]

However, during consideration in 1974 of a bill to amend the Higher Education Act of 1965, the purpose of which was provision of authority to assist training of disadvantaged students for the legal profession (CLEO program), an amendment was proposed which stipulated that:

No fellowship shall be awarded for graduate and professional study under this part which is found to have any criteria for admission which accord any preference or pose any disadvantage to any applicant on account of race, color, national origin, or sex.[70]

The amendment would have had the practical effect of terminating the specific program, since many law schools offered admission to students who had participated in the special summer programs that were targeted to minorities. In subsequent discussion before the Special Subcommittee on Education, U.S. House of Representatives, it was agreed that the philosophical issues were so important that it would be inappropriate to attempt to address them in what was a rather minor piece of legislation, and the amendment was withdrawn with respect to the bill at hand. Members of the subcommittee clearly indicated, however, that consideration of the question was merely being deferred, not dismissed.

In 1975, an amendment was offered to a bill revising the Public Health Service Act, which declared that no medical or public health school receiving assistance under the provisions of the act could:

discriminate, on the basis of race, color, national origin, or sex, in the admission of individuals to any of its training programs for any academic year.[71]

---

[68] Funding decisions as well.

[69] 45 *Code of Federal Regulations,* Section 80.3(b)6(ii).

[70] U.S. Congress, House, Special Subcommittee on Education of the Committee on Education and Labor, *Hearing on H.R. 14673,* 93d Cong., 2d Sess., June 5, 1974, p. 7.

[71] U.S. Congress, House, *Health Manpower Act of 1975,* H.R. 5546, 94th Cong., 1st Sess., 1975, p. 14.

138

The intent of this amendment was to abolish all preferential treatment in the admissions policies at medical schools. Although this amendment was subsequently voted down, the very existence of these types of actions suggests the strong possibility of congressional involvement in resolution of these questions.

Other legal challenges involving these issues are already en route to the U.S. Supreme Court. In *Bakke v. The Regents of the University of California,* an applicant to the University of California (Davis) Medical School claimed that he was denied admission to the school because minority students were given preference on the basis of race. The applicant alleged that a specific quota of 16 spaces in the first-year class was allotted to persons from economically and disadvantaged backgrounds,[72] that persons included in this category were given special treatment in the admissions process, and that all of those admitted through that process were members of ethnic and racial minority groups. The university acknowledged that it did have a special admissions program under which minority status was a consideration, the purpose of the program being to promote:

diversity in the student body and the medical profession and expanding education opportunities for persons from economically or educationally disadvantaged backgrounds.[73]

However, minority persons who were not from disadvantaged backgrounds were excluded from the special program and referred to the regular admissions program. The trial court ruled in favor of the applicant and explained that it:

cannot conclude that there is any compelling or even legitimate public purpose to be served in granting preference to minority students in admissions to the medical school when to do so denies white persons an equal opportunity for admittance.[74]

Accordingly it found the university to be in violation of the "equal protection" clause of the Fourteenth Amendment.

Although similar cases are likely to be presented to the U.S. Supreme Court in the near future, it is uncertain when and if the Court will choose to rule on the substantive issues. In the meantime, questions about the constitutionality of a broad spectrum of targeted programs remain unanswered. As long as such legal uncertainties exist, implementation of special programs for minority students will continue to be inhibited—but, on the other hand, they need not be precluded. At present we face a

---

[72] In the academic year 1974–75 there were approximately 3,737 applications for the 100 places in the first year class. *Bakke v. The Regents of the University of California,* No. 31,287 (Yolo County Super. Ct., November 28, 1974).

[73] *Ibid.,* p. 4.

[74] *Ibid.,* p. 22.

situation of "muddling through." There is no obvious "best way" to achieve what most believe to be valid and important goals without facing legal ambiguities. Some persons recommend definition of programs in such a way as to minimize or avoid the use of racial criteria as a means of avoiding legal controversy. There is concern, too, about the possibility of unprincipled extension of the use of racial classifications, if judicially validated. Others doubt the efficacy of nonracial alternatives and counsel candor about the explicit racial nature of programs. They believe that deception and evasiveness can only serve to intensify the divisiveness and bitterness that have been characteristic of much of racial relations in the past. Open, forthright expression of the importance of increased minority participation in graduate and professional education and the professions can contribute to improved understanding and public support, essential to achievement of this goal in the long run.

While it is clearly beyond the intention and capability of this report to offer advice on matters that will ultimately be resolved by the U.S. Supreme Court, we will restate our belief in the importance to the entire nation of promoting minority participation in graduate education. The socioeconomic, intellectual, and ethical fabric of our society will be strengthened when the talents of the minority population are more fully utilized. We approve sincere, thoughtful efforts by government, institutions, and others directed to this end, when applied in as just and reasonable manner as is possible.

5 Activities and Concerns of Graduate Schools

Universities are complex organizations with behavior patterns about which it is difficult to generalize. It is useful, however, to point out certain patterns in the actions of individuals and units within universities to aid in understanding and predicting responses to efforts to improve minority participation.

The signal feature of universities pertinent to minority concerns is the decentralized nature of decision making in matters affecting graduate work, differing significantly from undergraduate education. The central role and relative autonomy of faculty in graduate education are predominant; decisions about admissions, award of financial support, and curricular and degree requirements are generally the prerogative of faculty in individual departments with limited direction by the university administration or graduate school. While it is feasible to implement a single, institutionwide program for undergraduate minority students, a parallel effort at the graduate level is more difficult for several reasons.

The personal involvement of faculty in graduate education is key. Typically, more time and energy are enlisted in decisions about individual students; and faculty, over time, have developed a clear image of what kinds of graduate students they would like to have in a department. From their perspective, the most desirable student is one who will perform well academically, appears most able to fulfill their needs for research and teaching assistants, and whose interests closely approximate those of current faculty members. The type of academic credentials presented by past students who have been successful in the program serve as a logical model for predicting the performance of applicants. A minority student

141

who may not score highly on standardized tests or who received a bachelor's degree from a college unknown to the faculty may simply not appear to be the most qualified candidate in terms of a department's expectations and experience. A related concern is what may be called the "standards" question. While a minority student may fully meet requirements for admission to a graduate program, the student may have academic interests peripheral to those of the faculty or may not fit the faculty's conceptions of the "best" type of student, according to traditional criteria.[1]

Because of the relatively recent presence of significant numbers of minority students on university campuses, many graduate departments are in the process of learning how to react and respond to enrolled minority students. One outcome of this inexperience is a tendency on the part of some faculty to perceive minority students as a homogeneous whole, giving rise to a "Pygmalion" effect wherein all minority students, intellectually superior or marginal, well-prepared or ill-prepared, of high or low socioeconomic status, are perceived as disadvantaged. While faculty may be interested and willing to help minority students, they may not identify a particular minority student as eligible for the highest intellectual opportunities, awards, or guidance. It has been demonstrated, moreover, that a teacher's perception of a student's capabilities can have a strong effect on that student's performance.[2]

At the Ph.D. level, there is a unique "apprenticeship" relation between the student and dissertation professor. This can create psychological and educational dilemmas for the student who may, for cultural, social, or other reasons, feel distant or unable to communicate easily with a faculty member whose background and academic style differ from his or her own. In addition, the strong control exercised by faculty over the student's career in graduate school may make a minority student uneasy. For minority persons who are just beginning to enjoy recently won autonomy and status, this "student-mentor" relationship may prove confining.

The significance of the above is amplified through comparison of selected organizational and educational characteristics of graduate and professional schools.

STRUCTURAL CONTRASTS BETWEEN GRADUATE SCHOOLS AND PROFESSIONAL SCHOOLS

The effectiveness of special programs to promote minority participation in professional schools has led many to contemplate using these program

[1] This is probably a less serious problem in science and engineering than in other fields.
[2] Robert Rosenthal and Leonora Jacobson, *Pygmalion in the Classroom* (New York: Holt, Rinehart, and Winston, 1968).

models in graduate schools of arts and sciences. But in trying to emulate the successes of these programs, it should be emphasized that certain characteristics inherent in the organization and practices of professional schools appear to aid development of special activities. As such, professional schools represent the "easy" case in contrast to graduate schools. Several characteristics of professional *vis-à-vis* graduate schools may be compared to demonstrate this point.[3]

In professional schools administrative decisions pertaining to recruitment, admissions, and financial aid are centralized rather than divided between the graduate school or university and individual departments. Implementation of new programs is facilitated by the economies of scale made possible by the larger size of professional schools. Moreover, since the span of administrative control is synonymous with the scope of the educational program, decisions such as development of broader admissions criteria may be implemented with less difficulty.

The relative autonomy and greater cohesion of professional schools are reinforced by the existence of a well-articulated, formal curriculum, through which all students must proceed with only limited freedom to pursue individual intellectual interests. Concomitant with a well-defined curriculum is a set of formal evaluation processes. In graduate schools of arts and sciences, especially Ph.D. programs, academic requirements are less specific. Examinations and a dissertation based on a student's interests and background are the standard academic requirements that a student must fulfill in order to earn a doctoral degree. But the substantive content of programs varies from institution to institution and department to department, as do the educational goals of individual students. While judgments of student performance in professional schools are based on explicit evaluation criteria available to all students, this is only partly so in graduate schools, wherein one or two faculty members may be influential in assessing a student's performance and individual faculty members may evaluate students differently. And finally, the professional certification examination serves as the final standard for assessing educational achievement, one that must be achieved by all students from all schools. No such ultimate judgment exists for doctoral students. Whether or not one receives a degree is obviously one criterion, but many students do not complete their degree programs (in fact, roughly one out of two never do).

The intellectual rigor and content of Ph.D. programs vary, and one of the means used to judge a new Ph.D.'s capabilities is evaluation of both his or her teachers and their recommendations of the student.

---

[3] For illustrative purposes an extreme dichotomy between graduate schools of arts and sciences and professional schools awarding first professional degrees such as law and medicine is characterized. Clearly, such fields as business or public health exemplify characteristics of both.

Given the substantial subjective and personal element invoked in evaluation in graduate education, one can expect a natural conservatism to be built into the admissions process and selection of students to work with faculty in teaching and research. A Ph.D.'s performance after the completion of graduate work, particularly in the academic world, reflects on the reputation of the student's mentor. The faculty member has participated in examining the student, directed and certified his or her research, and when all is said and done, the professor is asked to give a personal opinion of the student's intellectual competence. In professional schools the subjective, personal element is much reduced, and the certification exam is intended as neutral instrument for determining competence. While faculty may be asked to personally recommend a student for employment, that student's future career performance does not reflect directly back on an individual faculty member.[4]

Several other distinctions can be drawn. The existence of a relatively standardized curriculum throughout the discipline simplifies the task of implementing special programs to assist disadvantaged students, as well as acquaints such students with the activities and academic expectations of the school. While special programs may be suitable for some academic fields in graduate school, the possible content of summer pregraduate school programs would be difficult to specify for many academic disciplines apart from orientation functions or coursework to give students a "head start."

Another distinction between graduate and professional schools is the guildlike nature of the professional associations. Since associations have a strong voice in determining entrance requirements and professional standards in the disciplines, they can also provide leadership in promoting minority group participation in the field. The American Bar Association (ABA), for example, has provided strong professional and financial support to the Council on Legal Education Opportunities (CLEO), which has the goal of encouraging and assisting minority/disadvantaged students in entering the legal profession. The analogous professional societies in the arts and science disciplines do not exhibit this strong guild role, nor do they exert the degree of influence over their membership as does the ABA. (The activities of professional societies are discussed further in Chapter 6.)

A final difference, related in part to the guild character of professional education, is the existence of a strong, well-defined, nonacademic employer constituency in certain fields. The Consortium of Graduate Man-

---

[4] The overall performance of professional school graduates, i.e., percentage passing the bar or working in prestigious firms, does, of course, reflect on the collective reputation of the faculty.

144

agement Education (CGME) has relied on financial contributions from business firms to support its program to expand minority involvement in business. The Committee on Minorities in Engineering of the National Academy of Engineering, which is concerned with increasing the number of minority engineers, has received grants from businesses and industries that employ engineers. With commitment and assistance from employers and leadership from the disciplinary societies, the professional schools are in a sound position to work actively to increase minority participation. For the graduate schools who have traditionally sent most of their graduates to teach in colleges and universities and now are faced with a declining academic labor market, the strong employer support is missing, and the professional societies lack the leadership capability and resources to implement major minority programs.

PATTERNS OF ACTIVITIES

During the course of this study, the staff of NBGE visited 14 graduate institutions to learn of their activities pertaining to minority participation. An effort was made to talk with several individuals holding a variety of positions at each institution. In general, the individual responsible for the graduate minority program or the dean in the graduate school charged with overseeing minority student concerns, if such a position existed, was contacted first. Then, both minority and nonminority faculty, and deans of various schools or colleges, were interviewed, depending on suggestions from administrators and faculty within the institutions and other persons knowledgeable about specific schools. In some instances, more than 20 persons met to discuss minority group activities in an institution, and in a few other schools only a single individual was available. A concerted effort was made, however, to meet with several individuals in order to obtain a balanced view of institutional activities. In some instances, outside opinions of specific institutional programs were obtained.

A number of other schools were visited briefly. The brevity of these discussions was often dictated because of time limitations or because of prior indications that the institution had not expressed special concern about minority group participation. Finally, several institutions were contacted by telephone or through correspondence in order to inquire about specific aspects of their minority group programs.

Discussions at these institutions were relatively unstructured, but attempted to obtain answers to a few specific questions: Was there a special effort to recruit and assist minority group students? If there were no special activities, why not? The availability of funds and mechanisms for

145

student support, organizational status of individuals or programs concerned about minority students, and problems affecting enrolled students were discussed. The extraordinary diversity of interest in and responses to minority group concerns made systematic analysis of findings impossible. Nonetheless, definite patterns of responses did emerge, and the discussions included comparisons of activities and problems of other institutions. On the whole, there was strong interest and cooperation on the part of the individuals contacted, although many universities did not have special activities. One spillover benefit of these visits was a stimulus to some institutional representatives to initiate further dialogue and action. Many individuals were interested and sympathetic but uncertain as to effective ways to proceed. A not uncommon response was: "Tell us how to do it." We hope that the following discussion will be useful in development of a better understanding of effective strategies for addressing these issues.

Perhaps the most fundamental characteristic observed was the ordinary sounding concept of "commitment." Institutions that were sensitive to minority group concerns and where significant numbers of minorities enrolled *and graduated* displayed strong public commitment and leadership from the central campus administration. In schools where this did not exist, no activities, or only a few scattered efforts in individual departments, were evident, generally initiated by a minority group faculty member. These were, on the average, small-scale efforts with a few faculty informally contacting colleagues who might recommend potential students, and occasionally, funds for a small number of support stipends were drawn from existing department resources. Such activities were constructive and effective within their limited scope, but generally existed in single departments or, in one case, a small graduate school. Ideally, every department in every school should take the initiative in encouraging minority participation, but this has not occurred.

The nature and intensity of concern about minority group participation in graduate schools were characterized as taking one of three forms. The first was a strong, large-scale, and comprehensive institutional commitment. Typically, this "active" type of institution had a graduate minority student program office, sometimes as part of the graduate dean's area of responsibility, in other instances as a separate program accountable to the graduate dean or central administration at the vice-presidential level. Several subprograms or formal activities, often with extramural funding, might exist within individual departments or schools. An "active" institution employed significant numbers of minority faculty, as well as other minority personnel specifically responsible for recruitment and other activities. Minority group participation was a publicly articulated priority of the central campus administration. And without

146

exception, these "active" institutions had allocated substantial amounts of their own institutional resources toward support of minority graduate students. Several large doctoral schools award one to three million dollars annually from their own funds to minority/disadvantaged graduate students. A caveat must be inserted lest it be inferred that every faculty member, student, and department was in full agreement as to the importance of encouraging minority group participation or how to implement these kinds of activities. Strong administrative leadership is a necessary, but not sufficient, condition for effectively encouraging minority group participation. Faculty involvement is central to any truly successful effort. A minority program isolated from the mainstream of the institution, in turn, isolates its students.

A very different situation was present in the "nonactive" type of institution. Few minority graduate students were enrolled, and there were few or no minority faculty. Several reasons were advanced for an institution's lack of action. General financial constraints were commonly cited. An institution could not provide special support funds for minority students or compete financially with other schools in attracting minority faculty. (One school was prohibited by state law from awarding any fellowships to students; state funds could be paid to students only for services rendered, primarily research and teaching assistantships. However, in this university students and faculty had initiated extensive fundraising activities for minority scholarships.) The general impression gained from discussions with faculty, administrators, and minority spokesmen in these schools was clear—minority graduate participation was not a high priority. These schools did not appear to have financial constraints more severe than those of the "active" schools. In fact, one large public school with stable enrollments had received large budgetary increases well in excess of inflationary rises, yet individuals there related a long list of other budgetary priorities; support for minority concerns was just too far down the list. The importance of minority participation was stated formally but not reflected in financial decisions.

Another reason articulated by the "inactive" schools for little central administration recognition and commitment to minority group concerns was that faculty and departments had traditionally taken the initiative in new programs and activities. It was perceived to be an intrusion on faculty prerogatives to urge or require faculty to become active in recruiting and assisting minority students. The NBGE staff, however, did not observe a single instance wherein several departments throughout an institution, individually and concurrently, became active in these concerns without strong institutional leadership. Some sincere, effective departmental efforts were observed, but those did not have widespread effects in stimulating other departments to initiate similar activities. Overall, the "inactive" schools were uninformed about recruitment techniques, emphasized no special support personnel, had little or no financial support available for minorities, recorded only very fragmented data on minority enrollments, and enrolled few minority graduate students.

I. Bruce Hamilton characterized one model of graduate school activities and minority participation that he termed the "natural flow" situation. Given a substantial minority population in the local geographical areas, a number of low-tuition, public institutions were able to attract a significant number of minority students with a minimum of special activities. The enrolled students appeared to be successful in and satisfied with the institution's programs and general environment. A public urban institution with a large minority population resident in nearby geographical areas should not have the problem of social and geographical isolation that acts as a disincentive to enrollment in some institutions. The presence of a local minority population provides important social support for students.

We cite, however, the example of a state institution located near the center of a large metropolitan area in which 70 percent of the public elementary/secondary students were from minority groups. This is the only public doctoral institution in the entire area, but minorities represent only 9 percent of the total graduate enrollment. The graduate school is making little effort to improve minority participation and, moreover, senses reluctance on the part of the faculty to move in this direction. A contributing factor is that the institution does not perceive itself to be an urban university; its programs and aspirations emphasize research and Ph.D. education and are oriented toward a national rather than regional perspective. This experience suggests that the "natural flow" component has not been sufficient in and of itself and indicates a need for positive action to attract minority students and to provide programs appropriate to their educational goals.

The third type of institutional response to minority group participation originates from the dedicated efforts of a few individuals within an institution. These individuals may obtain extramural funds to support a special program or work with a small pool of institutional resources to undertake personnel recruitment efforts or fund a few minority fellowships. This type of activity may be very successful within its immediate focus, but its drawback lies in dependence on the intense and continuing personal effort of its sponsors.

While most agree that the goal of increasing minority participation is laudable, there is disagreement about the appropriate allocation of responsibilities for efforts necessary to achieve this goal. Some institutions consider this to be entirely an obligation of the federal government. Others hold that the primary responsibility falls directly to the institution,

148

with or without federal assistance. Clearly, the particular viewpoint adopted is a prime determinant of the extent of institutional actions. Unless an institution makes a genuine public commitment to equal opportunity with strong faculty involvement, and that may mean making difficult choices in assigning budgetary priorities, it is unlikely that other activities and attitudes will be influenced in ways that create an institutional environment supportive of minority student achievement. We believe that:

Graduate institutions must assume the primary responsibility for encouraging and assisting minority students in attaining a high-quality graduate education. Initiative must derive from the institutions themselves, since they have the fundamental responsibility for selecting those who will receive the benefits of advanced education and enabling those persons to realize their educational goals. While government and other organizations must provide assistance of various kinds, such support should be viewed as a complement, not a substitute, to existing institutional activities.

Opinions about the appropriate focus of programs to improve minority participation are sharply divided. Should programs be directed toward students who are believed to have the potential to succeed in graduate school but, for a variety of reasons, might not meet standard admissions criteria or, if admitted, would be high-risk students in the absence of special assistance? Acceptance of this approach assumes that not all minority students require financial and academic support and thus should not be eligible. Alternatively, should attention be limited to minority students who have already demonstrated outstanding academic ability, with the goal being to ensure their representation among those qualified to enter top-level academic and professional positions? This division of opinion is further complicated by controversy surrounding the legitimacy of ethnic and racial criteria. Some institutions have "graduate opportunity" programs for persons with strong potential but who come from educationally, financially, or culturally disadvantaged backgrounds, regardless of ethnic or racial identity. While most students in these programs are of minority heritage, others are not necessarily excluded. Since this approach implies remediation and therefore, in the view of some, is inconsistent with the merit principle, the debate comes full circle.

RECRUITMENT

Many graduate schools have undertaken special efforts to recruit minority students; these take many forms and serve several purposes. Fundamental to any recruitment effort is the need to identify potential students, motivate

149

such students to apply to graduate school, and to inform them of the basic admissions requirements and the academic programs available at the institution. A less obvious, but equally important, purpose of recruitment is to assist applicants in evaluating their academic qualifications and goals in relation to the expectations and resources of individual departments. While most schools and departments engage in the identification, motivation, and information functions, efforts in the second area are less satisfactory.

Some institutions—because of geographic location, small size, or inexperience in enrolling minority students—have viewed identification of potential minority students as their first concern. Large-scale mailings and visits to black colleges and other undergraduate schools with large minority enrollments are common practices that serve this purpose. In response to the frequently heard question a few years ago, "How can we find potential minority students?," the Graduate Record Examinations Board established the Minority Graduate Student Locator Service in 1972–73.[5] Through this service, a graduate school may obtain a list of minority students who meet criteria specified by the institution, such as discipline, geographic region, and degree objective. For institutions, especially those whose other recruitment resources are limited, this type of service is an inexpensive, efficient way of identifying potential students; the effectiveness of the follow-up is, of course, a separate issue. Since successful recruitment involves more than identification, use of this service should be viewed as only one of a variety of initial steps.

The need to provide *general* encouragement and information about the benefits of graduate study has declined in recent years because of increasing minority student sophistication. Some students may, however, be apprehensive about the genuineness of institutional interest and commitment to minority education. Faculty receptivity to students' academic and professional interests is a related concern. For these reasons, impersonal forms of contact with students, such as mass mailings, may not be productive, especially for institutions that have enrolled few or no minority students in the past.

Whatever the particular mechanism for recruiting students, a key element in an effective recruitment effort is the ability to discern and match a student's interests and qualifications with the expectations and academic emphases of individual departments. Some recruitment procedures may interest and motivate potential students but neglect the "matching function." Two examples are offered.

One public research university reported that the use of professional (nonuniversity) recruiters had been effective in identifying and encourag-

[5] In fall 1974, 86 institutions and 4,550 students participated in the service.

ing students to pursue graduate work—but not at the school that employed the recruiters. The recruiters were only minimally knowledgeable about specific academic programs offered by the university and thus failed to convey a convincing picture of the available opportunities. A social science department in another institution narrated an unhappy experience in which a burst of departmental enthusiasm, combined with failure to provide adequate information and counseling, had resulted in the admission of several students whose career objectives differed sharply from the academic orientation of the department. The faculty were, moreover, unprepared to respond to the educational needs of this sudden influx of students. As a consequence, bitterness and frustration arose among faculty and students, and, ultimately, several students either transferred from or failed the program.

The use of faculty, students, or alumni to locate, inform, and recommend students is another common practice. If links between faculties in undergraduate and graduate institutions are developed, then the motivation, identification, information, and matching functions are facilitated. Similarly, a current graduate student or alumnus may interest other minority students in graduate study. Various cooperative programs for faculty–student exchanges between undergraduate and graduate schools—some funded through federal programs—have resulted in the development of personal ties that are helpful in recruitment and admissions procedures.

An example of a recruitment program that seeks to address all of these concerns is sponsored by the graduate school of The Ohio State University. Through this activity, the predominately black colleges and several other institutions are asked to recommend three or four of their talented seniors who might be interested in attending Ohio State for graduate work. These students are then invited to participate in the Graduate School Visitation Days Program. Students spend two days at Ohio State, during which time they receive information about admissions procedures, housing, financial aid, and student services. They also meet with faculty members in academic departments of their interest to discuss their individual qualifications and educational objectives, as well as departmental requirements and resources. The program concludes with a banquet "In Recognition of Those Who Are Young, Gifted and Black," attended by several hundred business, community, and professional leaders. A number of distinguished state and national leaders are invited to speak, and the banquet is highlighted by the presentation of distinguished service awards to two or three Ohio State black alumni.

Throughout these activities, stress is placed on the fact that black Americans have been successful at Ohio State. Attention is directed to the presence of 160 black faculty and more than 600 black graduate students at the university. In addition, the graduate school has published

151

a book containing short biographies of 72 distinguished black alumni, each of whom contributed a statement on the importance of advanced education to black youth. Thus, potential students are encouraged to view the graduate school as a place that offers genuine opportunity for achieving their educational objectives.

ADMISSIONS

There is a dichotomy in philosophies and attitudes about the appropriateness of special attention to minority applicants. Some institutions affirm nondiscrimination policies, while others lean toward affirmative practices. While nearly all schools approve special efforts to encourage, inform, and assist minority students in application to graduate study, there is less agreement about modification of admissions procedures.

In general, special attention to minority applicants takes the form of permitting flexibility in the interpretation of certain requirements supplemented by information from other sources, such as personal interviews and recommendations. On the basis of a midpoint review of its minority fellowship program, The Ford Foundation concluded that interviews were considered critical to the selection process, especially with respect to younger candidates, not only because of the additional insights gained about the applicants, but also because of the opportunity the interviews provided to advise the students.[6] The aim is to liberalize certain requirements as a means of enabling a broader (often more intensive) examination of academic potential. In most instances these procedures would be desirable for evaluation of all applicants (minority and nonminority), although they are often more time-consuming and costly.

The most common practice is the waiving of a specified minimum score on the Graduate Record Examinations tests. Hamilton reported that 97 percent of graduate schools that normally required a minimum score were willing to liberalize that requirement for minority/disadvantaged students.[7] Several schools were also willing to waive or modify the application fee and the requirement of a minimum undergraduate grade point average. Formal procedures to give explicit preference to minority applicants, if such students were considered less qualified than nonminority students, were rare and extremely controversial.

Admissions decisions focus on assessment of intellectual potential and academic qualifications. While the two are closely related, they are not

[6] The Ford Foundation, *The Ford Foundation Minority Fellowship Programs: A Midpoint Review* (forthcoming).
[7] I. Bruce Hamilton, *Graduate School Programs for Minority/Disadvantaged Students* (Princeton, N.J.: Educational Testing Service, 1973), p. 39.

identical, especially in the situation of minority students, many of whom have experienced socioeconomic and educational disadvantages. A student with strong potential and motivation may have uneven academic preparation, thus diminishing prospects for success in the degree program. Thus, recruitment and admissions processes involve two sequential tasks: first, the problem of identifying high academic aptitude from what may be mediocre past performance, and second, determining if resources are (or should be made) available to assist a student in strengthening selected areas in which his or her preparation may be inadequate.[8]

A useful analogy may be drawn with the experience of foreign graduate students. For many years, foreign citizens have received about one out of every six Ph.D.'s awarded by U.S. universities; in 1974, over 16 percent of total Ph.D.'s were conferred to non-U.S. citizens. In the social science fields, noncitizens received 12 percent of doctorates awarded, while in the natural sciences, foreign citizens earned one out of four degrees awarded.[9] On the basis of conversations with several graduate school faculty and administrators, we may speculate that many of these students may have scored poorly on standardized aptitude tests, were recommended from institutions often unknown to the graduate school, presented academic records with unfamiliar evaluation systems, or had language problems. Nonetheless, relationships and familiarity with certain high-quality schools were developed over time, letters of recommendation were carefully evaluated, and courses to improve the English skills of foreign students were developed. Admissions errors may have been made, and many foreign students did not fare well in graduate school. Despite these difficulties, foreign students remain a large component of the graduate school population. The foreign student experience might serve as a constructive example for graduate schools in responding to minority student applicants.

Several graduate departments reported that initial efforts in recruitment and admission activities had been acceptable but not outstanding. However, after 2 or 3 years of experience, their effectiveness improved sharply, as did the performance of the enrolled minority students. The number of "admissions mistakes" was minimal and compared favorably with that of nonminority students. Although the changes in criteria used in recruitment and student evaluation were difficult for institutions to articulate, they centered on improvement of the match between student goals and academic needs and the understanding and ability of the faculty to respond to these needs.

Ideally, admissions decisions represent the middle link of a coordinated

[8] Counseling, financial assistance, and other support may also be necessary.
[9] National Research Council, Commission on Human Resources, *Summary Report 1974: Doctorate Recipients from United States Universities* (Washington, D.C.: National Academy of Sciences, June 1975), Table 2.

continuum from recruitment, admissions, financial support, and supportive services. If a student is well informed about the opportunities and expectations of a graduate department and the department is cognizant of the student's academic background and objectives, then the admissions decision is simplified, since guesswork is reduced. A department can decide whether it has the capability to assist a talented student in strengthening his or her academic background in certain areas if necessary. Clearly the "sink-or-swim" attitude resulting from a guesswork admissions mode is costly, both to the student and school, if the student is unsuccessful in graduate study.

SUPPORTIVE SERVICES

Supportive services is an ambiguous term that can be interpreted in many ways. To some it evokes "remedial graduate education," a concept certain to incite controversy. To avoid red herring semantics, it is useful to sketch broad conceptual outlines for those kinds of supportive services appropriate at the graduate level and to consider briefly the scope and characteristics of existing programs. First, however, we will point out examples of supportive services that are available to *all* graduate students in universities and have been well established and accepted practices for many years.

Perhaps the most common practice is to allow graduate students to enroll in undergraduate courses (either for credit or noncredit) in order to remove some deficiency in their undergraduate preparation. In general, such enrollments are not in the major field, but rather in disciplines in which specific competencies are prerequisite to advanced work in the major discipline. For example, many social science graduate students require study at an elementary or intermediate level in statistics. Another common practice is a special 1-year curriculum as part of a 2-year program leading to a Master of Business Administration degree for students with baccalaureates in nonbusiness fields. Students with no previous work in business administration may be required to take a 1-year set of special core courses that provide basic work in the field, although such courses are not credited toward an M.B.A. or Ph.D. degree. A third type of special study is coursework to improve the English reading and writing skills of foreign students.

What is not generally acceptable as supportive services at the graduate level are special courses in the area of specialization geared at a slower than normal pace, enrollment in major course for which the expectation is that a student will need extensive tutoring or that a student will be admitted to graduate study with recognition that he or she will need

154

substantial undergraduate coursework in the major field in order to "catch up."

What kinds of supportive programs do exist for minority graduate students? Hamilton found that a substantial proportion of graduate schools provided services such as summer programs to remedy academic deficiencies, reduced course loads, special tutoring, and assistance in adjusting to the college or community to all graduate students. Many schools did, however, provide these same services "in a special manner above and beyond that given regular students." [10] The need to strengthen the basic quantitative and writing skills of minority students was commonly cited. Several institutions stressed that many nonminority students would also benefit from assistance in these areas.[11]

Summer programs offer another means of bridging the gap between undergraduate and graduate study. Their advantages are several; they permit an opportunity to carefully evaluate a student's academic preparation, sharpen study skills, introduce the methods and concepts of a discipline, raise intellectual self-confidence, and enrich academic background. While effective within their scope, they do have limitations. First, a period of 6 or 8 weeks is inadequate to provide remedial work for students with serious academic deficiencies. Second, students are unlikely to enroll in a summer program after college graduation unless there is a high probability that they will be admitted to advanced study upon completion of the program. As a consequence, most graduate-level activities of this type focus on students who would benefit from such a program but who are not unprepared for graduate study.[12]

Perhaps the most frequent form of assistance available only to minorities was the presence of a minority advisor. This individual undertook a wide range of counseling duties, both academic and nonacademic (employment, housing, financial, etc.), bolstering the minority student's feeling of security and confidence within the university. He or she was available to examine and assist in resolving minority student complaints. However, special counseling should be a complement to, rather than substitute for, a student's interaction with the individual department.

The graduate student's social and academic home is his major department and the majority of the student's campus experiences will evolve around that department. Thus, the student's major department must be regarded as the first line of response

[10] I. Bruce Hamilton, *op. cit.*, p. 47.
[11] For example, one graduate school of public policy offered an intensive 8-week summer course in quantitative methods in which all students were urged to enroll, although tuition was waived for minority students.
[12] A few programs are geared to students with marginal credentials, although this approach has been the subject of serious controversy.

to his needs and dialogue between him and his departmental advisor and staff must be encouraged. . . . Special minority counselors whenever possible should attempt to encourage those faculty student relationships and only intervene when circumstances deem it necessary.[13]

The need for this kind of sociocultural counseling from a minority spokesman is greatest on a campus with few minority faculty and a small-to-medium-sized minority student enrollment. Paradoxically, the schools characterized as "inactive" do not have, but need, this kind of service, whereas those schools that are "active" should be striving to reach a position in which they no longer require this kind of activity.

Very few institutions have reached the point of real integration of minority students into the institution. Nearly all of the "active" schools remain in a transition phase with special support personnel to assist graduate minority students. And, clearly, a delicate balance must be maintained between provision of special support sensitive to minority students' sociocultural and academic needs while avoiding minority student isolation in the university.

The most productive and enduring programs are those which are integrated into the mainstream of the university organization. Isolation is certain death during periods of austerity and political upheaval. The institutional community as a whole must share the success and failures of the established policies and objectives of minority student programs.[14]

FINANCIAL AID

Disadvantaged minority students need financial assistance to attend graduate schools—substantially more so on average than do other graduate students. Graduate schools, accepting this situation as a fact of life that must be dealt with if more minorities are to enter graduate education, have responded in a variety of ways in terms of dollar commitments and mechanisms for providing financial support. The availability of funds to provide financial support is considered a fundamental constraint to increasing minority participation.[15] Several institutions have appropriated $1 to $3 million annually from their own funds for support of graduate minority students; others have been unable to or chosen not to target monies specifically for minority student aid. While some schools have in the past received special funds from the federal government or

[13] Correspondence with Merritt J. Norvell, Jr., Assistant Dean, The Graduate School, University of Wisconsin, July 17, 1974.
[14] *Ibid.*
[15] But graduate schools also indicated that it is a major source of concern to *all* students, both minority and nonminority, in terms of being able to attract the most qualified students.

156

private foundations to initiate financial assistance programs for minorities, relatively few have such funds now.[16] Clearly, most institutions are straining under the burden of providing special support for minorities, particularly those allocating large amounts. Some schools certainly do face very stringent limitations and cannot allocate large sums to these concerns, while additional monies would enable others to substantially expand their minority enrollments. It cannot be concluded, however, that federal funds are indispensable, since several institutions *have* funded and implemented large-scale minority programs. The practical problem remains—how to distinguish those institutions that could allocate funds to minority student assistance if they so chose from those whose financial position is too precarious to do so.

Apart from the level of available support, the mechanism for providing assistance affects minority participation. While undergraduate aid programs focus on promoting access for needy students, philosophies of graduate student assistance (for all students) are very different. At the graduate level, there is debate about the appropriateness of a needs test in award of financial support from institutions *vis-à-vis* the merit principle, the traditional criterion. Departments strive to attract those students whom they regard as the most academically promising through offers of departmental support. This is especially critical in the present times of waning extramural resources. Currently, most institutions continue to compete, in effect, for the "best" students without regard to financial need. There is some sentiment among institutions toward greater emphasis on need in allocating student support, but it has not yet become a widespread practice.

Other considerations are introduced at the graduate level in the award of financial assistance. Graduate education is closely linked to the undergraduate educational process and the production of research.

Graduate students, serving as undergraduate teaching assistants and as research assistants, are central to the university's economy; the cost at which the university can produce undergraduate education and research depends critically upon the number and quality of graduate students present, and their forms of support.[17]

In concert with the federal government's interest in assisting the development of highly educated manpower related to national objectives, a large proportion of graduate students receive financial stipends as compensation for research and teaching responsibilities within universities. In re-

[16] In general, extramural funds now appear to be used for supportive services and special programs in contrast to general minority student assistance.

[17] National Board on Graduate Education, *Comment on the Newman Task Force Report on the Federal Role in Graduate Education* (Washington, D.C.: National Board on Graduate Education, 1973), p. 1.

TABLE 46   Full-time Graduate Students in Doctorate Science Departments by Source and Type of Major Support, 1973, U.S. Citizens [a]

Major Sources of Support	Total	Fellowships & Traineeships	Research Assistantships	Teaching Assistantships	Other Types of Support
U.S.	30,432	13,850	13,551	157	2,874
government	(27.6%)	(12.6%)	(12.3%)	(0.1%)	(2.6%)
Institutional	48,312	7,062	8,040	30,717	2,493
support	(43.6%)	(6.4%)	(7.3%)	(27.9%)	(2.3%)
Other outside	6,927	2,670	2,067	188	2,002
support	(6.3%)	(2.4%)	(1.9%)	(0.2%)	(1.8%)
Self-support	24,608	—	—	—	24,608
	(22.3%)				(22.3%)
Total	110,279	23,582	23,658	31,062	31,977
	(100.0%)	(21.4%)	(21.5%)	(28.2%)	(29.0%)

[a] Includes engineering and social and natural science departments. National Science Foundation, "Graduate Science Education: Student Support and Postdoctorals," Detailed Statistical Tables, Appendix III, 1975, Table E-10A (U.S. Citizens only).

cent years there have been drastic cutbacks in federal fellowships and slowed growth in research expenditures. While graduate institutions have compensated in part for drops in external aid through increases in teaching assistant positions and allocation of institutional funds to support graduate students, an increasing number of students now finance their own graduate education. Table 46 shows that in 1973 the major sources of support for over 64 percent of all full-time graduate students enrolled in doctoral science departments were federal fellowships or traineeships, both institutional and federal assistantships, and research and teaching assistantships. About one in five students relied on personal funds to finance graduate education, while the remaning 14 percent of students received the major share of their support from other sources, including the U.S. government and other institutional funds. In principle, research and teaching assistantships are awarded to the students best qualified to perform the required duties. Similarly, federal fellowships are awarded competitively, and recipients of traineeship positions are selected for their potential research contributions. The interrelation between graduate education programs, research activities and undergraduate teaching, and reliance on the merit principle are demonstrated by these funding patterns.

Equally important is evidence that within institutions minority students do not appear to be supported by the same means as nonminority students.[18] Minority students are generally not concentrated in the natural

[18] See Birt L. Duncan, "Minority Students: No Longer Separate but Still Not Equal," in *Scholar in the Making* (forthcoming).

science and engineering fields in which the greatest amount of financial assistance from the federal government is available. Several graduate school administrators indicated that by and large minorities do not receive assistance from departmental sources, such as teaching and research assistantships, proportionate to their enrollments in individual disciplines.

Institutions desiring to increase minority student participation may find themselves in a "catch-22" dilemma. Realizing that minority students require substantial financial aid, special monies may be appropriated and distributed from a central office. Supplemental funds are often effectively used as an incentive to stimulate departments to recruit actively and admit more minority students. In some cases, a department may be given an extra enrollment slot if a minority student is admitted; in others, extra- mural or university support of a minority student releases limited depart- ment funds for another student, thus expanding a department's total available resources. In a sense, minorities become, in the language of the economist, a "free good," not charged against a department's own limited funds. Several institutions indicated that departments would be less active in recruitment and admissions of minority students if the institutions did not provide special minority support funds. Some institutions reported that even this strategy met with disfavor from many faculty. Efforts to allocate special stipends were viewed as a zero-sum situation; money for a minority student meant less support money for nonminorities. This attitude was especially common in institutions that could not offer support to all their students and were experiencing difficulties in maintaining en- rollments. Some suggested that the existence of various national fellowship programs may have been ineffectual in expanding the total number of minority students in graduate education. Rather the availability of extra- mural funds has allowed institutions to reduce their own financial commit- ment to minority education. Substitution effects are a major concern.

But even when special monies were effective in promoting minority group participation, the success of the strategy was double-edged. As indicated above, over three-fifths of doctoral students in the sciences are supported in ways that complement their studies, and special nondepart- mental support may reinforce the student's isolation from the department, depriving him or her of valuable research and teaching opportunities. It is important for all students and critical for the success of minorities to be integrated into the mainstream of departmental concerns. In nearly every institution visited, a central problem was how to motivate departments to commit a proportionate share of their resources—fellowships, research assistantships, and teaching positions—to minority students. In attempts to remedy this situation, some institutions have monitored the allocation of departmental funds to minorities and nonminorities; others have estab- lished procedures for matching departmental funds with separate institu- tional funds. A willingness to allocate a share of existing departmental

159

monies to the support of minorities can be interpreted as one measure of departmental commitment to minority group participation.[19]

There is another widely debated consideration in award of special fellowships relative to teaching and research assistantships. Fellowships have been viewed as helpful in allowing the student entering with weaker undergraduate preparation to pursue his or her studies without added work responsibilities. However, the educational advantages of enabling the student to devote maximum time to coursework must be weighed against those to be gained from encouraging the student to become involved in the teaching and research activities of the department. One desirable resolution of this issue appears to be a combination of both, perhaps providing financial support without work requirements during the initial years of graduate school, with opportunities for teaching and research provided later in doctoral study.

---

[19] Many graduate departments, particularly in the prestigious private universities, normally support almost all their students. Provision of stipends for minorities in these schools should not, in principle, impose an *additional* financial burden.

6 Current Efforts to Promote Minority Participation

Only through the combined efforts of both the public and private sectors can change be realized. Many individuals and organizations are working toward the goal of increasing minority participation; others are not. Federal mission-oriented agencies, states, professional societies, philanthropic foun ations, and business and industry are among those that have initiated activities. In the following chapter, we will examine selected efforts—in terms of purpose, scope, and impact. It is not our intention to provide an exhaustive review nor an evaluation of current programs, but rather to set forth what we believe to be the responsibilities of and effective roles for various sectors in addressing these issues.

THE FEDERAL ROLE

Since the Higher Education Act of 1965, the federal government has shown a consistent, although uneven, commitment to equalizing educational opportunity in elementary, secondary, and baccalaureate education. With the passage of legislation establishing the Basic Educational Opportunity Grant (BEOG) program, the federal government has moved toward a quasi-entitlement concept in undergraduate financial aid. Other programs, such as College Work–Study, Supplemental Educational Opportunity Grant, Guaranteed Student Loan, and National Direct Student Loan, also assist the needy student. The expressed objective is to provide every high school graduate, regardless of financial circumstance, with an opportunity to attain postsecondary education if he or she chooses.

Supplementing the goal of removing financial barriers is the view that past educational performance should not deter access to postsecondary education. The TRIO programs, authorized under Title IV of the Higher Education Act of 1965, focus on the educational needs of disadvantaged students.[1] Federal efforts are complemented by a variety of state, private, and institutional programs that award aid on the basis of demonstrated need, encourage access through "open admissions," and offer remedial educational and supportive services to disadvantaged students.[2] Although federal programs are not targeted by racial and ethnic criteria, their impact on minority participation is positive, since a large proportion of minority students may be classified as disadvantaged.[3]

The federal role in support of graduate students is very different. Present federal programs are directed toward serving the broad national interest through ensuring a supply of highly educated persons to fulfill manpower and research needs. Commitment to equal opportunity is limited at best at the graduate level. Reduction of financial barriers is not considered a primary objective, since justification for a federal role based on a socioeconomic mobility argument is weak. Although persons holding a bachelor's degree may not enjoy the advantages of inherited wealth, neither are they likely candidates for poverty. Admission to graduate study and award of financial support are based on demonstrated academic merit.[4] "Open admissions" philosophies are not accepted, and graduate opportunity programs analogous to those in undergraduate education are rare. While the criteria used for federal assistance to undergraduate students have been favorable to minority students, the opposite holds for graduate education. For various reasons, minority graduate students have not benefited widely from current forms of federal support.

A few federal programs targeted to minorities do exist, although the

[1] *Upward Bound* is intended to generate motivation and strengthen the preparation of disadvantaged students for postsecondary training. *Talent Search* seeks to provide qualified students with information about career options and available financial resources. *Special Services* assist students with cultural, economic, or physical handicaps in need of remedial or supportive services to successfully complete postsecondary education. The *Educational Opportunity Centers* have the goal of improving college entrance and retention rates of residents within specified geographic regions.

[2] However, admission to many undergraduate schools remains highly selective, and numerous state and institutional scholarships are awarded on the basis of academic promise without consideration of need.

[3] Another program warrants comment in this context. Title III of the Higher Education Act of 1965 provides funds for "developing institutions" to strengthen their academic, administrative, and student services. The traditionally black colleges have been the major beneficiaries of this program.

[4] There is also the practical problem of how to determine financial need for graduate students, many of whom are financially independent.

162

rationale for such programs is not based solely on equity considerations, but, rather, relates primarily to manpower objectives. The federal mission-oriented agencies have implemented activities to increase the involvement of minorities in their research and training activities. The Council on Legal Education Opportunity, for example, is a federally funded program designed to increase the number of persons from disadvantaged backgrounds in the legal profession.[5]

We believe there is a clear federal responsibility to support efforts directed toward facilitating the participation of minority persons in graduate education. Present support of research and advanced training should be extended to recognize the importance of involving minority persons since the talents of minority men and women as scholars, professionals, scientists and teachers constitute a valuable national resource. Individual equity is another concern. Distinctions that confer status and opportunity on the basis of race or ethnic identity must be removed. The federal government, through its authority and resources, is best able to redress social inequities. Executive Order 11246, calling for affirmative action in higher education employment, and various directives stemming from the Civil Rights Act of 1964 exemplify the federal government's broad obligation to foster social justice. Yet requirements for affirmative action cannot be achieved without concurrent efforts to increase the number of minority persons with advanced degrees. A strong federal role is critical to attainment of these objectives. Two recommendations are advanced:

We urge the executive and congressional branches to express a resolution for federal support of and increased concern for minority participation in graduate education. Strong national leadership is essential to achievement of equal opportunity goals in graduate education.

The U.S. Office of Education should implement a program of competitive institutional grants for the purpose of supporting efforts to increase minority participation in graduate education. Funds should be provided for a broad range of activities, including student aid, tuition, supportive services, and administrative costs. Selection of grant recipients should be based on evaluation of institutional commitment and program effectiveness.

The approach embodied in current federal training grant programs is suggested as an appropriate model for implementation of this recommendation. Institutional initiative and flexibility as to program scope, emphasis, and organization should be encouraged. Accordingly, funds should be

[5] The program has, in effect, been limited to ethnic and racial minority persons.

available for a variety of purposes—tuition, student stipends, additional support personnel, special summer programs, and research and evaluation directly related to program effectiveness. An 8 percent administrative allowance should be provided.[6] Some provision for maintenance-of-effort should be a condition of the award. Initial grants should cover a 3- to 5-year period, with renewal contingent upon demonstration of program success as measured by student achievement. An obvious cost-effective use of these funds would be expansion of existing institutional programs that have demonstrated success. Graduate schools and departments that desire to initiate such activities would be eligible, although institutional plans for a continuing commitment upon termination of federal funding should be indicated.

Award of approximately 30–40 grants to institutions would result in an average of 150–200 students supported per institution. The existence of a "critical mass" is a significant consideration, although institutions with small graduate programs or low minority enrollments because of geographic location should be eligible to receive assistance. An annual appropriation of $50 million would permit support of a total of 6,500 students or about 1,500–2,500 new entrants each year, depending on the number of years students are supported through the program. This figure represents less than 1 percent of total graduate enrollments in U.S. colleges and universities.

The following distribution of funds is suggested as appropriate for implementation of a balanced program of activities although considerable variation in individual grants should be permitted:

1. Student assistance and tuition   65–70 percent
2. Special new programs and supportive services   25–30 percent
3. Research and evaluation   5 percent

Student assistance should be awarded on the basis of demonstrated financial need and academic merit. Financial support available through this program should be closely linked with existing institutional mechanisms for student support, such as departmental fellowships and research and teaching assistantships. For example, if a doctoral student receives finan-

---

[6] Alternatively, if an institution with ongoing activities only requires funds for student assistance in order to expand minority participation, a cost-of-education allowance of $4,500 per additional full-time student might be allocated. The National Board on Graduate Education recommended in an earlier report that the institutional allowance accompanying student fellowships should be increased to $4,500 to reflect in part the sharp increases in costs of education that have occurred in recent years. See Natioinal Board on Graduate Education, *Federal Policy Alternatives toward Graduate Education* (Washington, D.C.: National Board on Graduate Education), p. 77.

cial aid through the federal grant for the first and fourth years of graduate study, a department might be asked to provide support funds during the intervening period.

Examples of special, new programs that might be funded through an institutional grant include:

1. Activities designed to identify, motivate, and prepare talented under-graduate students for advanced study;
2. cooperative recruitment, admissions, and financial aid programs involving departments in a specific field of study administered by several graduate institutions; and
3. summer institutes to strengthen preparation for graduate work.

Funds should be available for research pertinent to minority student achievement. In addition, mechanisms for evaluation by individual institutions of their activities should be required.

Legislative authority for implementation of this program is provided under Title IX of the Higher Education Act of 1965, as amended in 1972. Part A presently authorizes grants to institutions for "(1) faculty improvement; (2) the expansion of graduate and professional programs of study; (3) the acquisition of appropriate institutional equipment and materials; (4) cooperative arrangements among graduate and professional schools; and (5) the strengthening of graduate and professional school administration." Research pertinent to the improvement of graduate programs is also allowed. Authorization for fellowships is specified under Part B of Title IX and stresses "the need to prepare a larger number of teachers and other academic leaders from minority groups." Part C provides public service graduate or professional fellowships, and Part D authorizes fellowships for "persons of ability from disadvantaged backgrounds as determined by the Commissioner, undertaking graduate or professional study." Technical amendment of this legislation would permit implementation of our program as proposed.

Many have contended that direct federal awards to students are preferable to assistance channeled through institutions. Portable fellowships maximize student freedom of choice in selection of discipline and school. This is clearly the philosophy prevailing in the federal BEOG program. We have previously stated our support of the "free-choice principle." [7] However, in defining a basic federal role in promoting equal opportunity, we believe that a program of competitive institutional grants is preferable for several reasons.

First, while direct financial assistance to minority students is a major

[7] National Board on Graduate Education, *Doctorate Manpower Forecasts and Policy* (Washington, D.C.: National Academy of Sciences, 1973), p. 5.

component of successful efforts to improve minority participation, it is not sufficient in itself. Broad institutional concern and supportive services are central to minority student success. Through evaluation of proposed and existing institutional activities, graduate schools with the strongest commitment to and effectiveness in facilitating minority student achievement would receive monies. Excessive student attrition that might occur in the absence of a supportive environment would be diminished. Second, a maintenance-of-effort provision in award of grants would reduce substitution effects wherein federal monies complement rather than supplant institutional funds directed to minority concerns. Moreover, although we propose that this program serve as the foundation of the federal role to increase minority participation, it should not be the only activity. Accordingly, we have stressed the importance of encouraging diversity in programmatic efforts by government, institutions, and others. Given this pluralistic approach, student freedom of choice should not be precluded. In sum, we believe the advantages of the recommended competitive institutional grants clearly outweigh those of a "portable" fellowship program.

Federal Mission-Oriented Agencies

It is far simpler to suggest a federal responsibility for promoting equal opportunity objectives than to specify the content of the federal role in their achievement. Given the pluralistic nature of the issues, a single federal role is, moreover, inappropriate. In accord with our position that efforts to increase minority participation should be integrated into the mainstream of teaching, research, and employment, involvement of minorities in the research and training programs of the mission-oriented agencies is essential.

The mission-oriented agencies of the federal government—such as the National Institutes of Health (NIH); the Atomic Energy Commission (AEC), now the Energy Resource and Development Administration (ERDA); and the National Space and Aeronautics Administration (NASA)— provide substantial support for graduate education. Support may be specifically directed to graduate students in the form of fellowships and traineeships. Often graduate students receive stipends for involvement in a federally sponsored research project. To the extent that graduate education is closely linked to research, federal contracts and grants represent a major, although less direct, source of support for the education of graduate students.

As stated in their statutory foundations and annual authorizations, implementation of the missions of these agencies is directed toward support of technical programs, such as health, space, energy, environment, and transportation. As such, specific commitment to the involvement of

166

minority persons in research and graduate education is not included. It is only through legislation and executive orders that attention to equal opportunity and affirmative action is officially required. Some agency activities are intended to have a specific impact on minority participation. A brief examination of selected programs may indicate problems and strengths and suggest directions for future efforts.

One of the first and most significant difficulties in formulating a new program is deciding how to provide aid to minority students. Most minority institutions do not offer graduate study—with the exception of teacher education—and few have major research programs. Consequently, activities involving aid to minority institutions will be of greater benefit to undergraduate students than graduate students. Most federal funds find their way into universities through research grants and contracts that are awarded on the basis of competitive peer review. Minority institutions receive an extremely small percentage of such awards. During FY 1973, 12 percent of the federal funds received by black colleges were for research and development, while R&D accounted for 43 percent of federal funds awarded to all colleges and universities. In contrast, student assistance represented 33 percent of the federal funds received by black colleges, whereas all colleges received only 22 percent of their funds for this purpose.[8]

There is one certain way of designing a program to aid minority graduate students directly—a fellowship or traineeship program limited by virtue of racial or ethnic criteria. However, because of uncertainty about the legality of allocating funds to minority students compounded by the recent reductions in all fellowship funds, few federal agencies award aid directly to minority graduate students; such programs are the exception rather than the rule.

The National Institute of General Medical Sciences (NIGMS) within NIH sponsors a training grant program for specific graduate departments at three predominately black institutions (Howard University, Meharry Medical College, and Atlanta University). The program has been operating for about 2 years but has supported more than 60 graduate students from a total funding of $3 million. The grant provides released time from teaching duties for some faculty to allow them to expand their research activities. One aim of the grant is to upgrade Ph.D. education in several health sciences departments during a transition period of 5 to 8 years, after which the departments and faculty will be in a position to compete more effectively for training grants available to all institutions.

NIGMS responds to charges of discrimination by observing that research and training have always been provided to a variety of institutions of

[8] Unpublished data provided by the Federal Interagency Committee on Education.

167

nonuniform quality. This program hopes to capture and develop a resource that has been previously neglected. Justification for the program emphasizes the precedent of funding a broad range of institutions and research areas. A training program for undergraduate students in minority colleges and universities is under consideration by NIGMS. It would support basic science departments, such as physics, chemistry, psychology, and mathematics, and thus influence undergraduate education students in other science fields.

Fundamental to this departmental training grant program is the assumption that the minority institutions would improve if they become more similar to majority institutions with respect to research and graduate education. Faculty should be given the opportunity to "sink or swim" in the arena of federal research and training grants. This assumption has not gone uncriticized when explicitly stated. Some argue that minority institutions perform a unique and valuable service to society and that an emphasis on teaching, with a concomitant deemphasis on research, is a characteristic worth preserving in these schools (and in many others). Moreover, as a consequence of increased involvement in sponsored research, undergraduate education in majority institutions has suffered relative to research and graduate training. The conclusion follows that minority institutions should not repeat the errors of the majority universities. To the extent that training grants assume a transition of minority institutions to a research institution model, arguments exist about the desirability of such grants.

The Minority Biomedical Support (MBS) program within NIH provides support for research projects in institutions with a significant commitment to the education of minorities. The goals of this program are to increase the number of minority persons working in biomedical research and to upgrade the research capability of faculty in institutions with substantial minority student enrollments. Project proposals are evaluated both on scientific merit and relevance to the program objectives. The MBS program focused initially on the historically black colleges, but was later broadened to take into account geographic considerations and to include persons from other minority groups. At the end of 5 years, institutions are eligible for renewal grants; however, selection of recipients becomes more competitive. Institutions must demonstrate progress in development of their biomedical research capability. During 1975, NIH awarded $8 million to 80 institutions, providing support for 499 faculty, 906 undergraduates, and 145 graduate students.

The National Institute of Mental Health (NIMH) sponsors several programs designed to expand the involvement of minority persons in its research and training activities. The need for increased minority participation is linked to the capability of the institute's more than 500 community mental health centers to provide services appropriate to local communities. Clearly, understanding of minority mental health needs and the availability of qualified professionals to respond to those needs are fundamental to the effectiveness of the community mental health program. The Health Revenue Sharing and Health Services Act of 1975 specifically includes a provision stating that a community mental health center serving a population with a substantial number of limited English-speaking persons must have:

(i) developed a plan and made arrangements responsive to the needs of such population for providing services to the extent practicable in the language and cultural context most appropriate to such individuals, and (ii) identified an individual on its staff and whose responsibilities shall include providing guidance to such individuals and to appropriate staff members with respect to cultural sensitivities and bridging linguistic and cultural differences.

One of the first activities initiated by the NIMH was a program of grants to colleges and universities to train minority professionals. These were minitraining grants that supported both students and faculty. Subsequently, funds were made available to community mental health organizations to develop centers that would be closely tied to university programs in social welfare. Student fieldwork experiences were provided through these centers, which frequently also offered special courses. This effort was viewed as one means of encouraging a stronger community-based component in university curricula.

Recognition of the need for more minority research investigators led to the establishment of a fellowship program within the Alcohol, Drug Abuse, and Mental Health Administration of NIMH, administered by professional associations.[9] The professional associations in turn provide the mechanism for selecting students who are interested in graduate study in mental-health-related disciplines. The agency sees several advantages to using a professional organization as an intermediary in awarding fellowships. The first is that it does not have the auxiliary costs, such as support for faculty, research, and teaching, and overhead normally associated with institutional training grants. Second, the associations can be asked to monitor the fellows more easily than could a number of institutions due to federal constraints and controls on the use of surveys by agencies. The program at NIMH is being extended and will award more than $5 million to the professional organizations over a 5-year period to provide graduate fellowships for minority students in sociology, social welfare, psychiatry, psychology, and nursing.

[9] During its first year, the National Institute of Education (NIE) "piggybacked" on this program by providing $100,000 to the American Sociological Association. Program support from NIE has been discontinued.

The program succeeded on the modest scale of 30 fellowships during its first year. Part of the reason for its effectiveness is that faculty provide advisory services to professional organizations, usually without remuneration. If the number of fellowships handled by one association expands appreciably, such a "bootleg" operation may not succeed. The success of this fellowship program has depended on the intense commitment of a limited number of faculty who work through the professional association. These faculty become personally involved with the identification of prospective minority graduate fellows and provide advice on the selection of programs and schools. The program is currently sufficiently small such that concern by the faculty, many of whom are minority group members, is an effective catalyst for a limited infusion of minority graduate students into a discipline. It is not clear, therefore, whether such a program would be as effective if substantially expanded.

NIMH has also allocated funds for establishment of six minority research and development centers. A premise underlying the implementation of these centers is that the minority populations should be able to define their own mental health needs and suggest appropriate solutions. Each of the centers is funded at $200,000 annually for 5 years to undertake research, technical assistance, and dissemination activities. Although some of the centers are affiliated with universities, proposals for establishment of the centers and substantive direction are initiated by minority mental health organizations.

A very significant action taken by NIMH is its stated goal that 25 percent of the trainees in its Social Sciences Research Training Grant program should be minority persons. Institutions are asked to indicate their plans to involve minority persons as faculty and trainees and to provide detailed information about minority participation—recruitment activities, financial aid, departmental policies, and supportive services—in existing grants.

NIMH justifies its minority programs by presenting data on the amount of support given to majority students and that to minority students. The high proportion of aid to majority students is used to refute any claims that they are victims of discrimination. A query about the means (an ethnically targeted program) receives a response about the ends (removing a current imbalance), as well as the necessity of such action for provision of NIMH's services.

A program of graduate traineeships at minority institutions sponsored by the National Science Foundation (NSF) was not funded in 1975. This cutback in minority traineeships was part of a 50 percent overall reduction in traineeships awarded by NSF. The remaining such awards are targeted toward energy programs, with no funds available for minority traineeships.

A number of agencies provide support for faculty members at minority institutions. As indicated earlier, such support is of benefit to graduate

170

students at those institutions, who profit both directly and indirectly from any research support received by faculty. Most of these programs are transitional. Support is provided for 1 to 3 years, at which point the faculty recipient should be able to develop a research program and compete successfully in the wider arena of federal research grants. Faculty need not be members of a minority group, but must be affiliated with a minority institution.

NASA has a program for research at minority institutions. Grants to faculty at minority institutions enable involvement in research at a NASA center or in areas related to work at a center. The local center is expected to monitor the project. There are currently about 5 such grants, averaging about $20,000 per year, principally at black institutions.

NSF sponsors a Research Initiation Grant for Minority Institution Improvement program. The purpose of this activity is to improve science education at minority institutions through support of research by faculty members. Science teaching faculty with no previous substantial research experience may receive project support for approximately 15 months, up to $20,000 total. In 1975, NSF awarded 48 grants, totalling almost $1 million.

NIGMS offers 1-year fellowships available to faculty at minority institutions, thus enabling faculty to complete work on a terminal degree. A related program within NIGMS supports a visiting scientist (not necessarily a minority person) for up to 1 year at a minority institution; such visiting scholars may assist an institution to strengthen or expand its programs.

Several agency programs are directed to strengthening the undergraduate education of minority students, since improvement of undergraduate preparation is an essential component of efforts to increase minority participants at the graduate level. NASA has a National Aerospace Fellowship program, which, despite its title, provides scholarships to minority undergraduate students as well as a summer internship at a NASA center. NSF sponsors a Minority Institution Science Improvement program to improve the quality of undergraduate science education. Annual funding of about $6 million provides support for curricula, facilities, and faculty at predominately minority institutions.

Most agencies that seek to improve minority group participation do so by channeling funds through minority institutions. This avenue avoids legal challenge, because minority institutions themselves do not discriminate among students on the basis of race or ethnic origin. In the past several years, agencies that support minority institutions in a specific program have expanded their definitions of such institutions to include many schools with less than a majority of minority group students. A strict definition of a minority institution as one with 51 percent or more minority groups students would generally limit such schools to the traditionally black colleges. Current definitions, however, are broad enough to include any institution that enrolls a substantial number of minority students and has shown a strong commitment to upgrading the educational performance of these students. This includes about 400 institutions, ranging from community and junior colleges to 4-year schools and a few universities.

Those agencies with the most successful programs have at least a few individuals strongly committed to equal educational opportunity and prepared to defend and implement a specific program. There are always reasons—political, tactical, legal, and fiscal—for lack of action. There are always conflicting priorities for use of limited agency funds. In general, the mission-oriented agencies have recognized the importance of developing the talents of minority men and women through graduate education and research. While almost all support the objective of greater minority participation, the means for implementing programs to accomplish their objectives are unclear. The most obvious method—direct student support targeted to minorities—is also the most difficult politically and legally. Therefore, most agencies focus on strengthening the educational and research capabilities in areas relevant to the individual agency's mission through support to minority institutions.

Such programs are effective yet necessarily limited in scope. While they may have a significant impact on the undergraduate education of minority students (half of black baccalaureates are conferred by the black colleges), at the graduate level minority institutions comprise only a small part of total graduate enrollments. Moreover, the scientific research capabilities of minority graduate schools are not comparable to those of the most prestigious research universities in this country, and few offer doctoral work. Consequently, the significance of these programs for promoting minority participation in graduate level education and research activities is minimal. Political and legal uncertainties compounded by the absence of clear national leadership on these issues both limit the scope and inhibit the potential for expansion of these efforts—and will continue to do so in the foreseeable future.

We believe it fundamental to the national interest to encourage the development and involvement of underutilized minority talent in scientific and research activities. Accomplishment of these goals requires that attention be directed to three broad areas:

1. Early identification, motivation, and preparation of talented undergraduate students for graduate study in science;

2. increased opportunities for advanced (primarily doctoral) training of minority persons leading to careers in science and research; and

3. strengthening of the academic credentials and research capabilities of minority scientists and faculty.

Initiative and diversity of approaches in resolution of these underlying problems should be encouraged. For this reason, we urge that a variety of programs such as those described above be sustained insofar as their effectiveness is demonstrated and the need for these activities remains. There are, however, striking omissions in the array of programmatic efforts sponsored by the mission-oriented agencies.

First and foremost is the lack of activities directed toward increasing the involvement of minority students in scientific research and training in Ph.D.-granting institutions. We believe that this area deserves the highest priority. Second, greater efforts to prepare and assist talented undergraduates in nonminority institutions for advanced study are essential in view of the extensive curricular prerequisites for graduate work in science.

A number of alternatives are proposed for consideration:

1. As one means of encouraging graduate faculty to identify and involve talented minority graduate students in research activities (primarily at the doctoral level), the federal mission agencies should provide unrestricted supplemental funds to graduate institutions, earmarked to reimburse principal investigators who employ minority students on research grants. Funds would be allocated as a share of the normal stipend paid to minority students for their services, thus partially reimbursing the project for costs of employing these students. This activity would complement the institutional grants program previously recommended (pp. 163–166), since all institutions and departments would be eligible to receive such reimbursements, given the voluntary, decentralized nature of the program. Combined funding from several agencies at a level of $5 million per year would permit support of 2,000 students with an average reimbursement of $2,500.

2. Cooperative programs between undergraduate and graduate institutions would facilitate a developmental approach in motivating, preparing, and assisting undergraduate minority students to enter and successfully complete advanced study in the scientific disciplines. Mechanisms to gain exposure to and experience in research projects prior to entry in graduate school might be one component of this kind of effort.

3. Early identification of undergraduates who show extraordinary promise in science and engineering, complemented by undergraduate honors or research assistant opportunities, offers another means of in-

creasing the pool of minority students who are interested in, qualified for, and aware of opportunities for graduate study in science.

4. The consortium model exemplified by existing efforts in the fields of law and business administration may be effectively used for the scientific disciplines. Through this approach, graduate departments in a single discipline or a group of related disciplines may consolidate their identification, recruitment, financial assistance, and supportive service activities. Resources and expertise would be pooled for the benefit of all participating institutions and departments, and the importance of faculty involvement emphasized. Joint summer institutes and exchange of undergraduate students among institutions for graduate study are possible features of this activity.

5. The tendency for many minorities with undergraduate training in the natural sciences to shift into other fields for doctoral study has been documented. Alteration of this trend would sharply expand the supply of new candidates for graduate study in the scientific disciplines. Programs to strengthen and update the scientific background of minority persons— many of whom may have completed their bachelor's degrees some years previously—who wish to undertake graduate work would address this problem.

PROFESSIONAL SOCIETIES

Professional societies have initiated a number of programs to increase the participation of minority group persons in activities of the profession and of the society. Despite a broad range of activities among societies, these programs have met with only a limited amount of success. The professional societies are not unlike most other traditional organizations in our country, in that their reaction to a growing national awareness about problems of minority persons has been to initiate a variety of activities— activities that are, however, *ad hoc,* temporary, underfunded, and not integral to the mainstream organizational structure. Consequently, the impact of such programs has been minimal; minority persons constitute a very small percentage of professional society memberships and play a minor role in the leadership of these associations.

The health of a disciplinary professional society is dependent on the general health of the discipline itself. It is thus not surprising that the societies, too, are suffering budgetary constrictions and reevaluating their program priorities. In such an environment, recently initiated programs with fledgling staff and support and often with outside support funds are among the first casualties. As foundation or federal support wanes, the "special" program likewise becomes moribund if the society is unable to divert funds to its operation.

Current Responses

Nearly every professional association has acknowledged the need to broaden minority involvement in its discipline, although few have designed programs to remedy low levels of minority group participation. Attention to minority group issues (their overall representation in higher education, achieving a "minority viewpoint") began in the late 1960's and in some instances died in the early 1970's. Some committees have disbanded after completion of a survey or publication of a report; others have been rendered ineffective by lack of association support, philosophical and fiscal. Activities range from inclusion of racial and ethnic information on membership surveys, whose results are simply distributed to members without any follow-up effort, to well-articulated, comprehensive programs that monitor involvement in graduate school and in the profession. Many professional societies are also constrained by the very real problem of attaining a "critical mass" for special programs in general and for minority activities in particular. Although many society members are broadly sympathetic to the special needs of minority persons, some do not fully understand the priorities of these needs. Unfortunately, growing divisions among many association memberships regarding their role in advocacy of minority group concerns in concert with waning external financial support impede broad-based support for these activities.

Most professional associations see their primary role as one of disseminating academic developments and research results through their journals and of providing a forum for the exchange of ideas at annual and special meetings. More recently, the associations have been concerned about the economic welfare and the job-seeking activities of their members. Again, concerns about minority group members are viewed as a lower priority than either of the above roles. In general, professional societies in which the subject matter of the discipline is oriented toward social issues—urban planning, public administration, etc.—tend to be more active in promoting minority concerns in contrast to purely "academic" disciplines.

Surveys

A common professional association activity has been the membership and departmental surveys, which include questions on enrollments, degrees awarded, faculty rank, and salary, etc. Within the past 2–4 years, nearly all groups have included one or more questions on ethnicity in their surveys. Occasionally, a separate survey or analysis has been carried out in order to measure participation and relative progress of minority groups and women within distinct professions. The results of these surveys are later disseminated through association newsletters and journals along with other survey findings. In one inventory undertaken by the American Sociological Association, survey findings over a 3-year period were examined in light of affirmative-action progress within graduate sociology departments, as well as in society membership, including discussion of the availability of financial aid, incidence of minority hiring, and rates of promotion. This practice highlights the size of the available pool, need for financial aid, rapid promotion opportunities, and the like; it also can stimulate new activities within university departments. Moreover, a disciplinary status report conveys a situation not readily evident from the perspective of individual institutions. However, this activity has little chance of succeeding unless findings are given prominent visibility by the association leadership.

Of course, a membership survey has the fundamental defect that the membership roster may reflect a disproportionately small number of minority persons. Other minority group professionals (and potential society members) may believe that the society does not reflect their interests as minority persons and thus do not join.

Committees

Over half of the societies have created committees on the status of minorities, both in graduate school and the profession at large. Committee activities have ranged from *pro forma* efforts (periodic meetings, minimal funding for staff or program activities, and no clearly defined approach to addressing minority group concerns from a disciplinary standpoint) to development of reports on such issues as minority views of the profession and education for minority needs.

Such committees face a variety of problems, not the least of which is their *ad hoc* nature. The problems of minority persons in professional activities are profound and are not likely to be solved by an *ad hoc* effort. The temporary status may point to a lack of real commitment by the society to resolving these problems. In most cases such committees never achieve the "critical mass," visibility, or active participation that are necessary to make significant progress.

A related development has been the formation of minority caucuses. In some instances, associations of minority professionals parallel to the established disciplinary society have been formed. These have been per-

176

ceived as a means of facilitating communication among minority professionals and developing a political influence.

Fellowship Programs

A very few associations have initiated graduate fellowship programs of one variety or another targeted to minorities. Most are merit-based and quite small (ranging from five to 40). Virtually all of the programs are funded by outside sources, and thus any association commitment of time and talent is tentative. While the principal purpose of these efforts is to increase the pool of qualified minorities in the disciplines, these activities also serve as potential models for implementation of programs geared to the needs of minority populations. Documentation of successful efforts assists in answering questions such as: How were students located and recruited? How were talented students identified? What placement strategies were used? How were local funding agencies involved? Many departments, reluctant to undertake special efforts in an air of uncertainty over effective ways of implementing programs, are more likely to respond once a viable pattern has been established and publicized by these "seed" efforts. Although the association fellowship programs are well intentioned, few have built-in mechanisms for sustaining long-term institutional commitment. As the external funding ends (as it often does), the program disappears.

In general, the professional societies exercise little control over the profession or its members. But their most valuable assets—membership and prestige—offer a unique opportunity to exercise leadership in the discipline. An unambiguous statement of support for equal opportunity and increases in minority participation in the profession could have a substantial impact on the attitudes and perceptions, perhaps even the behavior, of the members.

Effective leadership requires neither control nor an opinion survey of the membership. The most respected members of a discipline are usually elected as officers of a professional society. Their established reputations in the disciplines provide a strong basis for "candidacy" for national office. These officers have a unique opportunity to prod the interest of the membership on almost any issue, including that of minority participation in the discipline.

As long as equal opportunity efforts are located solely in special offices, commissions, or committees, the membership of the society will view them as peripheral to the interest of the leaders. Only when the established leaders of the society—its successful researchers, Nobel laureates, prize

177

winners, officeholders—become centrally concerned and involved with equal opportunity programs will the members view these programs as important enough to require action and commitment to complement rhetoric and good intentions.

In addition to the significant leadership role available to it, the professional society has a crucial function as a communicator among elements of the discipline. The scholarly journals provide one facet of this intradisciplinary tie; newsletters and magazines constitute media for more informal exchanges. These less-formal publications may be used to exchange information about programs for involving more minorities in the disciplinary affairs. The professional society offers the most direct and efficient mechanism for communication with faculty and departments; such interdepartment exchanges are crucial in sharing and sustaining innovations in many aspects of graduate education. Using the society mechanism not only facilitates communication but also creates an environment of concern, interest, and acceptability of innovative attempts to increase minority participation in graduate education. If such attempts are initiated and/or supported by prestigious members of the discipline, the communication is clearly more effective and more likely to be adopted elsewhere in the discipline.

We urge professional associations to draw upon the prestige and talents of members and to assign a high priority to promoting increased opportunities for minority men and women in graduate study and in the professions. Such efforts should be central, not peripheral, to the mainstream of association activities to ensure the sustained commitment essential to their viability and success. The professional societies should facilitate communication and serve in a coordinating role among departments and among faculty to:

1. Disseminate and publicize successful program models designed to promote minority group participation;

2. encourage leadership and commitment from members with the highest standing in the discipline in addressing these concerns;

3. provide administrative support to facilitate cooperation among institutions and departments to implement special programs; and

4. continue to monitor and evaluate the status of minority persons in the discipline.

A variety of activities should be implemented with the encouragement and involvement of professional societies, including short-term summer workshops to strengthen student preparation in specific subject areas prerequisite to work in the major discipline, i.e., quantitative skills for advanced study in the social sciences, cooperation among institutions and

178

departments for the recruitment and financial support of minority students, and association-sponsored fellowship programs.

OTHER EFFORTS: THE STATES, PHILANTHROPIC FOUNDATIONS, AND BUSINESS AND INDUSTRY

Throughout this report we have emphasized the complex, interlocking character of the problems encountered by minority persons aspiring to advanced study. Accordingly, it has been stressed that no single solution can encompass the extraordinary sensitivity, expertise, commitment, and resources necessary to deal with these issues. Rather, the combined efforts of government, institutions, and the private sector are required. The following section provides a brief discussion of the states, philanthropic foundations, and business and industry. This is not intended as a definitive review of their activities. We do, however, suggest responsibilities and actions that we believe represent constructive contributions to expanding opportunities for minority men and women in graduate study.

The States

The report of the Education Commission of the States' Task Force on Graduate Education declared that:

While graduate education with its attendant research, including master's and doctoral programs, is clearly a national resource, it is also a regional, state and local resource. Primary responsibility for providing educational opportunity constitutionally and historically rests with the states.[10]

The contributions flowing from graduate education and research to the states resemble those at the national level—the education and development of skilled individuals, production of new knowledge through research, preservation and transmission of knowledge, and improvement of the quality of life in our society.[11] Similarly, while equal educational opportunity is a central concern of the federal government, the states also have both an obligation and special capabilities to address this issue. The necessity of a state role in facilitating minority student access and achievement in graduate education is dictated by two broad considerations. First,

[10] Education Commission of the States, *The States and Graduate Education,* Report of the Task Force on Graduate Education, (Denver: Education Commission of the States, February 1975), p. 1.
[11] National Board on Graduate Education, *Graduate Education: Purposes, Problems and Potential* (Washington, D.C.: National Board on Graduate Education, November 1972), pp. 3–6.

within states, the specific emphases and forms of advanced training may be modified in accord with state and regional manpower and research needs, as well as public attitudes toward graduate education and general resource constraints. Second, the history, size, and composition, as well as the economic, educational, and cultural circumstances, of the minority populations within individual states are diverse and affect participation throughout higher education.

Doctoral education and research are generally considered a national resource, thereby justifying substantial federal support for these activities, since doctorate recipients are mobile and the benefits of research are available to the entire nation. However, as the task force of the Education Commission of the States pointed out, most higher education institutions are "responsive to the needs of the states in which they are located. They provide assistance in identifying state-level issues, training individuals to investigate these issues and conducting research activities to resolve state-level problems." [12] Moreover, state manpower requirements may be quite different from the aggregate national demand. State and regional manpower needs may also derive, in part, from the skills and training required to address issues pertinent to the resident minority communities. Highly educated persons in urban planning, public health, and other professional areas are important to improvement of the quality of life of both the minority communities and all persons in the state.

The size and character of the resident minority population vary among states. For example, while blacks, Chicanos, and Asian Americans comprise 30 percent of the population in California, in some New England states minority persons represent less than 1 percent of the residents.[13] Chicanos are concentrated in the five southwestern states, while Puerto Ricans reside primarily in New York and New Jersey. The American Indian population is most numerous in the mountain, southwestern, and south central states. The impact of the variation in geographic distribution upon access to graduate study warrants examination.

A large proportion of graduate students attend graduate school in their home state, especially in public universities.[14] Low tuition in public institutions is a strong incentive for persons to attend graduate study in

[12] Education Commission of the States, *op. cit.*, p. 11.
[13] U.S. Bureau of the Census, 1970 Census of Population, vol. I, *Characteristics of the Population*, part 1, "United States Summary" (Washington, D.C.: U.S. Government Printing Office, 1973), Table 60.
[14] In New York State, three-fourths of graduate students were state residents, although this proportion showed wide variation according to the particular institution attended. New York State Board of Regents, *Meeting the Needs of Doctoral Education in New York State* (Albany: Regents Commission on Doctoral Education, January 1973), pp. 58–59.

180

their home state, since, for many, high tuition fees would preclude attendance. Participation in programs with a professional career orientation, especially those which award a terminal master's degree, is likely to be affected by geographic proximity. The growth of such programs, as well as opportunities for extended study and other nontraditional forms, points to a demand for graduate education that is compatible with current employment in making such opportunities available in new forms, new times, and at new locations. Most graduate students attend on a part-time basis. Although it is difficult to differentiate master's from doctoral students in aggregate enrollment statistics, in 1971, 59 percent of first-year graduate students in doctorate institutions were full-time students, while only 26 percent of first-year students in other institutions attended on a full-time basis. It is probable that the difference in these figures would be more striking if a clean distinction between master's and doctoral students in Ph.D. schools could be drawn.[15]

Cultural factors also influence the effect of geographic proximity upon access to graduate education; for example, minority persons who plan to attend graduate education in order to obtain skills that may be applied to improvement of the status of the minority community may be reluctant to attend graduate study at great distance from their homes. It has been suggested that Native American students, in particular, are unwilling to break close ties with the tribal community in order to obtain advanced study.

Although equalizing educational opportunity is a widely accepted objective of the state role in postsecondary education, the basic philosophies and programmatic efforts adopted by individual states are diverse. This is not surprising since "the 50 states differ greatly on a variety of important variables: legislation, the mix of public and private institutions, student migration patterns, arrangements for financing postsecondary education, and level of support for the total systems."[16] At the graduate level, this issue is further complicated by the conceptual debate about the propriety of treating a student who holds a bachelor's degree as disadvantaged, as well as the legal and political controversies over use of race or ethnic criteria. Although a detailed review of the current activities of each of the states is beyond the scope of this report, it is useful to identify general trends and highlight a few significant developments.

Most states have expressed concern about the importance of ensuring

---

[15] Figures calculated from U.S. Department of Health, Education, and Welfare, National Center for Educational Statistics, *Students Enrolled for Advanced Degrees, Fall 1971* (Washington, D.C.: U.S. Government Printing Office, 1974), Table 7.
[16] American Council on Education, Policy Analysis Service, *Federal–State Responsibility for Facilitating Student Access* (Washington, D.C.: American Council on Education, March 1975), p. 1.

equal opportunity in their master plans or other statewide policy documents; many have included an explicit reference to the circumstance of ethnic and racial minority persons. At the undergraduate level, a direct state role in provision of student assistance is common; eligibility for state aid is determined on academic merit, financial need, or a combination of both. For educationally and financially disadvantaged students, several states have implemented or supported educational opportunity programs (EOP), designed to ameliorate barriers to access and completion of undergraduate study.

At the graduate level, there are few direct statewide programs to assist students with financial need (loan programs are an exception), and we are not aware of any state program that assists educationally disadvantaged graduate students comparable to activities widespread at the undergraduate level.

State higher education programs that use ethnic or racial criteria in determining eligibility are rare. There are, however, notable exceptions. Several states award scholarships to persons of American Indian ancestry. In general, such programs have been authorized by the state legislatures in recognition of long-standing social, educational, and economic deprivations that have affected the resident Indian populations.

Other programs represent a response to the 1973 ruling upheld by the Court of Appeals for the District of Columbia in which 10 states were ordered to take steps to desegregate their systems of higher education. In one state, as a component of the statewide equal educational opportunity plan, fellowships are awarded to black college faculty seeking to pursue a terminal degree. Financial aid is also available to nonminority students entering an historically black college. Although not restricted to ethnic or racial minority individuals, programs to train personnel to implement federal and state bilingual–bicultural requirements have benefited the minority population.

The biennial survey of racial and ethnic enrollments in higher education institutions conducted by the Office for Civil Rights, Department of Health, Education, and Welfare, has stimulated a number of states to take a central role in coordinating or supplementing that survey. In several instances, collection of additional statistics on variables such as degree attainment, financial aid, attrition, and academic performance, by race and ethnic identity, forms the core of an extensive data base that permits detailed examination of minority participation throughout the state system of higher education.

While programs directed to either financially disadvantaged or minority graduate students are uncommon, it should be stressed that the reference here is to statewide, centralized programs in contrast to programs administered by individual public institutions, although the latter activities may be supported through state funds. In some instances institutions have requested specific state appropriations to support disadvantaged or minority graduate students, often implemented through a graduate opportunity program, and many public institutions have provided assistance to minority students from general operating funds.

In our view there appear to be advantages to encouraging individual institutions, and departments within institutions, to undertake efforts to advance minority participation in contrast to direct statewide initiatives. The decentralized nature of graduate education is key. Programmatic efforts conceived and administered external to individual institutions and lacking strong faculty participation may be ineffective in involving minority students in the mainstream of departmental teaching and research activities. We affirm our belief that:

The states have both an obligation and special capabilities to address issues affecting minority participation at the graduate level. Insofar as master plans have been developed in individual states, such plans should specify a concern for equality of opportunity in graduate education. States should encourage and respond to institutional initiatives in development of efforts directed to this end. We recommend that states provide support to institutions for:

1. Financial assistance for disadvantaged graduate students to advance the participation of minority persons;

2. provision of supportive services within institutions; and

3. development of cooperative programs between undergraduate and graduate institutions to identify, encourage, and strengthen the academic preparation of talented minority undergraduates for entry to graduate study.

Business and Industry

The minority population continues to lag far behind whites in the proportion holding high-paying, high-status jobs. In 1974, blacks comprised 6 percent of professional and technical workers and 3 percent of persons holding managerial and administrative positions.[17] In recent years a clear trend of occupational upgrading has occurred among blacks and other races. As more minority men and women earn college degrees, they are joining the nation's work force at career entry levels that typically require a higher education. The national commitment to facilitate equal educational opportunity for minority persons parallels a similar objective in the

[17] U.S. Bureau of the Census, Current Population Reports, Series P-23, no. 54, *The Social and Economic Status of the Black Population in the United States, 1974* (Washington, D.C.: U.S. Government Printing Office, 1975), p. 75.

employment sector. Business and industry are required by federal and state civil rights legislation to take positive actions to ensure nondiscriminatory hiring and promotion policies. Accordingly, firms are seeking to attract qualified minority graduates for administrative, professional, and research positions much as colleges and universities have broadened their recruitment efforts to include more minority Ph.D.'s among the pool of candidates considered for faculty appointments. However, while openings are available at levels requiring undergraduate and graduate degrees, there is a shortage of minority persons with the appropriate educational qualifications, especially in technical areas.[18]

The paucity of minority persons holding advanced degrees is compounded by another factor. Evidence from a survey of doctoral scientists and engineers suggests that blacks, Hispanic persons, and American Indians are less likely to hold positions in business and industry than are white or Oriental persons. In 1973, about one-fifth of doctoral-level scientists and engineers were employed by business and industry. Of these, less than 8 percent were members of a racial or ethnic minority group. While the proportion of Orientals employed by business or industry was surprisingly large, the percentage of doctorate scientists and engineers that were blacks, Hispanic persons, and American Indians totaled only about 1 percent.[19] A 1969 survey of black doctorates reported that only 2.7 percent of the 1,096 respondents indicated that they were currently employed in industry.[20]

Recognition of this situation has stimulated business and industry to support a variety of efforts to assist minority persons to attain an advanced degree, especially in professionally oriented fields where a large percentage of the graduates enters nonacademic positions. Numerous companies have provided scholarships for minority individuals, and many have contributed funds to aid minority institutions. At the graduate level, cooperative efforts between institutions and the private sector have enjoyed considerable success. Two consortia of business schools that seek to recruit and assist minorities in entering graduate study in business and management have received substantial funding from the private sector. A newly organized consortium committed to increasing the number of minorities earning graduate degrees in engineering has sought significant

[18] See "College Recruitment," *Black Enterprise,* March 1973, p. 37, and "Engineering Field Openings for Blacks in Midst of Job Revival," *Black Enterprise,* March 1973, p. 34.
[19] National Research Council, Commission on Human Resources, *Minority Groups Among Doctorate Level Scientists, Engineers, and Scholars* (Washington, D.C.: National Academy of Sciences, 1974), p. 30.
[20] James W. Bryant, *A Survey of Black American Doctorates* (New York: The Ford Foundation, 1970), p. 7.

involvement of the private sector; industry research centers have agreed to provide summer work experiences for program participants. The possibilities for effective participation by the private sector are many; grants to support individual students or existing institutional activities, as well as a more active partnership in the educational process (such as internships, summer programs, or research), are central.

Business and industry have a fundamental interest in and responsibility for increasing the supply of highly educated minority persons. Two strategies are advanced:

Provision of financial support to graduate institutions or a consortium of graduate departments that normally provide personnel with advanced degrees to particular business or industrial firms. A more active partnership with educational institutions through provision of internship or research experiences in the private sector should be encouraged.

Identification, encouragement, and financial assistance for promising minority employees to undertake advanced study that will enable them to move into high-level positions.

This recommendation has particular significance in view of the economic forces tending to encourage minority baccalaureates to accept immediate employment upon graduation. Promising minority students may be diverted from graduate study although their long-run career goals may be best served by undertaking advanced study.

Foundations

Philanthropic foundations have been in the forefront of those dedicated to advancement of equality of educational opportunity. The leadership exercised by foundations, complemented by their greater flexibility relative to other institutions in funding decisions, represents a major contribution to the national commitment to improve the educational status of minority men and women. The private foundations have supported numerous activities benefiting minorities, including fellowship awards to aid minority persons in doctoral study, grants to strengthen the black colleges and universities, educational leadership programs, summer institutes, and pertinent research. Some have chosen to focus their attention and resources on specific disciplinary fields with the aim of increasing the number of minority persons represented in those areas. Business and management, engineering, and medicine are three fields in which foundations have been active. In several instances, specific numerical targets, i.e., number of graduates, have been established, and projects directed to those goals were supported. Foundations have provided "seed money" for experimental programs, and successful programs initiated by foundations have often been continued by government and other institutions.

185

Foundation commitment initiated in the past decade was instrumental in promoting the first significant influx of minority students into graduate and professional schools through fellowship awards to minority individuals. One outcome of these efforts was to clearly demonstrate to higher education institutions and to the broader society that highly motivated minority students, despite gaps in educational preparation, could realize high levels of academic achievement in advanced study. Moreover, those students who earned graduate degrees also became role models for encouragement of future classes of minority students.

Whereas earlier foundation endeavors led the way and signaled the need for broader societal action, the current situation marks a transition period. In our view the present approach should be directed to institutionalizing or normalizing minority participation such that minority access and achievement will not be solely dependent on special efforts. The magnitude of the problem and the concomitant resource expenditures implied necessarily mean that foundations must focus on areas in which they can have a measurable impact. In this context we stress the critical role of foundations in providing selective support to promising efforts that will serve as a catalyst in creation of an educational environment conducive to minority student achievement.

Overall, private foundations continue active in promoting social justice and expansion of higher education opportunities for minorities. However, total foundation grants in this area are expected to decline in the near future with the phasing out of two of the largest programmatic efforts. While significant gains have been realized in the past decade, unresolved problems remain. Therefore:

We urge foundations to initiate, develop, and sustain commitment to and support of selected programs to improve minority participation in graduate education, as an important complement to federal, state, institutional, and other activities.

Through broad and varied experience with minority efforts, foundations have developed a high level of insight into these issues. Informal evaluation of alternative approaches has enabled foundation personnel to understand which kinds of programs are effective (as well as those that are ineffective). Yet relatively little of this knowledge is shared among foundations or with external agencies, institutions, or researchers on a systematic basis. Mechanisms for disseminating information gained from these activities can assist others in improving the effectiveness of existing programs and preclude the necessity of others having to "reinvent the wheel."

We recommend that foundations consider various means of sharing the insights gained through their individual experiences in minority concerns. Two possibilities are suggested:

186

1. Periodic conferences sponsored either singly or jointly by foundations with relevant activities to exchange information about particular subject areas, with the aim of identifying effective program approaches. The proceedings of such conferences should be published and broadly disseminated.

2. Systematic codification and dissemination of knowledge derived from their activities in order to provide information about productive program efforts. The availability of such information would be useful to other institutions and individuals who are interested and involved in these concerns.

Supplement:

MISSION, STATUS, PROBLEMS, AND PRIORITIES
OF BLACK GRADUATE SCHOOLS

Black graduate schools constitute a valuable resource in the provision of opportunity for advanced education. Presently 28 black graduate schools offer graduate study leading to a master's degree, four of whom offer doctoral programs. About one-fifth of all black students enrolled in graduate education nationwide attend a predominately black institution. Graduate enrollments in these schools have grown rapidly, having more than doubled in the 6 years from 1967 to 1973.

In light of the significance of their role, NBGE concluded that a report on the subject of minority participation in graduate education would be severely deficient without discussion of the role, status, and priorities of black graduate institutions, as viewed by the schools themselves. During a meeting of the newly established Conference of Deans of Black Graduate Schools in Dallas, Texas, in February 1974, the possibility of preparation of a statement by the conference was discussed. In September 1974, a meeting with representatives of the conference and other distinguished black educators in Atlanta, Georgia, was cosponsored by NBGE and the Conference of Deans of Black Graduate Schools, at which time final approval of the focus and organization of such a statement was agreed upon by the group. Under the leadership of Henry E. Cobb of Southern University, a report on the "Mission, Status, Problems, and Priorities of Black Graduate Schools" was developed by the conference. The statement provided here represents an abridgement of a more comprehensive report to be published separately by the conference.

We believe this statement to be of special significance in view of three concerns. First, there has been almost no discussion or research on the

189

status and contributions of the black graduate schools within the wider higher education context. Second, most analyses to date have not focused on the concerns and views of faculty and administrators currently working in these schools. Third, the effects of the historical isolation of these institutions from the mainstream educational system have been intensified by the fact that there has been little cooperation and communication among the black graduate schools. This statement prepared by the Conference of Deans of Black Graduate Schools speaks to all of these issues. As such it provides valuable information about the role and priorities of these schools in light of the rapidly changing context of higher education, as perceived by individuals in these schools themselves. This discussion is, moreover, an important first step in developing constructive ties among these institutions to assist in strengthening opportunities for graduate education at black colleges and universities. We are pleased to present this thoughtful and illuminating statement and believe its conclusions and recommendations merit the most careful consideration.

Mission, Status, Problems, and Priorities of Black Graduate Schools

BY CONFERENCE OF DEANS OF
BLACK GRADUATE SCHOOLS [1]

Compiled and Edited by Henry E. Cobb

INTRODUCTION

For nearly a half century a number of black institutions of higher education have offered systematic programs leading to graduate degrees. The
early programs moved slowly through a period of gradual evolution from
what was called "graduate work" to the full-fledged status of graduate
schools.[2] Black graduate schools seemed to have been founded in clusters
and tended to follow a pattern set by that cluster. Fisk (which initiated
its program in 1927), Hampton, Atlanta, Xavier, and Howard all had
programs by 1934. The establishment of graduate programs at the black
public colleges followed. Some were responses to the inability of their
graduates to secure aid for out-of-state graduate study, through provisions
that operated in some states in the 1940's and early 1950's.[3] About one-
half of the black graduate schools were established prior to the *Brown* v.
Board of Education decision in 1954.

---

[1] Contributors are listed on pp. 216–217.
[2] Rayford W. Logan, *Howard University: The First Hundred Years, 1867–1967*
(New York: New York University Press, 1969), pp. 275, 314; Clarence A. Bacote,
The Story of Atlanta University: A Century of Service, 1865–1965 (Atlanta: Atlanta
University Press, 1969), pp. 278–279. Fisk University announced a program of
graduate studies in 1889, but its operation was only temporary.
[3] A graduate program was set up in 1945 at Florida A&M University after considerable pressure from this source. Leedell W. Neyland and John W. Riley, *The History
of Florida Agricultural and Mechanical University* (Gainesville: University of
Florida Press, 1963), p. 184.

It is clear from the above that graduate programs, as functional units of the institutions onto which they were grafted, began many years after these institutions were founded. The purpose and function of the graduate programs at many of these institutions are leavened by influences arising out of the institutional histories. The facts that (1) many of these institutions were chartered for the education of those now called the disadvantaged and (2) many of those under public control have operated as land-grant colleges since 1890 have helped to shape the course of their development in terms of the realities associated with these designated missions.

Largely because of these two statutory injunctions and the decidedly unfriendly atmosphere in which, for most of their existence, these colleges and universities have operated, they have been compelled to be relevant, not so much eschewing the ivory tower as bending to the winds of necessity. The clienteles of these institutions have not been, for the most part, those with traditional academic credentials. These institutions, however, accepted this condition as a point of departure; they fashioned programs, developed materials, and assigned faculty to transform their students, or an astonishingly large percentage of them, into creditable graduates.

THE MISSION OF BLACK GRADUATE SCHOOLS

The purpose of graduate education has been stated many times, but its socializing, humanizing, and tooling functions remain preeminent. A recent statement of purposes suggested four major functions. First, the development of highly skilled individuals; second, the production of knowledge; third, the preservation and transmission of knowledge; and, fourth, improving the quality of life in American society.[4] Conceptually, graduate programs in the black institutions lean heavily on the time-honored dictum that the university of which they are a part is a community of scholars, that the central focus of that community is the discovery and growth of ideas, and that the finest expression of this entire concept is the spirit of free inquiry, which is a necessary condition in a search for truth.

Any valid attempt to assess the past and present missions of black graduate schools must consider the four functions of graduate education in America stated above. A precondition for assessment of the future roles of these schools is a clear recognition of the program diversity and hence

[4] National Board on Graduate Education, *Graduate Education: Purposes, Problems, and Potential* (Washington, D.C.: National Board on Graduate Education, 1972), pp. 4–6.

192

functional differences that exist among these institutions. But as is often the case with majority institutions, black graduate schools are treated as one institutional archetype and "a single standard is sometimes invoked across the board." [5]

Black graduate schools, while sharing with other institutions the universal concerns of higher education, serve an additional function in their distinctive ability to fulfill a role oriented toward the needs of a defined cultural community. Black graduate schools provide an avenue of cultural mobility for those people who have had constrictive experiences of success in the traditional educational systems of the country. Black schools have had to be responsive to the special social and educational problems of their student population. The black graduate school has become especially adept at providing motivational bridges and models for the "disadvantaged student" and has gained a significant degree of expertise that is either lacking or of low priority in other institutions.

While the universal mission of graduate education should be responsive to the dominant needs and themes of the total society, the manner in which the black graduate school can be most responsive to this universal mission, and at the same time true to its particular role, is one that involves deliberate choice. The black graduate school must enhance the effectiveness and efficiency of its programs of scholarship and research as these respond to career and professional needs of its students. As an agent of social change, the black graduate school must bridge the educational gaps of black students and it must also be the vehicle by which talented students may gain access to graduate programs often denied them in other schools.

The stability of American society depends, in large measure, upon progress in raising the proportion of minority people pursuing careers for which graduate education is a prerequisite. It is only by increasing the numbers in the professions that we will be able to tap a large reservoir of unused talent. Medicine, dentistry, college teaching, and science and engineering are areas where minorities are grossly underrepresented.[6] The black graduate school properly utilized can serve an important role in filling this talent gap.

Indeed, a crucial role that the black college and the black graduate school have played and are now playing is that of providing an ambience in which blacks and other disadvantaged students may take tentative steps toward acquiring or furthering their education without being exposed immediately to the full competitive rigor and impersonal, even sometimes

[5] See Panel on Alternative Approaches to Graduate Education, *Scholarship for Society* (Princeton, N.J.: Educational Testing Service, 1974), p. 10.
[6] For pertinent data see National Research Council, Commission on Human Resources, *Minority Groups among United States Doctorate Scientists, Engineers, and Scholars, 1973* (Washington, D.C.: National Academy of Sciences, 1974).

unfriendly, atmosphere in a large and highly selective institution. Many students who achieve a significant degree of success in a black graduate school would be foredoomed to failure or constant frustration in a less supportive environment. This does not mean that the standards of black schools are necessarily lower than those of other institutions, but rather, in highly selective schools with deliberately limited enrollments, many applicants of various ethnic and racial backgrounds capable of performing satisfactorily must be arbitrarily denied admission. The disproportionately low percentage of blacks and other minorities among the holders of advanced degrees argues for the black graduate school to continue and to enlarge its function of increasing the numbers of those pursuing graduate work, especially in disciplines of high societal need.

Many of the graduates of black colleges and black graduate schools who are currently making indispensable contributions to the nation in the arts, sciences, business and professions would have been excluded from higher education by the normal admissions policies of the nonminority institutions. If black institutions did not exist, many of the current generation of black applicants to higher education would suffer the same fate. Existing evidence suggests that the black graduate school can be more adaptive to the particular needs of black students. This would include developing special programs to serve both part-time and older students, as well as those who are prepared to work in the traditional model as full-time students.

It must also be borne in mind that the role of the black graduate school, like that of any educational institution, cannot be separate from the aspirations, needs, and cultural development of its constituency. As W. E. B. DuBois observed more than 40 years ago, "The proper education of any people includes sympathetic touch between teacher and pupil; knowledge on the part of the teacher, not simply of the individual taught, but of his surroundings and background, and the history of his class and group." [7] It is undeniable that the black graduate school can and must serve as an interpreter and translator of the ethnic and cultural experience of black people in America. This role is too often overlooked or understressed.

The black graduate school should be the critical locus of original research and investigation about the black graduate experience in America. Let it be clear that this special mission of black graduate schools is no less universal nor any more parochial than any other graduate school. The uniqueness lies in the fact that the black graduate school starts from a different beginning as it moves toward an understanding of the universe of activities between and among mankind and the environment. That beginning determines the way in which the world of pure fact will be re-

[7] W. E. B. DuBois, "Does the Negro Need Separate Schools?" *Journal of Negro Education,* July 1935, p. 278.

duced to described fact. This is not to say that the black graduate school should be limited in the subjects taught or the students recruited. At a black graduate school all subjects should be "black" only to the extent that all subjects at mainstream American colleges are "white." The black graduate school, as do all graduate schools, seeks to attract the brightest and most creative minds—but without eschewing its obligation to salvage and polish those minds that have been callously crippled by the existing inequities of the American system of education.

Finally, the mission of black graduate schools is closely related to the black community. Although, like its undergraduate counterpart, it has been seriously criticized for not serving its constituency, the black college and the black graduate school are the black community's most conspicuous and prestigious features. Part of the misunderstanding or, more precisely, the lack of understanding regarding this phenomenon stems from the fact that the ties that bind the two entities are not always readily visible. Many observers assume that the lack of clearly discernible programmatic links between black institutions of higher education and the black community indicates the absence of a relationship. In fact the nexus is organic. If there had been no black community, there would be no black schools. Given the social, political, and economic realities associated with the origin and development of these institutions, without black colleges and black graduate schools the black community, as we now know it, could hardly have existed.[8] As the black community again becomes self-conscious and turns in on itself, it is to black institutions that blacks are likely to turn for reinforcement.

Black graduate schools, once limited in their clientele by externally imposed constraints, must now transcend this condition and prepare to become multicultural centers of excellence. They must also prepare to provide the necessary leverage for impacting both minority and majority communities with highly skilled personnel from among their graduates. As some already have done, black graduate schools must also become places where the finest minds—faculty and students—may pursue the truth in a climate of freedom and curiosity.

CURRENT STATUS OF BLACK GRADUATE SCHOOLS

Twenty-eight black institutions currently offer systematic programs leading to graduate degrees. All schools offer the master's degree, and four

[8] See Mack H. Jones, "The Responsibility of the Black College to the Black Community," *Daedalus,* Summer 1971 (special issue on "The Future of the Black Colleges"), and Ernest Patterson, "Political Socialization and the Survival of Black Graduate Schools," in *Proceedings of the Conference of Deans of Black Graduate Schools* (Atlanta: 1973).

have doctorate programs. For those with master's study, a wide variation in programmatic structures exists, ranging from the single-degree structures in some institutions to the comprehensive scheme of offerings found at Howard University. Of the three institutions that award doctoral degrees, Howard University has the most comprehensive program, offering doctoral work in approximately 20 areas. Atlanta University confers the Ph.D. in three disciplines and the Ed.D. in one. Meharry Medical College awards the Ph.D. in three fields, the focus of which is biomedical sciences, and Texas Southern University recently established an Ed.D. program in educational administration.

A brief review of the magnitude of graduate education in the black colleges is in order. In fall 1973 the historically black graduate schools enrolled 19,919 students,[9] and in 1972–73 they conferred 5,545 master's degrees.[10] These schools awarded 43, or 5.7 percent, of the 760 doctorates earned by black U.S. citizens in 1972–73.[11] Data obtained from a 1973 survey of the 28 black graduate schools, in which all but five institutions participated, present a clearer pattern of enrollment and degree granting trends.[12] The data in Table 47 clearly indicate the tremendous growth in enrollment of these institutions. The change in the enrollment from spring 1969 to spring 1973 is just short of phenomenal, especially in light of highly publicized claims of increased ease of access to majority graduate institutions. Further inspection of Table 47 suggests that between 1972 and 1973 enrollments began to level off.[13]

Another parameter of institutional effectiveness is the achievement record. Only when enrollments are measured against exit patterns will the work of institutions be clearly seen. Table 48 shows that 21 black institutions conferred 3,864 master's degrees in 1972–73. If the corrections shown in the table notes are considered, a total of 4,500 degrees for all 28 institutions that year would not be an unreasonable estimate. The percentage increase for all degrees from 1971 to 1972 was 22 percent.[14]

[9] Elias Blake, Jr., Linda J. Lambert, and Joseph L. Martin, *Degrees Granted and Enrollment Trends in Historically Black Colleges: An Eight-Year Study* (Washington, D.C.: Institute for Services to Education, 1974), p. 26.
[10] *Ibid.*, pp. 47–48.
[11] National Research Council, Commission on Human Resources, *Minority Groups among Doctorate Level Scientists, Engineers, and Scholars, 1973* (Washington, D.C.: National Academy of Sciences, 1974).
[12] Twenty-two of the 23 participating schools reported enrollments. Of these, six privately controlled institutions reported 2,877 enrolled students and 16 publicly controlled institutions reported an enrollment of 11,516.
[13] Comparison of spring session enrollments for 1972 and for 1973 must consider the missing data as noted.
[14] This does not include the production accruing from the remarkable increase in enrollment for spring 1973 shown in Table 47. Pertinent enrollments are as follows: 1971 (15,505), 1972 (16,549), and 1973 (19,191). Blake, Lambert, and Martin, *op. cit.*, p. 21.

TABLE 47 Enrollment Patterns in Black Graduate Schools, Fall 1968–Spring 1973

| Year | Enrollment by Session [a] | | |
	Summer	Fall	Spring
1972–73	11,743	11,952 [b]	14,393
1971–72	11,677	11,339	10,365 [b]
1970–71	9,711 [b]	8,399 [b]	9,064 [b]
1969–70	11,008	6,744 [b]	7,835 [b]
1968–69	9,496	6,844 [b]	5,737

[a] Enrollment data provided by 22 institutions.
[b] Three of the reporting institutions were unable to provide data.

The increase in degrees granted in that period was also astonishingly large in every category. The increases in the "M.Ed." and "total degrees" categories were 34 percent and 108 percent, respectively.

Since the M.Ed. degree is only offered in education or through a dual program in education and another discipline, it is apparent that at least 60 percent of the degrees conferred were in education. In addition, some schools offer an M.A. and M.S. degree in education only, thus raising the number of education degrees as a proportion of total degrees granted.

In much of the sparse literature on blacks in graduate education, two points have been emphasized: the tendency of blacks to cluster in education and the tremendous underrepresentation in "respectable" disciplines like the sciences. First, it should be noted that the doctorates earned by blacks represent only 2.7 percent of all doctorates awarded to U.S. citizens,

TABLE 48 Degree-Granting Patterns in Black Graduate Schools, 1968–69 to 1972–73 [a]

| Year | Type of Degree Awarded [b] | | | | |
	M.A.	M.S.	M.Ed.	M.B.A.	Total Degrees
1972–73	708	750	2,319	87	3,864
	(18%)	(19%)	(60%)	(2%)	(100%)
1971–72	619	770	1,727	38	3,154
	(20%)	(24%)	(55%)	(1%)	(100%)
1970–71	476	524	1,357	15	2,372
	(20%)	(22%)	(57%)	(1%)	(100%)
1969–70	423	411	977	3	1,814
	(23%)	(23%)	(54%)	(0%)	(100%)
1968–69	397	470	987	—	1,854
	(21%)	(25%)	(53%)	—	(100%)

[a] Twenty-three institutions participated but two did not furnish degree granting data. Of these two, one awarded over 600 master's degrees in 1973.
[b] A significant number of M.S.W. (social work) and M.S.L.S. (library science) degrees awarded during this period are not included.

and there are too few blacks earning doctorates in every field. But even this meager production must be put in proper perspective if appropriate recommendations are to be made. The central question is: What should an appropriate distribution be? Should blacks strive to approximate the distributions indicated by the percentages for whites? But there is an overall Ph.D. "glut" it is said. Since this history of doctoral production of majority institutions is reasonably well documented, black institutions engaged in doctoral work or planning to engage in it are not doomed to repeat the errors of this history.

The concentration of black students in the field of education occurring at both the master's and doctoral level is partially a function of the history of black education and the atmosphere in which it has developed in this country. The marketability of educational skills looms large as a force directing curricular preferences. For many years, securing a teaching position in one of the black segregated schools was one of the most productive careers among a limited range of vocational options for blacks with college degrees. As career opportunities have increased, the percentage of bachelor's degree graduates in education has declined. For example, the production in education moved from 44.9 percent of the total in 1965–66 to 33.4 percent of the total in 1972–73 in the black colleges.[15] A sizeable proportion of blacks holding master's degrees earned their degrees at black institutions where education, in most cases, is the major field of enrollment. This situation reflects, in part, the rush for retooling that occurred among black precollege teachers when elementary and secondary desegregation plans were implemented in recent years. It also reflects the nexus between black educational institutions and the black community. Clearly, black graduate students must broaden the scope of their curricular and degree-seeking choices; however, this admonition should be accompanied by recognition of the important role that the schools and the teachers play in social change. There are not too many blacks with master's degrees in education; there are too few blacks with degrees in other fields. Indeed, for blacks to desert the classroom at this point in our history would be inconsistent with any reasonable prognosis of the future of black people or, indeed, the future of America.

As indicated above, the distribution of blacks in the education fields at the doctoral level differs only slightly from that at the master's level. While blacks receiving doctorates in education accounted for 59.5 percent of all black Ph.D.'s, black Ph.D.-granting institutions, as late as 1973, had not contributed to these figures. The black graduate schools have conferred few doctorates in education. A recent analysis of black doctoral recipients of 1972–73 revealed that "only 14 percent of blacks who later

[15] *Ibid.*, p. 38.

198

received a doctorate at a white university, received a master's from a black graduate school. Moreover, 70 percent of those doctorates who attended a black graduate school at the master's level received the Ph.D. in an education field, whereas 58 percent of black doctorates who attended only white graduate schools received their doctorates in education." [16] Two points immediately stand out: first, the percentage of those receiving master's degrees at black graduate schools is woefully small. Second, the selection of education as the field of concentration takes place mainly at white institutions. The small number of doctoral recipients receiving the master's degree at black institutions was only sufficient to raise the percentage from 58.0 percent to 59.5 percent.

The tendency for a large percentage of blacks especially and other minorities, with the exception of Orientals, to earn doctorates in education raises a problems for the distribution of minorities, not only in graduate education but also for the distribution of minorities in the labor market at levels requiring doctoral training. Again, why this tendency to cluster in education? The suggestion here is that both the problem and the solution can be found in the nature of the doctoral-granting institutions and the larger society itself. An important, perhaps even crucial, aspect of this amalgam is the intellectual and cultural background that the black student brings to the graduate school with him. This includes his perception of the nature and role of graduate education, as well as its impact for his career goals. The field of education with its emphasis on learning styles and psychosocial influences on achievements may offer the minority student an environment less alien and more supportive in which to learn. The answer, of course, is not to force all black graduate students into education or even the majority, but to apply the socializing processes apparently found in education to other areas. For some black graduate students, the black graduate school provides such a supportive environment.

I. Bruce Hamilton found that at a significant number of major graduate institutions there was a relationship between the number of minorities enrolling and activities to attract and retain minority students.[17] There are indications that students in black studies curricula and the programs themselves tend to thrive when such programs are linked with significant support services on the campuses of major universities.[18] In a perceptive

[16] Analysis by NBGE of data from National Research Council, National Academy of Sciences, Doctorate Records File, November 1974.
[17] See I. Bruce Hamilton, *Graduate School Programs for Minority/Disadvantaged Students* (Princeton, N.J.: Educational Testing Service, 1973).
[18] Elias Blake, Jr. and Henry J. Cobb *et al., Black Studies: Issues in Their Institutional Survival* (Washington, D.C.: Institute for Services to Education, 1974), pp. 23–26.

statement on the Chicano and graduate education, Rudolph de la Garza put these points in perspective. Describing the situation at major graduate schools, he commented that:

There is also an assumption shared by a great many graduate faculty and administrators that there is nothing left to be done once Chicanos have been admitted. That is, they have not internalized the need to change the content of their programs and the very objectives of graduate training if the changed admissions criteria are to have any effect.

Moreover:

Graduate schools, including both administrators and faculty, explain their response in traditional and, by our judgment, unacceptably naive language. Their explanation is grounded in the view of graduate schools primarily and sometimes exclusively serving academic and intellectual functions rather than as major structures intimately and directly affecting the economic, social and political processes of the nation. . . . Graduate schools are tied to the community in obvious and irrefutable ways. They are the training ground for decision makers, intellectual leaders and role models in all areas.[19]

Kent G. Mommsen, who surveyed black Ph.D.'s in American higher education, found that blacks perceived themselves as discriminated against. Thus, any assessment of doctoral achievement among them should weigh this factor. Mommsen concluded that "only weak support can be claimed for the . . . major hypothesis that institutional racism may be decreasing in American higher education." [20] For some black and other disadvantaged graduate students, the black graduate school may provide the kind of supportive environment needed to overcome these cultural discontinuities.

Since most black graduate schools offer only the master's degree, an examination of the nature and scope of their programs at that level should shed some light on their role and status. Figures 2–5 represent a graphic display of program structures according to type of degree, general area of knowledge, and number of institutions involved. The four areas of knowledge shown in the figures are the professional fields, social sciences, mathematics and sciences, and humanities.

For the most part, graduate programs in these institutions focus on the traditional disciplines and education. In schools where disciplines such

[19] Rudolph O. de la Garza, "A Chicano View of Graduate Education: Where We Are and Where We Should Be," *Proceedings of the Fourteenth Annual Meeting* (Phoenix, Ariz.: Council of Graduate Schools of the United States, 1974), pp. 80–81.
[20] Kent G. Mommsen, "Blacks in American Higher Education: A Cohort Analysis," *Journal of Social and Behavioral Sciences* 20, no. 2 (Spring 1974):110–111, 113.

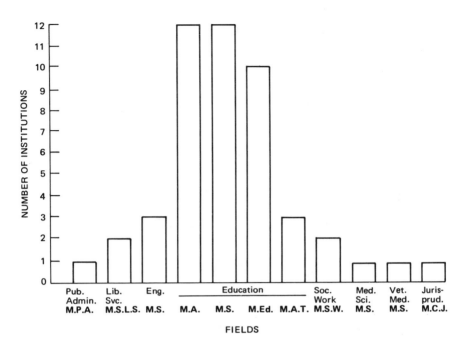

FIGURE 2   Type of degrees by number of institutions—professional fields.

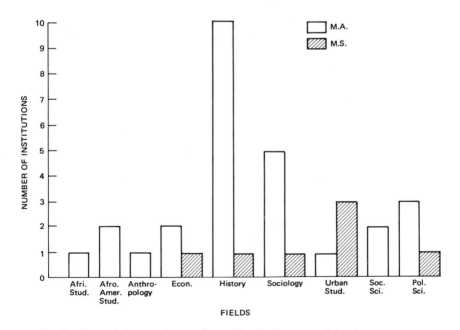

FIGURE 3   Type of degrees by number of institutions—social sciences.

201

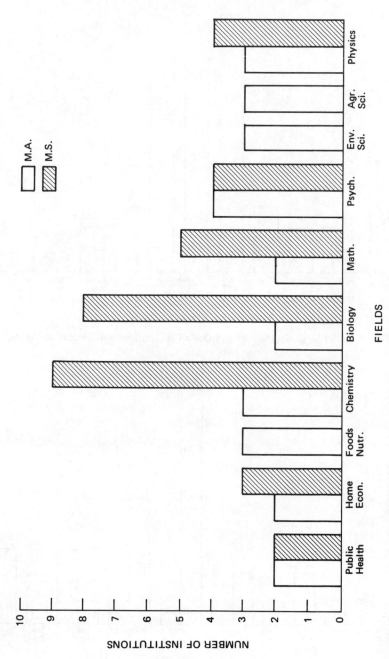

FIGURE 4 Type of degrees by number of institutions—mathematics and sciences.

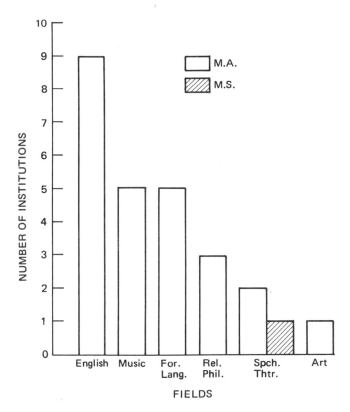

FIGURE 5 Type of degrees by number of institutions—humanities.

as urban affairs, computer science, and the health sciences are offered, the programs are new. Even for such traditional disciplines as English, history, biology, and chemistry, less than one-half of the institutions had programs in these areas. Only five institutions offered the master's degree in sociology, a surprising finding, given the social problems associated with the black community. Although the programs offered by these institutions have been diversified in recent years, the conclusion that they remain too narrow appears sound. Since 1973, many black graduate schools have undergone several positive changes. Some have added from one to seven new master's degree programs and recruited a new cadre of doctorates to their faculties.

Although we use the terminology "black graduate schools," most of these institutions enroll a substantial number of nonblack students. Table 49 provides an indication of the extent of the diversity of students.

TABLE 49 Distribution of Black Graduate Schools, by Racial Composition of Student Body, 1973

	White Students Enrolled		Other Nonblack Students Enrolled	
	No. of Schools	Percentage Distribution	No. of Schools	Percentage Distribution
0–19%	10	43.5	14	60.9
20–39%	3	13.0	3	13.0
40–59%	4	17.4	0	0.0
60–79%	1	4.3	1	4.3
No Response	5	21.7	5	21.7
Total N	23	100.0	23	100.0

SOURCE: Unpublished findings from 1973 survey by Conference of Deans of Black Graduate Schools.

TABLE 50 Distribution of Black Graduate Schools, by Proportion of Nonblack Faculty, 1972–73

	White and Other Nonblack Faculty	
	No. of Schools	Percentage Distribution
0–19%	7	30.5
20–39%	4	17.4
40–59%	5	21.7
60–79%	2	8.7
No Response	5	21.7
Total N	23	100.0

SOURCE: Unpublished findings from 1973 survey by Conference of Deans of Black Graduate Schools.

The ethnic composition of the faculties reveals greater diversity than is true for students, as shown in Table 50. Historically, one of the criteria for judging the quality of a graduate program has been the production of research and the preparation of researchers. While these activities are still prominent in certain areas, the preparation of practitioners and teachers is receiving greater attention.[21]

Of paramount importance in achieving either of the two objectives stated above is the educational qualifications of the faculty. More than four-fifths of the 21 respondent institutions have faculties in which over 70 percent of the faculty hold doctoral or other terminal degrees. Almost one-half of the institutions reported that between 90 and 100 percent of their faculty

[21] Mary J. Clark, "Dimensions of Quality in Doctoral Education," *Findings,* Educational Testing Service, vol. 1, no. 4, 1974.

members held terminal degrees, while seven institutions indicated that more than 95 percent of their faculty possessed terminal degrees. Further, in academe the origin of the terminal degree, or where it was earned, is a matter of unspoken prestige on small campuses where eminence seldom stems from research production. In the past leading eastern and mid-western universities, such as Cornell, Columbia, Ohio State, New York, and Indiana, ranked as the top producers of black doctorates. Only a handful of the present faculty of black colleges with graduate programs received their doctorates from black institutions.

In concluding this section, it is necessary to note that of the 28 black graduate schools, all but two, Meharry and Atlanta, are affiliated with a black undergraduate institution. They, therefore, suffer many of the same disabilities affecting the black colleges. Further, because of this synergistic relationship, they may rightfully claim the potential for making the same type of contribution. It must be emphasized that for a century the black college was the major avenue for blacks to higher education; they have continued to produce the majority of bachelor's degrees awarded to blacks. Significantly, most of the blacks holding doctorate degrees received their undergraduate education at black colleges. In other areas where blacks hold responsible leadership positions, an overwhelming majority received their first degrees at black colleges. Blacks who hold federal judgeships, ambassadorial posts, high-ranking government positions, and who are stars of sports and other areas of entertainment fit this model.[22]

SPECIAL PROBLEMS AND ALTERNATIVES

Black graduate schools, like other institutions of higher education today, are beset by a number of problems, many of which have a common origin and similar impact. Such problems arise from societal traumas resulting from social change or the failure of society to respond to the urgent need for change. Although of common origin, many of these problems strike the black institutions with greater force and exacerbate an already tenuous hold on existence. Among the problems that black graduate schools share with other institutions are those that relate to administrative and program imbalances and those that deal with financial support. As early as 1969, the Rivlin Report was warning educators about these imbalances.

The present system of giving aid for research to the leading scientists has certainly strengthened the outstanding institutions vis-à-vis those of lesser rank. This is generally desirable since these centers of excellence are national assets. But when excellence is concentrated in relatively few institutions, certain regions and centers

[22] Arthur E. Teele, "The Contributions of Black Colleges and Universities," *Vital Speeches* XL(April 1, 1974):361.

of population may lack the centers of graduate education and research required to upgrade their social, cultural, and economic development. Further, since the same faculty and graduate students usually participate in undergraduate instruction, the development of high quality undergraduate education in these regions and centers of population is often hindered.[23]

The relevance of this statement to the black graduate school situation is clear. The concentration of special federal funds for research and development in special institutions has had the effect of screening out most, if not all, black graduate schools on the basis of lack of demonstrated capability in outstanding research or public image as "centers of excellence" that would give them consideration as "national assets."

Responding to the question of the five major needs that must be met if black graduate schools are to survive and improve their performance, nearly all the deans participating in the 1973 survey listed financial support as the first or second choice, emphasizing the need for funds for (1) faculty development, (2) student support, (3) library holdings, and (4) research equipment. Consequently, plans for providing financial aid to these institutions should give high priority to these areas. Even those deans that advocated program changes as a matter of prime urgency did so in a framework of new outlays for program support. In his critique of major reports on graduate education, Charles V. Kidd summed up the matter of the importance of finance to graduate ventures cogently and succinctly:

An analysis of these reports on graduate education leads one to conclude that questions of principle and purpose are not in fact separable from questions of dollars, because some of the most important questions of principle can only be answered in budgetary terms.[24]

The black graduate school lacks the endowment, the gifts, or the funds within its operating budget to assist in financing graduate students. Financial assistance for the minority graduate student determines the success or failure of the graduate program in spite of adequate facilities and a competent faculty. These schools must compete with those institutions that have not historically trained minorities but that are currently engaged in affirmative-action programs to attract the top students from the traditional sources of the black graduate school. Programs are often competitive, but financial support for students is not. The real solution to the financial problems of black graduate schools lies in the recognition, by appropriate federal agencies, of these institutions as vehicles for achieving national educational goals that have been deemed valid. This requires the tre-

---

[23] U.S. Department of Health, Education, and Welfare, *Toward A Long Range Plan for Federal Financial Support for Higher Education.* A Report to the President (Washington, D.C.: U.S. Government Printing Office, 1969), pp. 18–19.
[24] C. V. Kidd, "Graduate Education: The Great Debate," *Change,* May 1974, p. 44.

mendous power and prestige of the national government to assure the success of these schools, as is done with other projects that operate in the national interest.

Federal aid to black colleges, down 2.7 percent from the previous year, totaled about 250 million for 114 institutions in 1972. A little more than 83.5 million or 33.4 percent of this amount went to 10 institutions.[25] Howard University was by far the largest recipient, receiving more than double the amount received by any other school except Meharry and Tuskegee. Funds for research and development at black colleges have increased, while funds for student aid and construction have declined. These 114 institutions enrolled some 247,207 students and received 5.5 percent of the total federal funds for institutions of higher education.[26] This is impressive by any method of calculation, but caution must be exercised in interpreting these figures. Financial statistics have real meaning only when measured against the job done, that is, characteristics of the student population and other special obligations that consume large blocks of the aid with little impact on institutional development. In many cases, the black colleges function largely as conduits through which federal funds pass to certain identified and designated populations. Guiding this query is the assumption that funds are linked to programs and that programs are linked to needs. The major question then becomes: "What does this allocation mean in relation to what was required to achieve the designated purpose?"

It seems unlikely that the federal role in relation to black institutions of higher education will change until they provide more effective input into national educational planning. At the first meeting of the Conference of Deans of Black Graduate Schools in October 1973, the need for carefully planned and concerted action was stressed in relation to problems of finance. If the needs of black institutions are to receive recognition, their cases must be advanced systematically, persistently, and early enough to be considered in the budgeting process.[27] As these schools develop greater expertise in seeking federal funds, however, there is the distinct possibility of the development of harmful competition, perhaps even a wild scramble, among black graduate schools for the scarce resources available, all of which may be further complicated by competition with majority schools. Consequently, other hard problems of choice must be dealt with at both institutional and program levels.[28]

---

[25] Federal Interagency Committee on Education, *Report,* vol. 1, no. 5, Nov. 1974.
[26] *Ibid.*
[27] Elias Blake, Jr., "Institutional Resources," in *Proceedings of the Conference of Deans of Black Graduate Schools,* Atlanta, 1973, pp. 91–92.
[28] Leonard H. O. Spearman, "Financing Black Graduate Education—A Public View," in *Proceedings of the Conference of Deans of Black Graduate Schools, op. cit.,* pp. 105–117.

Previous statements for an increased federal role indicate the pessimistic outlook for increased financial support. Kidd states the case concerning the ineffectual nature of a succession of major reports in this way:

They argued for stability of federal research support, and support has been cut. They have argued for aid to graduate students, and federal aid has been progressively reduced. They have argued for institutional support, and federal institutional support has been all but eliminated.[29]

Yet a very strong plea for an increased federal role must be made, first because it supports the general proposition for a more substantial, although more balanced, federal role in support of higher education, and second because the situation regarding black graduate schools is decidedly different. Despite the golden years of the 1960's and the increased attention to problems of access for minorities to higher education, the job simply has not been done. More alarming is the rate at which it is not being done. Federal aid policy formulators today searching for viable alternatives should be prepared to accept, at least experimentally, additional instruments for the achievement of educational goals. Thus, black graduate schools are recommended here as appropriate vehicles for that purpose and for the realization of America's commitment to equality of opportunity for all its citizens.

Even a cursory examination of the curricula of black graduate schools will reveal that the range of programs of study is exceedingly narrow. For most of these institutions, the only visible formal ties with the black community are education courses for in-service teachers who still live in the black community but quite possibly no longer work there. Attempts have been made in some cases to link courses of study with career opportunities, but often the curriculum has been overly influenced by traditional occupations. In order to discharge their responsibilities to minorities and to the educational community at large, it will be necessary for black graduate schools to expand their curricula both horizontally and vertically. In the first instance this is necessary to meet the breadth and depth of their students' interests and needs. And, in the second instance, this move is vitally necessary for institutional development. Development of the capability of producing research-oriented scholars and highly skilled practitioners is crucial to how black institutions are viewed by other faculty, students, and the broader society. The penalty for failing to change their image is consignment to a status of educational tutelage that will operate in perpetuity.

One influence that led to the founding of the Conference of Deans of Black Graduate Schools was the realization that most of these institutions

---

[29] Charles V. Kidd, *op. cit.,* p. 43.

existed in a state of isolation, not only from the mainstream but from each other. Few belonged to any national or regional organizations concerned primarily with the improvement of graduate instruction and research. While all had been visited by regional accreditation associations, these were primarily concerned with undergraduate training. As a consequence, black graduate schools were likely to know less about each other than about almost any other graduate institution. The Conference of Deans of Black Graduate Schools has not only attempted to breach this wall of isolation but also, as originally proposed, to provide a forum for the discussion of common problems. A concomitant development has been the increased participation of the black graduate school in the activities of the Conference of Southern Graduate Schools, thus expanding the professional affiliations of these schools. As the black graduate schools diversify their programs, more are joining the Council of Graduate Schools in the United States. These involvements have already provided a form of intellectual cross-fertilization that should eventually result in interinstitutional mutual support mechanisms for maximum utilization of the group's limited resources.

Meaningful cooperation will not emerge, however, until the administrations and faculties of the black institutions accept the cultural significance of their existence and identify and affirm a world view that emerges from their own experiences. Thus blacks must cease being satisfied with simply following standards and move toward maintaining and assessing standards of their own creation. Failure to do this is to deprive the larger educational community of a point of view derived, in many instances, from a different cognitive style. Blacks will have to accept the fact that the context for excellence does not depend on size and location of the institutions or the color of the participants. It does not depend entirely on the amount of science equipment, number of books in the library, or even the number of Ph.D.'s on the faculty, although all of these are important. It does depend on clearly defined and realistic goals zealously pursued, the strict administration of reasonable standards, and a system administered with integrity.

A deterrent to the visibility of black graduate schools has been the lack of readily available information on the nature of their concerns. Any change in mission, status, and posture of these institutions will necessitate the development of highly improved management information systems. An accurate data base is not only needed for both effective short- and long-range planning, but also for any definitive statements of needs.

Unquestionably, one of the problems that helps to create the cloud of impermanency around black graduate schools and other black educational institutions is the problem associated with desegregation and affirmative action policies of the federal government. Certainly one of the interesting paradoxes in the history of blacks in America relates to the reverberations from the passage of the Civil Rights Act of 1964 and the various court decrees designed to eradicate dual systems of education. As a result, black institutions have existed amid threats of role changes, mergers, and even closure. Much of the confusion stems from misunderstandings. The following discussion is designed to clarify this issue.

The historic *Adams* v. *Richardson* decision placed the Department of Health, Education, and Welfare under injunction to commence in June 1974 enforcement of Title VI of the Civil Rights Act in 10 states that were found to be operating a racially dual system of public higher education— Louisiana, Mississippi, Oklahoma, North Carolina, Florida, Arkansas, Pennsylvania, Georgia, Maryland, and Virginia.[30]

Interest in the legitimate role of black institutions of higher education has been a subject of great controversy motivated by a variety of factors, including the growing desire of black citizens to have a significant role in, and to share the fruits of, the American economy on the one hand and the national commitment to provide equality of opportunities for all citizens on the other. The contention here is that the *Adams* case has established a legitimate basis for the existence of predominately black colleges in an emerging desegregated society.

A close analysis of the decision will reveal in unmistakable terms that it is not intended that black colleges be dismantled or merged. This view is verified in the Court of Appeals' opinion:

A predicate for minority access to quality postgraduate programs is a viable, coordinated state-wide higher education policy that takes into account the special problems of minority students and of black colleges. As *amicus* points out, these black institutions currently fulfill a crucial need and will continue to play an important role in black higher education.[31]

The Department of Health, Education, and Welfare guidelines for the development of a statewide plan for higher education that would be in compliance support this view:

The plan and its implementation may not place a greater burden on black as compared to white students, faculty, or staff in any aspect of the educational process . . . the closing down or down-grading of an historically black institution in connection with desegregation would create a presumption that a greater burden is being placed on black students and faculty. . . .[32]

[30] *Adams* v. *Richardson,* United States Court of Appeals, District of Columbia Circuit. Federal Reporter 480, Second Series 1973, III, N 8, p. 1164.

[31] *Ibid.,* p. 1165.

[32] Department of Health, Education, and Welfare, Letter to Dr. Jesse Bankston, President, Louisiana State Board of Education, November 10, 1973, p. 8.

The operational goals of the *Adams* decision, as well as those of the Department of Health, Education, and Welfare guidelines, are clear. First, there is concern for the achievement of the desegregation of public higher education through the development of a unitary, nonracial system. As defined by the Southern Regional Education Board, a unitary system "provides maximum access to postsecondary education programs to all, without racial discrimination in admission, staffing, instructional support, and all other facets of operating a higher education enterprise." [33] The Court of Appeals concluded that correcting the constitutional wrongs of segregated school systems can be achieved only through a coordinated statewide plan rather than on the basis of a school by school plan. [34]

Second, there is concern for equalizing higher education opportunities for blacks. Stated operationally, the courts expect an expansion in the number of black students entering and graduating from desegregated undergraduate and graduate programs.

A third objective centers on enhancing the quality of black colleges, which traditionally have been underfunded, underdeveloped, and under-utilized. The impact of these handicaps has been restricted educational programs, limited research, and narrow graduate programs. If these deficiencies were corrected, students would then elect to apply for admission to black colleges on the basis of their quality rather than on the basis of racial factors. Undoubtedly, what has been said about black colleges also applies to their graduate schools. The *Adams* decision emphasized the importance of a statewide higher education policy relating minority access to postgraduate education taking into account the special problems of minority students and black colleges. The implication is that postgraduate programs must be funded at, or relocated in, existing black institutions.

In order to exploit the opportunity to be a component of a nonracial educational system, the elements of a quality graduate school must be present. Consistent with this view, a required goal would be the achievement of a nonracial or multiethnic character as reflected in the programs, personnel, and student body. Fortunately, the black graduate school, though generally chronologically younger than the black undergraduate college, has by virtue of its proximity to the college, and in the experiences of its faculty and students, an invaluable heritage of expertise in multi-ethnic or multicultural transactions. Even during the period of legally enforced segregation, black colleges and graduate schools included students from the Caribbean area and various colonies or countries of Africa and some of Asian origin. Since the abolition of enforced segregation,

[33] James J. Garland, *Suggestions for Achieving Unitary State Systems of Higher Education* (Southern Regional Education Board, October 1973), p. 4.
[34] *Adams* v. *Richardson, op. cit.,* p. 1165.

black colleges and graduate schools have continued to attract students of other racial or cultural backgrounds from abroad and, in addition, have begun to enroll greater numbers of students of native white American background.

Plans for achieving these purposes cannot be made in a vacuum. Empirical studies of the broad spectrum of manpower, economic, and social needs are required as a basis for developing the professional orientation. This is essential to the development of programs that will have multiracial attractiveness.

Although the 10 states are under mandate to assume responsibility for enhancing the quality of postgraduate education in predominantly black colleges, graduate deans and faculties must exercise aggressiveness and creativity in the development and implementation of programs that serve the needs of the individual states and that satisfy the expectation of the *Adams* v. *Richardson* case.

However, a recent discussion of the Florida Plan for Equalizing Educational Opportunity in Public Higher Education closed on an ominous note that had more economic than legal overtones. After reciting several economic woes the report concluded:

> The import of these developments upon the enhancement of educational opportunity for black post-high school students, whether at the community college level, or the level of the senior colleges and universities with their graduate and professional schools is, at this point, problematic; particularly, since many of the key provisions for supportive services to black students and for monitoring and measuring their rates of attrition, retention, program completion or graduation, both in the community colleges and in the predominantly white universities, are stalled in their implementation because of the exigencies of a faltering economy.[35]

Unfortunately, this situation is not atypical within a national context.

PRIORITIES FOR BLACK GRADUATE SCHOOLS

Priorities for black graduate schools arise as a result of a combination of aims, mandates, needs, opportunities, and the potential of the delivery systems of these institutions. As America moves toward the fulfillment of its commitment to promote equality of access for disadvantaged minorities to higher education, the black graduate school looms larger and larger as one of the viable options for achieving that purpose. The point concern-

[35] Charles Stanley, Joshua Williams, and Malcolm Barns, "The Impact of the Pratt Decision on Black Public Colleges: Florida's Commitment" (Paper read at the Annual Meeting of the American Educational Research Association, March 30–April 3, 1975), pp. 22–23.

ing access is equally valid for the labor market, which, at the higher positions of authority and trust, is replete with inequities.

One of the prime requisites for the effective functioning of a group in a technological society is having within its midst a sufficiently large cadre of individuals capable of operating effectively in the technological structure at various levels. Current efforts for achieving this purpose for minorities are simply inadequate. A recommendation for greater use of black graduate schools in pursuit of that objective seems to be strongly warranted. Programs must be developed that will include the aspirations of other minorities. But, as a case study, the focus is on blacks: "It is primarily blacks whom critics of minority programs have had in mind in implying that such programs have lowered the academic standards of institutions and seriously diminished the value of degrees" by their presence.[36]

Priorities for black graduate schools are essentially of two types: those that relate specifically to program design and operation and those that relate to overall institutional character. The distinction, however, is a matter of editorial convenience, since all of these priorities interface and overlap within the broad spectrum of intrainstitutional relationships.

1. Prime necessities for the development and conduct of quality graduate programs are equipment and facilities for the achievement of program goals. *Research efforts of the faculty and appropriate experiences for graduate students depend upon the presence of both basic and sophisticated research equipment, ample library resources, and adequate physical facilities.* This means that for courses of study in the sciences and engineering, up-to-date laboratories for basic experiments and computer support services must be readily available. In cases where such facilities do not exist, expenditures to provide them seems to be the most appropriate option for the creation of a pool of black scientists with doctoral certification.[37]

2. *Of primary importance to black graduate schools is financial assistance for institutional development and student aid.* If black graduate schools are to assume an educational responsibility consistent with their special potential for and their commitment to providing access to higher educational opportunity for qualified minority youth in particular and American youth in general, increased capability for providing a greater number of and more competitive types of student aid packages is essential.

3. *The retention and further recruitment of an appropriately trained*

[36] U.S. Department of Health, Education, and Welfare, *Report on Higher Education*, Frank Newman, chairman *et al.* (Washington, D.C.: U.S. Government Printing Office, March 1971), p. 44.
[37] See James Jay, *Negroes in Science: Natural Science Doctorates, 1876–1969* (Detroit: Balamp Publishing, 1971).

and dedicated faculty is one of the highest priority in any move to im-
prove the performance of black graduate schools. One of the key elements
in any learning equation is the faculty. Hence, black graduate schools
must solve the problem first of retaining their most productive faculty,
who are being lured away by higher salaries, opportunities for research,
and lighter teaching loads. Conditions of work must also be made sufficiently inviting to attract new and old faculty members who are suitable
to serve as models for the students enrolled in these institutions.

4. Although most of these schools were founded expressly for the
education of blacks, they have now reached that point in their history
where they must broaden their concerns to include other ethnic groups,
not simply in the passive sense of dropping barriers, but also in the active
sense of reaching out to embrace a pluralistic concept of society. *This
means that black graduate schools must, as some already have, become
multiethnic and multiracial educational centers for advanced study where
students from any cultural groups might pursue studies with or without
the self-consciousness of color or race.*

5. Pertinent to an enlargement of the role that black graduate schools
must now seek to play is their entrance into the educational mainstream.
A first priority in achieving that goal is breaking down or, at least, breach-
ing the wall of isolation by which most of these institutions are surrounded.
But this wall will not come down until the administrations and faculties
of the black institutions accept the cultural significance of their existence.
The wall will not come down until these principals identify and affirm a
world view that emerges out of the welter of their own experiences. *Trans-
lated into educational principles, this means that blacks will have to cease
being satisfied with simply following standards and move into areas of
maintaining and assessing standards of their own creation. Blacks will
have to accept the fact that the context for excellence does not depend on
size and location of the institution or even the color of the participants; it
does not depend entirely on the amount of science equipment, number
of books in the library, or even the number of Ph.D.'s on the faculty,
though all of these are important; it depends on clearly defined and
realistic goals zealously pursued, the strict administration of reasonable
standards, and a system administered with integrity.*

6. A pressing priority is the development, extension, or improvement
of programs in the basic areas of science, engineering, social science,
humanities, business and commerce, and teacher training concerns. All
of these areas are significantly related not only to effective functioning in
an industrial society but to survival as well. *A knowledge of the material culture, an understanding of social relationships and social control,
an appreciation for artistic and literary expression, the management of a*

214

people's affairs, and techniques for improving and transmitting the cultural heritage are valid concerns for all institutions of higher education. For black graduate schools whose clientele is often from the ranks of the disadvantaged, these concerns are operational musts. Quality programs in these fields are needed to provide the kind of prestige necessary to attract students and faculty who wish to pursue excellence in an atmosphere of scholarly inquiry.

7. *New program priorities must include such areas of high societal need as programs in various phases of urban affairs, allied health, recreation and leisure, and multicultural studies. All must be approached through the medium of time, space, social, and power relationships.* Central to the success of these studies is the appreciation of interdisciplinary techniques; also interinstitutional and intrainstitutional cooperation must be employed. Bringing the expertise of specialists in various fields to bear on a single problem is a new and more effective technique for solving societal problems.

The last point in this category of priorities is not so much a plea for a program as a plea for a condition. If the petition of black graduate schools for understanding and support is to be taken seriously (this petition receives much of its justification from the minority status of these institutions and their prior successful involvement in minority transactions), this principle must be expressed in the policies and programs of these institutions. Already active in training students in Euro-American and Afro-American concerns, these institutions must now both broaden and refine these interests. They must include and emphasize studies on Africa, Europe, and Asia. And, as a matter of intensive expansion, they must include studies that will provide options for Spanish-speaking and Native Americans. Again, as a matter of deliberate choice, they must lead the way in abolishing this baneful differential between men and women. Pernicious, wherever it exists, among American blacks where the woman is the culture-bearer, the time-binder, indeed the phylogenic key, the practice is not only wasteful and foolish, but a tendency toward self-destruction.

The major conclusion reached in this statement is that providing the nation with a pool of highly trained minority personnel has not and probably will not be accomplished through the instrumentality of majority institutions. This would seem to be sufficient basis for the expansion of the programs of black graduate schools both upward and outward. Resources, of course, must be adequate to implement the projected course of action. The task is hardly impossible. For example, a survey by the American Council on Education in 1973 found that on the faculties of higher educational institutions in the United States 37 percent of the men and 18 percent of the women possessed a terminal degree.[38] We suggest that this is not an impossible standard to meet.

Finally, if this has been, at least partially, a perceptual statement, this does not mean that it is not objective. It does mean that the authors attempted to look at educational realities through a framework not necessarily consistent with prevailing establishment views. Hence, the statement is not a part of the "great debate" on graduate education. That debate is among the "haves" largely on the question of the niceties of resource allocation. This statement about how to obtain resources is from the "have-nots."

CONTRIBUTORS

Although a list of contributors follows, it is useful to indicate the areas in which the various contributors worked. Ralph Hines, Mack Jones, Huey Charlton, Charles Stanley, and Wesley Elliott contributed to the statement on mission. Statements on faculty, students, and general program structure were submitted by Oscar Rogers, Virginia Jones, William Brooks, James Eaton, and Joseph Jones. Under special problems, the work on legal status was done largely by E. C. Harrison, although a paper by Charles Stanley, Joshua Williams, and Malcolm Barnes of Florida A&M University was helpful. Statements on financial problems were submitted by Zubie Metcalf and Joseph Jones. Two papers by Albert Spruill were used wherever the content fitted.

Papers on specific disciplines were submitted by four people. These papers, altered only slightly in the longer version of this statement, are presented here only in an abbreviated summary. The authors were: June Aldridge (humanities), Ransford Johnson (economics), Lafayette Fredericks (science), and Jewel Prestage (political science). Statistical advice was provided by John Moland and editorial assistance by Philip Butcher. The introductory statements and section on "Current Status" were written by the editor. Yet, in a sense, all the deans participated in the latter phase, since the data used were taken from questionnaires executed by them.

JUNE ALDRIDGE, Professor of English and Chairman of the Division of Humanities, Spelman College

WILLIAM BROOKS, Acting Chairman of the Graduate Council, Lincoln University, Missouri

[38] John Centra, *Women, Men and the Doctorate* (Princeton, N.J.: Educational Testing Service, 1974), pp. 51–52.

PHILLIP BUTCHER, Dean, Graduate School, Morgan State College

HUEY E. CHARLTON, Dean, School of Education, Atlanta University

HENRY E. COBB, Dean, Graduate School, Southern University at Baton Rouge

JAMES EATON, Associate Dean, Graduate Studies, Savannah State College

WESLEY ELLIOT, Director, Graduate Studies, Fisk University

LAFAYETTE FREDERICKS, Chairman, Department of Biology, Atlanta University

ELTON C. HARRISON, Vice President, Research and Planning, Southern University at Baton Rouge

RALPH HINES, Executive Vice President, Meharry Medical College

RANSFORD JOHNSON, Chairman, Department of Economics, Howard University

JOSEPH JONES, Dean, Graduate School, Texas Southern University

MACK JONES, Professor and Chairman of the Department of Political Science, Atlanta University

VIRGINIA L. JONES, Dean, School of Library Sciences, Atlanta University

ZUBIE METCALF, Assistant to the Vice President, Academic Affairs, Tuskegee Institute

JOHN MOLAND, JR., Professor of Sociology and Director of the Center for Social Research, Southern University at Baton Rouge

JEWEL PRESTAGE, Professor and Chairman, Department of Political Science, Southern University at Baton Rouge

OSCAR ROGERS, JR., Dean, Graduate School, Jackson State University

ALBERT SPRUILL, Dean, Graduate School, North Carolina A&T University

CHARLES STANLEY, Professor of Education, Florida A&M University

Appendix A: Reference Tables

TABLE A-1: Doctoral Degrees Awarded by Field of Study, Race and Ethnic Identity, and Citizenship Status, 1973–74 (U.S. Native-born Citizens)

TABLE A-2: Doctoral Degrees Awarded by Field of Study, Race and Ethnic Identity, and Citizenship Status, 1973–74 (U.S. Naturalized Citizens)

TABLE A-3: Doctoral Degrees Awarded by Field of Study, Race and Ethnic Identity, and Citizenship Status, 1973–74 (Noncitizens—Permanent Visas)

TABLE A-4: Doctoral Degrees Awarded by Field of Study, Race and Ethnic Identity, and Citizenship Status, 1973–74 (Noncitizens—Temporary Visas)

TABLE A-5: Doctorates Conferred, by Minority Status, by Field of Study, 1969–72 and 1972–75, (AAU Institutions)

TABLE A-6: Enrollments in Ph.D.-granting Institutions, by Field of Study, Race and Ethnic Group, Fall 1973

TABLE A-7: Bachelor's Degrees Awarded by Field of Study, Race and Ethnic Group, 1973–74

TABLE A-8: First-Year and Total Minority Enrollments in Medical Schools, 1970–71 to 1974–75

TABLE A-9: First-Year and Total Minority Enrollments in Law Schools, by Race and Ethnic Group, 1971–72 to 1974–75

TABLE A-10: Doctoral Degrees Awarded by Field of Study, Race and Ethnic Identity, and Citizenship Status, 1972–73 (U.S. Native-born Citizens)

TABLE A-11: Doctoral Degrees Awarded by Field of Study, Race and Ethnic Identity, and Citizenship Status, 1972–73 (U.S. Naturalized Citizens)

TABLE A-12: Doctoral Degrees Awarded by Field of Study, Race and Ethnic Identity, and Citizenship Status, 1972–73 (Noncitizens—Permanent Visas)

TABLE A-13: Doctoral Degrees Awarded by Field of Study, Race and Ethnic Identity, and Citizenship Status, 1972–73 (Noncitizens—Temporary Visas)

219

TABLE A-1 Doctoral Degrees Awarded by Field of Study, Race and Ethnic Identity, and Citizenship Status, 1973–74 (U.S. Native-born Citizens)

Field	Total[a]	U.S. Native-born Citizens					
		Black	Spanish American[b]	Puerto Rican	American Indian	Oriental	White
Physical sciences and mathematics	3,272	46	11	5	15	24	3,171
	(100.0%)	(1.4%)	(0.3%)	(0.2%)	(0.5%)	(0.7%)	(96.9%)
Men	3,042	43	11	5	14	20	2,949
Women	230	3			1	4	222
Physics and astronomy	862	3	5	1	4	7	842
	(100.0%)	(0.3%)	(0.6%)	(0.1%)	(0.5%)	(0.8%)	(97.7%)
Men	836	2	5	1	4	7	817
Women	26	1					25
Chemistry	1,266	28	4	3	3	10	1,218
	(100.0%)	(2.2%)	(0.3%)	(0.2%)	(0.2%)	(0.8%)	(96.2%)
Men	1,150	28	4	3	3	7	1,105
Women	116					3	113
Earth sciences	370	1	1	—	2	1	365
	(100.0%)	(0.3%)	(0.3%)	—	(0.5%)	(0.3%)	(98.6%)
Men	350	1	1	—	1	1	346
Women	20				1		19
Mathematics	774	14	1	1	6	6	746
	(100.0%)	(1.8%)	(0.1%)	(0.1%)	(0.8%)	(0.8%)	(96.4%)
Men	706	12	1	1	6	5	681
Women	68	2				1	65
Engineering	1,155	16	4	7	7	18	1,503
	(100.0%)	(1.0%)	(0.3%)	(0.5%)	(0.5%)	(1.1%)	(96.7%)
Men	1,542	16	4	7	7	18	1,490
Women	13						13

Life sciences	3,337	69	16	6	15	3,198
	(100.0%)	(2.1%)	(0.5%)	(0.2%)	(0.4%)	(95.8%)
Men	2,717	51	16	6	14	2,600
Women	323	8			1	598
Basic medical sciences	1,324	28	6	4	9	1,260
	(100.0%)	(2.1%)	(0.5%)	(0.3%)	(0.7%)	(95.2%)
Men	1,001	20	6	4	8	947
Women	323	8			1	313
Other biosciences	1,010	19	8	2	5	968
	(100.0%)	(1.9%)	(0.8%)	(0.2%)	(0.5%)	(95.8%)
Men	823	12	8	2	5	789
Women	187	7				179
Medical sciences	386	11	1	—	—	371
	(100.0%)	(2.8%)	(0.3%)	—	—	(96.1%)
Men	303	10	1			290
Women	83	1				81
Agricultural sciences	541	4	1	—	1	532
	(100.0%)	(0.7%)	(0.2%)	—	(0.2%)	(98.3%)
Men	522	4	1		1	513
Women	19					19
Environmental sciences	76	7	—	—	—	67
	(100.0%)	(9.2%)	—	—	—	(88.2%)
Men	68	5				61
Women	8	2				6

TABLE A-1—Continued

Field		U.S. Native-born Citizens					
	Total [a]	Black	Spanish American [b]	Puerto Rican	American Indian	Oriental	White
Social sciences	4,713	104	20	12	18	22	4,537
	(100.0%)	(2.2%)	(0.4%)	(0.3%)	(0.4%)	(0.5%)	(96.3%)
Men	3,549	71	14	7	15	14	3,428
Women	1,164	33	6	5	3	8	1,109
Psychology	2,188	50	6	6	8	13	2,105
	(100.0%)	(2.3%)	(0.3%)	(0.3%)	(0.4%)	(0.6%)	(96.2%)
Men	1,526	27	2	5	7	5	1,480
Women	662	23	4	1	1	8	625
Economics	541	4	3	1	2	5	526
	(100.0%)	(0.7%)	(0.6%)	(0.2%)	(0.4%)	(0.9%)	(97.2%)
Men	487	3	3	1	2	5	473
Women	54	1					53
Anthropology	772	22	3	1	2	2	742
	(100.0%)	(2.8%)	(0.4%)	(0.1%)	(0.3%)	(0.3%)	(96.1%)
Men	527	18	2		2	2	503
Women	245	4	1	1			239
Political science, public administra- tion, and inter- national relations	634	17	8	3	1	—	605
	(100.0%)	(2.7%)	(1.3%)	(0.5%)	(0.2%)	—	(95.4%)
Men	536	16	7	1	1		512
Women	98	1	1	2			93
Other social sciences	578	11	—	1	5	2	559
	(100.0%)	(1.9%)		(0.2%)	(0.9%)	(0.3%)	(96.7%)
Men	473	7			4	2	460
Women	105	4		1	1		99

Arts and humanities	3,950 (100.0%)	74 (1.9%)	21 (0.5%)	17 (0.4%)	17 (0.4%)	13 (0.3%)	3,808 (96.4%)
Men	2,809	43	16	10	8	6	2,726
Women	1,141	31	5	7	9	7	1,082
History	951 (100.0%)	22 (2.3%)	6 (0.6%)	3 (0.3%)	3 (0.3%)	1 (0.1%)	916 (96.3%)
Men	776	16	6	1	1		752
Women	175	6	6	2	2	1	164
English and American language and literature	1,130 (100.0%)	17 (1.5%)	2 (0.2%)	—	8 (0.7%)	4 (0.4%)	1,099 (97.3%)
Men	717	5	2	—	3	1	706
Women	413	12			5	3	393
Foreign languages and literature	611 (100.0%)	11 (1.8%)	10 (1.6%)	11 (1.8%)	2 (0.3%)	2 (0.3%)	575 (94.1%)
Men	358	8	5	8	2		335
Women	253	3	5	3		2	240
Other arts and humanities	1,258 (100.0%)	24 (1.9%)	3 (0.2%)	3 (0.2%)	4 (0.3%)	6 (0.5%)	1,218 (96.8%)
Men	958	14	3	1	2	5	933
Women	300	10		2	2	1	285
Professional fields	1,038 (100.0%)	31 (3.0%)	5 (0.5%)	1 (0.1%)	8 (0.8%)	4 (0.4%)	989 (95.3%)
Men	886	19	5	1	7	3	851
Women	152	12			1	1	138

TABLE A-1—Continued

Field	Total [a]	U.S. Native-born Citizens					
		Black	Spanish American [b]	Puerto Rican	American Indian	Oriental	White
Education	6,109 (100.0%)	493 (8.1%)	72 (1.2%)	11 (0.2%)	44 (0.7%)	28 (0.5%)	5,461 (89.4%)
Men	4,486	329	59	5	35	20	4,038
Women	1,623	164	13	6	9	8	1,423
Other or unspecified fields	26 (100.0%)	—	—	—	—	—	26 (100.0%)
Men	21	—	—	—	—	—	21
Women	5						5
TOTAL	24,000 (100.0%)	833 (3.5%)	149 (0.6%)	59 (0.2%)	124 (0.5%)	142 (0.6%)	22,693 (94.6%)
Men	19,052 (79.4%)	572 (68.6%)	125 (83.8%)	41 (69.4%)	100 (80.6%)	111 (78.1%)	18,103 (79.7%)
Women	4,948 (20.6%)	261 (31.4%)	24 (16.2%)	18 (30.6%)	24 (19.4%)	31 (21.9%)	4,590 (20.3%)

[a] Represents an 89 percent sample of total (33,000) doctorates awarded in 1973–74. Nonrespondents include persons who did not indicate their racial or ethnic identity or who used an out-of-date questionnaire lacking the racial/ethnic question.
[b] Includes Chicano, Mexican American, and Spanish American.

SOURCE: Special analysis by NBGE of data from National Research Council, National Academy of Sciences, Doctorate Records File, June 1975.

Field	Total [a]	U.S. Naturalized Citizens			
		Black	Spanish American [b]	Oriental	White
Physical sciences and mathematics	128	0	2	37	89
	(100.0%)	(0.0%)	(1.6%)	(28.9%)	(69.5%)
Men	113	—	2	30	81
Women	15	—	—	7	8
Physics and astronomy	40	0	0	13	27
	(100.0%)	(0.0%)	(0.0%)	(32.5%)	(67.5%)
Men	40	—	—	13	27
Women	—	—	—	—	—
Chemistry	40	0	2	9	29
	(100.0%)	(0.0%)	(5.0%)	(22.5%)	(72.5%)
Men	35	—	2	6	27
Women	5	—	—	3	2
Earth sciences	10	0	0	0	10
	(100.0%)	(0.0%)	(0.0%)	(0.0%)	(100.0%)
Men	9	—	—	—	9
Women	1	—	—	—	1
Mathematics	38	0	0	15	23
	(100.0%)	(0.0%)	(0.0%)	(39.5%)	(60.5%)
Men	29	—	—	11	18
Women	9	—	—	4	5
Engineering	116	0	3	46	67
	(100.0%)	(0.0%)	(2.6%)	(39.7%)	(57.7%)
Men	111	—	3	43	65
Women	5	—	—	3	2
Life sciences	113	0	6	18	89
	(100.0%)	(0.0%)	(5.3%)	(15.9%)	(78.8%)
Men	80	—	5	9	66
Women	33	—	1	9	23
Basic medical sciences	58	0	4	9	45
	(100.0%)	(0.0%)	(6.9%)	(15.5%)	(77.6%)
Men	42	—	3	5	34
Women	16	—	1	4	11
Other biosciences	25	0	2	4	19
	(100.0%)	(0.0%)	(8.0%)	(16.0%)	(76.0%)
Men	16	—	2	3	11
Women	9	—	—	1	8
Medical sciences	14	0	0	3	11
	(100.0%)	(0.0%)	(0.0%)	(21.4%)	(78.6%)
Men	8	—	—	1	7
Women	6	—	—	2	4
Agricultural sciences	13	0	0	2	11
	(100.0%)	(0.0%)	(0.0%)	(15.4%)	(84.6%)

225

Field	Total [a]	U.S. Naturalized Citizens			
		Black	Spanish American [b]	Oriental	White
Men	11	—	—	—	11
Women	2	—	—	2	—
Environmental sciences	3	0	0	0	3
	(100.0%)	(0.0%)	(0.0%)	(0.0%)	(100.0%)
Men	3	—	—	—	3
Women	—	—	—	—	—
Social sciences	155	3	7	13	132
	(100.0%)	(1.9%)	(4.5%)	(8.4%)	(85.2%)
Men	115	2	6	8	99
Women	40	1	1	5	33
Psychology	67	1	3	3	60
	(100.0%)	(1.5%)	(4.5%)	(4.5%)	(89.5%)
Men	42	—	3	1	38
Women	25	1	—	2	28
Economics	17	1	2	1	13
	(100.0%)	(5.9%)	(11.8%)	(5.9%)	(76.5%)
Men	17	1	2	1	13
Women	—	—	—	—	—
Anthropology and sociology	23	0	1	2	20
	(100.0%)	(0.0%)	(5.5%)	(11.1%)	(83.3%)
Men	18	—	1	2	15
Women	5	—	—	—	5
Political science, public administration, and international relations	29	0	1	4	24
	(100.0%)	(0.0%)	(3.4%)	(13.8%)	(82.8%)
Men	23	—	—	3	20
Women	6	—	1	1	4
Other social sciences	19	1	0	3	15
	(100.0%)	(5.3%)	(0.0%)	(15.8%)	(78.9%)
Men	15	1	—	1	13
Women	4	—	—	2	2
Arts and humanities	285	1	21	15	248
	(100.0%)	(0.4%)	(7.4%)	(5.3%)	(87.0%)
Men	148	—	16	11	121
Women	137	1	5	4	127
History	49	0	1	2	46
	(100.0%)	(0.0%)	(2.0%)	(4.1%)	(93.9%)
Men	33	—	1	1	31
Women	16	—	—	1	15

Field	Total a	U.S. Naturalized Citizens			
		Black	Spanish American b	Oriental	White
English and American language and literature	40	0	0	3	37
	(100.0%)	(0.0%)	(0.0%)	(7.5%)	(92.5%)
Men	17	—	—	2	15
Women	23	—	—	1	22
Foreign languages and literature	149	1	17	2	129
	(100.0%)	(0.7%)	(11.4%)	(1.3%)	(86.6%)
Men	67	—	13	1	53
Women	82	1	4	1	76
Other arts and humanities	47	0	3	8	36
	(100.0%)	(0.0%)	(6.4%)	(17.0%)	(76.6%)
Men	31	—	2	7	22
Women	16	—	1	1	14
Professional fields	35	1	1	6	27
	(100.0%)	(2.9%)	(2.9%)	(17.1%)	(77.1%)
Men	29	1	—	3	25
Women	6	—	1	3	2
Education	125	8	6	15	96
	(100.0%)	(6.4%)	(4.8%)	(12.0%)	(76.8%)
Men	78	5	5	8	60
Women	47	3	1	7	36
Other or unspecified fields	2	0	0	1	1
	(100.0%)	(0.0%)	(0.0%)	(50.0%)	(50.0%)
Men	2	—	—	1	1
Women	—	—	—	—	—
TOTAL a	959	13	46	151	749
	(100.0%)	(1.4%)	(4.8%)	(15.7%)	(78.1%)
Men	676	8	37	113	518
	(70.4%)	(61.5%)	(80.4%)	(74.8%)	(69.1%)
Women	283	5	9	38	231
	(29.6%)	(38.5%)	(19.6%)	(25.2%)	(30.9%)

a Represents an 89 percent sample of total (33,000) doctorates awarded in 1973–74. See Table A-1 for an explanation of survey coverage.
b Includes Chicano, Mexican American, and Spanish American.

SOURCE: Special analysis by NBGE of data from National Research Council, National Academy of Sciences, Doctorate Records File, June 1975.

TABLE A–3 Doctoral Degrees Awarded by Field of Study, Race and Ethnic Identity, and Citizenship Status, 1973–74 (Noncitizens—Permanent Visas)

Field	Total [a]	Noncitizens—Permanent Visas			
		Black	Spanish American [b]	Oriental	White
Physical sciences and mathematics	326	3	4	232	87
	(100.0%)	(0.9%)	(1.2%)	(71.2%)	(26.7%)
Men	284	3	4	199	78
Women	42	—	—	33	9
Physics and astronomy	83	1	1	54	27
	(100.0%)	(1.2%)	(1.2%)	(65.1%)	(32.5%)
Men	72	1	1	44	26
Women	22	—	—	10	1
Chemistry	140	0	1	110	29
	(100.0%)	(0.0%)	(0.7%)	(78.6%)	(20.7%)
Men	119	—	1	93	25
Women	21	—	—	17	4
Earth sciences	40	0	1	21	18
	(100.0%)	(0.0%)	(2.5%)	(52.5%)	(45.0%)
Men	36	—	1	20	15
Women	4	—	—	1	3
Mathematics	63	2	1	47	13
	(100.0%)	(3.2%)	(1.6%)	(74.6%)	(20.6%)
Men	57	2	1	42	12
Women	6	—	—	5	1
Engineering	427	4	2	306	115
	(100.0%)	(0.9%)	(0.5%)	(71.7%)	(26.9%)
Men	422	4	2	303	113
Women	5	—	—	3	2
Life sciences	278	5	2	169	102
	(100.0%)	(1.8%)	(0.7%)	(60.8%)	(36.7%)
Men	217	4	2	134	77
Women	61	1	—	35	25
Basic medical sciences	106	0	2	61	43
	(100.0%)	(0.0%)	(1.9%)	(57.5%)	(40.6%)
Men	79	—	2	46	31
Women	27	—	—	15	12
Other biosciences	54	1	0	29	24
	(100.0%)	(1.9%)	(0.0%)	(53.7%)	(44.4%)
Men	38	—	—	19	19
Women	16	1	—	10	5
Medical sciences	49	1	0	33	15
	(100.0%)	(2.0%)	(0.0%)	(67.3%)	(30.6%)
Men	38	1	—	28	9
Women	11	—	—	5	6

228

| Field | Total [a] | Noncitizens—Permanent Visas | | | |
		Black	Spanish American [b]	Oriental	White
Agricultural sciences	62	3	0	41	18
	(100.0%)	(4.8%)	(0.0%)	(66.1%)	(29.0%)
Men	55	3	—	36	16
Women	7	—	—	5	2
Environmental sciences	7	0	0	5	2
	(100.0%)	(0.0%)	(0.0%)	(71.4%)	(28.6%)
Men	7	—	—	5	2
Women	—	—	—	—	—
Social sciences	183	16	3	50	114
	(100.0%)	(8.7%)	(1.6%)	(27.3%)	(62.3%)
Men	139	16	2	41	80
Women	44	—	1	9	34
Psychology	37	2	1	8	26
	(100.0%)	(5.4%)	(2.7%)	(21.6%)	(70.3%)
Men	16	2	—	4	10
Women	21	—	1	4	16
Economics	44	1	2	14	27
	(100.0%)	(2.3%)	(4.5%)	(31.8%)	(61.4%)
Men	40	1	2	12	25
Women	4	—	—	2	2
Anthropology	38	4	0	5	29
	(100.0%)	(10.5%)	(0.0%)	(13.2%)	(76.3%)
Men	25	4	—	4	17
Women	13	—	—	1	12
Political science, public administration, and international relations	36	8	0	16	12
	(100.0%)	(22.2%)	(0.0%)	(44.4%)	(33.3%)
Men	35	8	—	16	11
Women	1	—	—	—	1
Other social sciences	28	1	0	7	20
	(100.0%)	(3.6%)	(0.0%)	(25.0%)	(71.4%)
Men	23	1	—	5	17
Women	5	—	—	2	3
Arts and humanities	209	6	9	47	147
	(100.0%)	(2.9%)	(4.3%)	(22.5%)	(70.3%)
Men	128	5	5	35	83
Women	81	1	4	12	64
History	27	4	0	12	11
	(100.0%)	(14.8%)	(0.0%)	(44.4%)	(40.7%)
Men	22	3	—	10	9
Women	5	1	—	2	2

Field	Total [a]	Noncitizens—Permanent Visas			
		Black	Spanish American [b]	Oriental	White
English and American language and literature	29	1	0	3	25
	(100.0%)	(3.4%)	(0.0%)	(10.3%)	(86.2%)
Men	19	1	—	2	16
Women	10	—	—	1	9
Foreign languages and literature	97	0	8	10	79
	(100.0%)	(0.0%)	(8.2%)	(10.3%)	(81.4%)
Men	49	—	5	6	38
Women	48	—	3	4	41
Other arts and humanities	56	1	1	22	32
	(100.0%)	(1.8%)	(1.8%)	(39.3%)	(57.1%)
Men	38	1	—	17	20
Women	18	—	1	5	12
Professional fields	56	1	0	18	37
	(100.0%)	(1.8%)	(0.0%)	(32.1%)	(66.1%)
Men	46	1	—	15	30
Women	10	—	—	3	7
Education	90	7	0	35	48
	(100.0%)	(7.8%)	(0.0%)	(38.9%)	(53.3%)
Men	67	6	—	26	35
Women	23	1	—	9	13
Other or unspecified fields	2	0	0	1	1
	(100.0%)	(0.0%)	(0.0%)	(50.0%)	(50.0%)
Men	2	—	—	1	1
Women	—	—	—	—	—
TOTAL	1,571	42	20	858	651
	(100.0%)	(2.7%)	(1.3%)	(54.6%)	(41.4%)
Men	1,305	39	15	754	497
	(83.0%)	(92.8%)	(75.0%)	(87.8%)	(76.3%)
Women	266	3	5	104	154
	(17.0%)	(7.2%)	(25.0%)	(12.2%)	(23.7%)

[a] Represents an 89 percent sample of total (33,000) doctorates awarded in 1973–74. See Table A-1 for an explanation of survey coverage.
[b] Includes Chicano, Mexican American, and Spanish American.

SOURCE: Special analysis by NBGE of data from National Research Council, National Academy of Sciences, Doctorate Records File, June 1975.

230

TABLE 4 Doctoral Degrees Awarded by Field of Study, Race and Ethnic Identity, and Citizenship Status, 1973–74 (Noncitizens—Temporary Visas)

Field	Total [a]	Noncitizens—Temporary Visas			
		Black	Spanish American [b]	Oriental	White
Physical sciences and					
mathematics	600	12	12	294	282
	(100.0%)	(2.0%)	(2.0%)	(49.0%)	(47.0%)
Men	543	12	11	261	259
Women	57	—	1	33	23
Physics and astronomy	180	1	5	99	75
	(100.0%)	(0.5%)	(2.8%)	(55.0%)	(41.7%)
Men	168	1	4	93	70
Women	12	—	1	6	5
Chemistry	150	5	1	99	45
	(100.0%)	(3.3%)	(0.7%)	(66.0%)	(30.0%)
Men	132	5	1	85	41
Women	18	—	—	14	4
Earth sciences	77	3	2	20	52
	(100.0%)	(3.9%)	(2.6%)	(26.0%)	(67.5%)
Men	73	3	2	20	48
Women	4	—	—	—	4
Mathematics	193	3	4	76	110
	(100.0%)	(1.6%)	(2.1%)	(39.4%)	(57.0%)
Men	170	3	4	63	100
Women	23	—	—	13	10
Engineering	559	14	16	252	277
	(100.0%)	(2.5%)	(2.9%)	(45.1%)	(49.5%)
Men	553	14	16	251	272
Women	6	—	—	1	5
Life sciences	584	26	34	263	261
	(100.0%)	(4.5%)	(5.8%)	(45.0%)	(44.7%)
Men	521	24	33	221	243
Women	63	2	1	42	18
Basic medical sciences	134	3	4	75	52
	(100.0%)	(2.2%)	(3.0%)	(56.0%)	(38.8%)
Men	110	2	3	59	46
Women	24	1	1	16	6
Other biosciences	128	4	6	58	60
	(100.0%)	(3.1%)	(4.7%)	(45.3%)	(46.9%)
Men	110	3	6	47	54
Women	18	1	—	11	6
Medical sciences	51	2	3	25	21
	(100.0%)	(3.9%)	(5.9%)	(49.0%)	(41.2%)
Men	45	2	3	21	19
Women	6	—	—	4	2

Field	Total [a]	Noncitizens—Temporary Visas			
		Black	Spanish American [b]	Oriental	White
Agricultural sciences	263	17	21	102	123
	(100.0%)	(6.5%)	(8.0%)	(38.8%)	(46.8%)
Men	248	17	21	91	119
Women	15	—	—	11	4
Environmental sciences	8	0	0	3	5
	(100.0%)	(0.0%)	(0.0%)	(37.5%)	(62.5%)
Men	8	—	—	3	5
Women	—	—	—	—	—
Social sciences	433	27	9	109	288
	(100.0%)	(6.2%)	(2.1%)	(25.2%)	(66.5%)
Men	374	25	8	92	249
Women	59	2	1	17	39
Psychology	74	1	0	10	63
	(100.0%)	(1.4%)	(0.0%)	(13.5%)	(85.1%)
Men	53	1	—	5	47
Women	21	—	—	5	16
Economics	156	12	3	49	92
	(100.0%)	(7.7%)	(1.9%)	(31.4%)	(59.0%)
Men	149	12	3	48	86
Women	7	—	—	1	6
Anthropology	69	4	4	17	44
	(100.0%)	(5.8%)	(5.8%)	(24.6%)	(63.8%)
Men	51	2	4	10	35
Women	18	2	—	7	9
Political science, public administration, and international relations	65	4	1	13	47
	(100.0%)	(6.2%)	(1.5%)	(20.0%)	(72.3%)
Men	59	4	1	11	43
Women	6	—	—	2	4
Other social sciences	69	6	1	20	42
	(100.0%)	(8.7%)	(1.4%)	(29.0%)	(60.9%)
Men	62	6	—	18	38
Women	7	—	1	2	4
Arts and humanities	187	19	3	40	125
	(100.0%)	(10.2%)	(1.6%)	(21.4%)	(66.8%)
Men	142	14	3	35	92
Women	45	5	—	5	33
History	33	8	0	4	21
	(100.0%)	(24.2%)	(0.0%)	(12.1%)	(63.6%)
Men	27	8	—	3	16
Women	6	—	—	1	5

TABLE A-4—Continued

Field	Total [a]	Noncitizens—Temporary Visas			
		Black	Spanish American [b]	Oriental	White
English and American language and literature	31	0	0	2	29
	(100.0%)	(0.0%)	(0.0%)	(6.5%)	(93.5%)
Men	24	—	—	—	24
Women	7	—	—	2	5
Foreign languages and literature	34	4	2	1	27
	(100.0%)	(11.8%)	(5.9%)	(2.9%)	(79.4%)
Men	19	1	2	—	16
Women	15	3	—	1	11
Other arts and humanities	89	7	1	33	48
	(100.0%)	(7.9%)	(1.1%)	(37.1%)	(53.9%)
Men	72	5	1	30	36
Women	17	2	—	3	12
Professional fields	105	7	1	20	77
	(100.0%)	(6.7%)	(1.0%)	(19.0%)	(73.3%)
Men	98	7	1	18	72
Women	7	—	—	2	5
Education	241	17	1	74	149
	(100.0%)	(7.1%)	(0.4%)	(30.7%)	(61.8%)
Men	182	15	1	48	118
Women	59	2	—	26	31
Other or unspecified fields	1	0	0	1	0
	(100.0%)	(0.0%)	(0.0%)	(100.0%)	(0.0%)
Men	1	—	—	1	—
Women	—	—	—	—	—
TOTAL	2,710	122	76	1,053	1,459
	(100.0%)	(4.5%)	(2.8%)	(38.9%)	(53.8%)
Men	2,414	111	73	925	1,305
	(89.0%)	(90.9%)	(96.0%)	(87.8%)	(89.4%)
Women	296	11	3	128	154
	(11.0%)	(9.1%)	(4.0%)	(12.2%)	(10.6%)

[a] Represents an 89 percent sample of total (33,000) doctorates awarded in 1973–74. See Table A-1 for an explanation of survey coverage.
[b] Includes Chicano, Mexican American, and Spanish American.

SOURCE: Special analysis by NBGE of data from National Research Council, National Academy of Sciences, Doctorate Records File, June 1975.

TABLE A–5 Doctorates Conferred, by Minority Status, by Field of Study, 1969–72 and 1972–75, (AAU Institutions) [a]

Field of Study	Period 1969–72			Period 1972–75		
	Total Doctorates	Total Minority Doctorates	% Minority of Total	Total Doctorates	Total Minority Doctorates	% Minority of Total
Physical sciences	7,628	213	2.8	6,673	259	3.9
Mathematics	2,565	59	2.3	2,353	81	3.4
Engineering	6,428	180	2.8	5,484	207	3.8
Life sciences	7,331	287	3.9	7,268	369	5.1
Social sciences	8,334	203	2.4	9,197	488	5.3
Arts and humanities	9,999	261	2.6	10,669	559	5.2
Education	8,132	447	5.5	8,344	926	11.1
Other professional fields	2,878	96	3.3	3,339	217	6.5
Total, all fields	53,295	1,746	3.3	53,327	3,106	5.8

[a] Includes Asians, blacks, Spanish-surnamed persons, and American Indians. Citizenship status is unknown.

SOURCE: Joseph L. McCarthy and Dael Wolfle, "Doctorates Granted to Women and Minority Group Members," *Science* 189 (September 12, 1975): 856–859.

TABLE A–6   Enrollments in Ph.D.-Granting Institutions, by Field of Study, Race and Ethnic Group, Fall 1973

| Field of Study | Total | Race or Ethnic Group [a] | | | | |
		Black	Spanish-Sur-named	Ameri-can Indian	Asian	Minor-ity Sub-total
Physical sciences and mathematics	34,075 (100.0%)	604 (1.8%)	218 (0.6%)	72 (0.2%)	827 (2.4%)	1,721 (5.1%)
Engineering	31,273 (100.0%)	368 (1.2%)	263 (0.8%)	37 (0.1%)	1,020 (3.3%)	1,688 (5.4%)
Life sciences	40,879 (100.0%)	1,146 (2.8%)	411 (1.0%)	138 (0.3%)	779 (1.9%)	2,474 (6.1%)
Social sciences	35,583 (100.0%)	1,471 (4.1%)	426 (1.2%)	110 (0.3%)	380 (1.1%)	2,387 (6.7%)
Arts and humanities	53,920 (100.0%)	1,516 (2.8%)	794 (1.5%)	164 (0.3%)	484 (0.9%)	2,958 (5.5%)
Other fields	80,666 (100.0%)	4,146 (5.1%)	769 (1.0%)	276 (0.3%)	999 (1.2%)	6,190 (7.7%)
Education	96,568 (100.0%)	6,990 (7.2%)	1,113 (1.2%)	384 (0.4%)	587 (0.6%)	9,074 (9.4%)
Total, all fields	372,964 (100.0%)	16,241 (4.4%)	3,994 (1.1%)	1,181 (0.3%)	5,076 (1.4%)	26,492 (7.1%)

[a] Includes only U.S. citizens and noncitizens holding permanent visas.

SOURCE: Elaine H. El-Khawas and Joan L. Kinzer, *Enrollment of Minority Graduate Students at Ph.D. Granting Institutions,* Higher Education Panel Reports, no. 19 (Washington, D.C.: American Council on Education, 1974).

TABLE A–7   Bachelor's Degrees Awarded, by Field of Study, Race and Ethnic Group *a*

| Field of Study | Total Baccalaureate Recipients *b* | | Percentage Distribution of Minority Baccalaureate Recipients | | | | |
	No.	%	Sub-total	Black	Spanish Sur-named	Asian	Ameri-can Indian
Total, all fields	989,200	100.0	7.8	5.3	1.3	.9	.3
Arts and humanities	139,900	100.0	6.1	3.3	1.8	.7	.2
Biological sciences	53,500	100.0	6.6	3.6	1.1	1.7	.1
Business and manage-ment	133,300	100.0	7.6	4.9	1.2	1.2	.3
Education	177,800	100.0	9.6	7.9	1.1	.3	.3
Engineering	62,500	100.0	5.1	1.8	1.4	1.5	.4
Mathematics	24,500	100.0	7.2	4.6	.7	1.7	.1
Physical sciences	26,400	100.0	5.3	2.7	1.3	1.1	.2
Psychology	52,100	100.0	7.4	4.8	1.4	1.0	.3
Social sciences	158,800	100.0	9.7	7.2	1.4	.8	.3
All other fields	158,400	100.0	7.9	5.2	1.1	1.2	.4

a The above figures represent population estimates based on a stratified sample of all institutions that confer a bachelor's degree. In view of variations in response rates among institutions and other factors that affect the accuracy of the survey findings, caution should be exercised in interpretation of these data. Problems in compiling minority statistics are more fully described in the forthcoming report of the Higher Education Panel of the American Council on Education on bachelor's degrees awarded to minority students, 1973–74.

b Includes U.S. citizens and foreign nationals holding permanent visas.

SOURCE: Higher Education Panel, 1976 (unpublished figures).

236

TABLE A-8 First-Year and Total Minority Enrollments in Medical Schools, 1970-71 to 1974-75

Race or Ethnic Group	Enrollments									
	1970-71		1971-72		1972-73		1973-74		1974-75	
	1st Year	Total	1st Year	Total	1st Year	Total	1st Year	Total	1st Year	Total
Black American [a]	697 (6.1%)	1,509 (3.8%)	882 (7.1%)	2,055 (4.7%)	957 (7.0%)	2,582 (5.4%)	1,023 (7.2%)	3,045 (6.0%)	1,106 (7.5%)	3,355 (6.3%)
American Indian	11 (0.1%)	18 (0.04%)	23 (0.2%)	42 (0.1%)	34 (0.2%)	69 (0.2%)	44 (0.3%)	97 (0.2%)	71 (0.5%)	159 (0.3%)
Mexican American	73 (0.6%)	148 (0.4%)	118 (1.0%)	252 (0.6%)	137 (1.0%)	361 (0.8%)	174 (1.2%)	496 (1.0%)	227 (1.5%)	638 (1.2%)
Puerto Rican—mainland	27 (0.2%)	48 (0.1%)	40 (0.3%)	76 (0.2%)	44 (0.3%)	90 (0.2%)	56 (0.4%)	123 (0.2%)	69 (0.5%)	172 (0.3%)
American Oriental	190 (1.7%)	571 (1.4%)	217 (1.8%)	647 (1.5%)	231 (1.7%)	718 (1.5%)	259 (1.8%)	883 (1.7%)	275 (1.9%)	959 (1.8%)
Total, U.S. minority	998 (8.8%) [b]	2,294 (5.7%)	1,280 (10.4%)	3,072 (7.1%)	1,403 (10.3%) [b]	3,820 (8.1%)	1,556 (11.0%) [b]	4,644 (9.2%) [b]	1,748 (11.8%) [b]	5,283 (9.9%)
Total, all students	11,348 (100.0%)	40,238 (100.0%)	12,361 (100.0%)	43,650 (100.0%)	13,677 (100.0%)	47,366 (100.0%)	14,124 (100.0%)	50,716 (100.0%)	14,763 (100.0%)	53,554 (100.0%)

[a] Black Americans in Howard and Meharry medical schools represented about 45 percent of total enrollments in 1970-71 and 20 percent of enrollments in 1974-75.

[b] Percentage total does not add because of rounding.

SOURCE: Data made available by the Association of American Medical Colleges, Division of Student Studies, Washington, D.C., December 1974.

237

TABLE A-9   First-Year and Total Minority Enrollments in Law Schools, by Race and Ethnic Group, 1971–72 to 1974–75 [a]

Race or Ethnic Group	1971–72		1972–73		1973–74		1974–75	
	First Year	Total	First Year	Total	First Year	Total	First Year	Total
Black American	1,716 (4.7%)	3,744 (4.0%)	1,907 (5.4%)	4,423 (4.3%)	1,943 (5.2%)	4,817 (4.5%)	1,910 (5.0%)	4,995 (4.5%)
Chicano (Mexican American)	4.03 (1.1%)	883 (0.9%)	480 (1.4%)	1,072 (1.1%)	539 (1.5%)	1,259 (1.2%)	559 (1.5%)	1,357 (1.2%)
Puerto Rican	49 (0.1%)	94 (0.1%)	73 (0.2%)	143 (0.1%)	96 (0.3%)	180 (0.2%)	117 (0.3%)	263 (0.2%)
American Indian	71 (0.2%)	140 (0.1%)	79 (0.2%)	173 (0.2%)	109 (0.3%)	222 (0.2%)	110 (0.3%)	265 (0.2%)
Asian American	254 (0.7%)	480 (0.5%)	298 (0.8%)	681 (0.7%)	327 (0.9%)	850 (0.8%)	429 (1.1%)	1,063 (1.0%)
Other Hispanic American	74 (0.2%)	179 (0.2%)	96 (0.3%)	231 (0.2%)	94 (0.3%)	261 (0.2%)	182 (0.5%)	387 (0.3%)
Total minority	2,567 (7.1%) [b]	5,520 (5.8%)	2,933 (8.3%)	6,723 (6.6%)	3,108 (8.4%) [b]	7,589 (7.2%) [b]	3,307 (8.7%)	8,330 (7.5%) [b]
Total, all students	36,171 (100.0%)	94,468 (100.0%)	35,131 (100.0%)	101,707 (100.0%)	37,018 (100.0%)	106,102 (100.0%)	38,074 (100.0%)	110,713 (100.0%)

[a] Includes all ABA-approved law schools.
[b] Percent total does not add due to rounding.

SOURCE: American Bar Association, *Law Schools and Bar Admission Requirements, A Review of Legal Education in the United States—Fall 1974* (Chicago: American Bar Association, 1975), pp. 36, 39.

238

TABLE A-10 Doctoral Degrees Awarded by Field of Study, Race and Ethnic Identity, and Citizenship Status, 1972–73 (U.S. Native-born Citizens)

Field	Total [a]	Black	Spanish American [b]	Puerto Rican	American Indian	Oriental	White
		U.S. Native-born Citizens					
Physical sciences and mathematics	3,051 (100.0%)	32 (1.0%)	12 (0.4%)	3 (0.1%)	10 (0.3%)	18 (0.6%)	2,976 (97.5%)
Physics and astronomy	876 (100.0%)	9 (1.0%)	0 (0.0%)	0 (0.0%)	3 (0.3%)	2 (0.2%)	862 (98.4%)
Chemistry	1,122 (100.0%)	18 (1.6%)	7 (0.6%)	1 (0.1%)	3 (0.3%)	7 (0.6%)	1,086 (96.8%)
Earth sciences	334 (100.0%)	0 (0.0%)	1 (0.3%)	2 (0.6%)	3 (0.9%)	3 (0.9%)	325 (97.0%)
Mathematics	719 (100.0%)	5 (0.7%)	4 (0.6%)	0 (0.0%)	1 (0.1%)	6 (0.8%)	703 (97.8%)
Engineering	1,546 (100.0%)	17 (1.1%)	1 (0.1%)	3 (0.2%)	6 (0.4%)	14 (0.9%)	1,505 (97.3%)
Life sciences	2,923 (100.0%)	51 (1.7%)	15 (0.5%)	6 (0.2%)	17 (0.6%)	44 (1.5%)	2,790 (95.4%)
Basic medical sciences	1,144 (100.0%)	27 (2.3%)	5 (0.4%)	6 (0.5%)	5 (0.4%)	22 (1.9%)	1,079 (94.3%)
Other biosciences	901 (100.0%)	10 (1.1%)	6 (0.7%)	0 (0.0%)	5 (0.5%)	13 (1.4%)	867 (96.0%)
Medical sciences	304 (100.0%)	8 (2.6%)	2 (0.7%)	0 (0.0%)	2 (0.7%)	6 (2.0%)	286 (94.1%)

TABLE A-10—Continued

Field	Total [a]	U.S. Native-born Citizens					
		Black	Spanish American [b]	Puerto Rican	American Indian	Oriental	White
Agricultural sciences	512 (100.0%)	5 (1.0%)	2 (0.4%)	0 (0.0%)	5 (1.0%)	3 (0.6%)	497 (97.1%)
Environmental sciences	62 (100.0%)	1 (1.6%)	0 (0.0%)	0 (0.0%)	0 (0.0%)	0 (0.0%)	61 (98.4%)
Social sciences	3,745 (100.0%)	59 (1.6%)	16 (0.4%)	8 (0.2%)	21 (0.6%)	22 (0.6%)	3,619 (96.6%)
Psychology	1,691 (100.0%)	23 (1.4%)	7 (0.4%)	4 (0.2%)	9 (0.5%)	10 (0.6%)	1,638 (96.9%)
Economics	481 (100.0%)	2 (0.4%)	1 (0.2%)	1 (0.2%)	3 (0.6%)	3 (0.6%)	471 (97.9%)
Anthropology	587 (100.0%)	19 (3.2%)	2 (0.3%)	2 (0.3%)	6 (1.0%)	5 (0.8%)	553 (94.2%)
Political science, public administration and international relations	547 (100.0%)	6 (1.1%)	3 (0.5%)	1 (0.2%)	2 (0.4%)	3 (0.5%)	532 (97.2%)
Other social sciences	439 (100.0%)	9 (2.0%)	3 (0.7%)	0 (0.0%)	1 (0.2%)	1 (0.2%)	425 (96.8%)

Field	Total						
Arts and humanities	3,512 (100.0%)	50 (1.4%)	19 (0.5%)	6 (0.2%)	18 (0.5%)	10 (0.3%)	3,409 (97.1%)
History	835 (100.0%)	17 (2.1%)	2 (0.2%)	2 (0.2%)	3 (0.4%)	1 (0.1%)	810 (97.0%)
English and American language and literature	1,035 (100.0%)	12 (1.1%)	3 (0.3%)	0 (0.0%)	6 (0.6%)	3 (0.3%)	1,011 (97.7%)
Foreign languages and literature	513 (100.0%)	6 (1.2%)	11 (2.1%)	4 (0.8%)	1 (0.2%)	2 (0.4%)	489 (95.3%)
Other arts and humanities	1,129 (100.0%)	15 (1.3%)	3 (0.3%)	0 (0.0%)	8 (0.7%)	4 (0.3%)	1,099 (97.3%)
Professional fields	873 (100.0%)	17 (1.9%)	0 (0.0%)	0 (0.0%)	1 (0.1%)	3 (0.3%)	852 (97.6%)
Education	4,991 (100.0%)	346 (6.9%)	30 (0.6%)	10 (0.2%)	34 (0.7%)	12 (0.2%)	4,559 (91.3%)
TOTAL	20,641 (100.0%)	572 (2.8%)	93 (0.5%)	36 (0.2%)	107 (0.5%)	123 (0.6%)	19,710 (95.5%)

[a] Represents a 75 percent sample of total (33,727) doctorates awarded in 1972–73. Nonrespondents include persons who did not indicate their racial or ethnic identity or who used an out-of-date questionnaire lacking the racial/ethnic question.
[b] Includes Chicano, Mexican American, and Spanish American.

SOURCE: Special analysis by NBGE of data from National Research Council, National Academy of Sciences, Doctorate Records File, November 1974.

TABLE A–11 Doctoral Degrees Awarded by Field of Study, Race and Ethnic Identity, and Citizenship Status, 1972–73 (U.S. Naturalized Citizens)

Field	Total [a]	U.S. Naturalized Citizens			
		Black	Spanish American [b]	Oriental	White
Physical sciences and mathematics	130	0	5	34	91
	(100.0%)	(0.0%)	(3.8%)	(26.2%)	(70.0%)
Physics and astronomy	54	0	3	12	39
	(100.0%)	(0.0%)	(5.6%)	(22.2%)	(72.2%)
Chemistry	37	0	1	14	22
	(100.0%)	(0.0%)	(2.7%)	(37.8%)	(59.5%)
Earth sciences	8	0	0	1	7
	(100.0%)	(0.0%)	(0.0%)	(12.5%)	(87.5%)
Mathematics	31	0	1	7	23
	(100.0%)	(0.0%)	(3.2%)	(22.6%)	(74.2%)
Engineering	108	1	1	39	67
	(100.0%)	(0.9%)	(0.9%)	(36.1%)	(62.0%)
Life sciences	110	1	6	18	85
	(100.0%)	(0.9%)	(5.5%)	(16.4%)	(77.3%)
Basic medical sciences	55	1	2	9	43
	(100.0%)	(1.8%)	(3.6%)	(16.4%)	(78.2%)
Other biosciences	26	0	2	5	19
	(100.0%)	(0.0%)	(7.7%)	(19.2%)	(73.1%)
Medical sciences	15	0	0	1	14
	(100.0%)	(0.0%)	(0.0%)	(6.7%)	(93.3%)
Agricultural sciences	11	0	2	3	6
	(100.0%)	(0.0%)	(18.2%)	(27.3%)	(54.5%)
Environmental sciences	3	0	0	0	3
	(100.0%)	(0.0%)	(0.0%)	(0.0%)	(100.0%)
Social sciences	147	2	7	18	120
	(100.0%)	(1.4%)	(4.8%)	(12.2%)	(81.6%)
Psychology	57	0	5	4	48
	(100.0%)	(0.0%)	(8.8%)	(7.0%)	(84.2%)
Economics	27	0	1	4	22
	(100.0%)	(0.0%)	(3.7%)	(14.8%)	(81.5%)
Anthropology and sociology	18	1	1	3	13
	(100.0%)	(5.6%)	(5.6%)	(16.7%)	(72.2%)
Political science, public administration, and international relations	31	1	0	4	26
	(100.0%)	(3.2%)	(0.0%)	(12.9%)	(83.9%)
Other social sciences	14	0	0	3	11
	(100.0%)	(0.0%)	(0.0%)	(21.4%)	(78.6%)

Field	Total [a]	U.S. Naturalized Citizens			
		Black	Spanish American [b]	Oriental	White
Arts and humanities	236	2	19	10	205
	(100.0%)	(0.8%)	(8.1%)	(4.2%)	(86.9%)
History	34	0	1	4	29
	(100.0%)	(0.0%)	(2.9%)	(11.8%)	(85.3%)
English and American language and lit-erature	23	0	0	1	22
	(100.0%)	(0.0%)	(0.0%)	(4.3%)	(95.7%)
Foreign languages and lit-erature	139	2	16	2	119
	(100.0%)	(1.4%)	(11.5%)	(1.4%)	(85.6%)
Other arts and humanities	40	0	2	3	35
	(100.0%)	(0.0%)	(5.0%)	(7.5%)	(87.5%)
Professional fields	23	0	1	5	17
	(100.0%)	(0.0%)	(4.3%)	(21.7%)	(73.9%)
Education	95	2	3	4	86
	(100.0%)	(2.1%)	(3.2%)	(4.2%)	(90.5%)
TOTAL	849	8	42	128	671
	(100.0%)	(0.9%)	(4.9%)	(15.1%)	(79.0%)

[a] Represents a 75 percent sample of total (33,727) doctorates awarded in 1972–73. See Table A–10 for an explanation of survey coverage.
[b] Includes Chicano, Mexican American and Spanish American.

SOURCE: Special analysis by NBGE of data from National Research Council, National Academy of Sciences, November 1974.

243

TABLE A–12 Doctoral Degrees Awarded by Field of Study, Race and Ethnic Identity, and Citizenship Status, 1972–73 (Noncitizens—Permanent Visas)

| Field | Total [a] | Noncitizens—Permanent Visas | | | |
		Black	Spanish American [b]	Oriental	White
Physical sciences and mathematics	317	2	2	222	91
	(100.0%)	(0.6%)	(0.6%)	(70.0%)	(28.7%)
Physics and astronomy	96	1	1	66	28
	(100.0%)	(1.0%)	(1.0%)	(68.8%)	(29.2%)
Chemistry	127	0	0	102	25
	(100.0%)	(0.0%)	(0.0%)	(80.3%)	(19.7%)
Earth sciences	31	1	0	14	16
	(100.0%)	(3.2%)	(0.0%)	(45.2%)	(51.6%)
Mathematics	63	0	1	40	22
	(100.0%)	(0.0%)	(1.6%)	(63.5%)	(34.9%)
Engineering	383	1	3	259	120
	(100.0%)	(0.3%)	(0.8%)	(67.6%)	(31.3%)
Life sciences	274	11	1	165	97
	(100.0%)	(4.0%)	(0.4%)	(60.2%)	(35.4%)
Basic medical sciences	102	3	1	65	33
	(100.0%)	(2.9%)	(1.0%)	(63.7%)	(32.4%)
Other biosciences	55	3	0	29	23
	(100.0%)	(5.5%)	(0.0%)	(52.7%)	(41.8%)
Medical sciences	43	1	0	25	17
	(100.0%)	(2.3%)	(0.0%)	(58.1%)	(39.5%)
Agricultural sciences	67	4	0	43	20
	(100.0%)	(6.0%)	(0.0%)	(64.2%)	(29.9%)
Environmental sciences	7	0	0	3	4
	(100.0%)	(0.0%)	(0.0%)	(42.9%)	(57.1%)
Social sciences	163	5	0	66	92
	(100.0%)	(3.0%)	(0.0%)	(40.5%)	(56.4%)
Psychology	38	0	0	9	29
	(100.0%)	(0.0%)	(0.0%)	(23.7%)	(76.3%)
Economics	52	1	0	25	26
	(100.0%)	(1.9%)	(0.0%)	(48.0%)	(50.0%)
Anthropology	27	1	0	10	16
	(100.0%)	(3.7%)	(0.0%)	(37.0%)	(59.3%)
Political science, public administration, and international relations	23	2	0	12	9
	(100.0%)	(8.7%)	(0.0%)	(52.2%)	(39.1%)
Other social sciences	23	1	0	10	12
	(100.0%)	(4.3%)	(0.0%)	(43.5%)	(52.2%)

244

Field	Total [a]	Noncitizens—Permanent Visas			
		Black	Spanish American [b]	Oriental	White
Arts and humanities	184	10	8	27	139
	(100.0%)	(5.4%)	(4.3%)	(14.7%)	(75.6%)
History	29	2	0	10	17
	(100.0%)	(6.9%)	(0.0%)	(34.5%)	(58.6%)
English and American language and literature	21	2	0	4	15
	(100.0%)	(9.5%)	(0.0%)	(19.0%)	(71.4%)
Foreign languages and literature	86	4	8	4	70
	(100.0%)	(4.7%)	(9.3%)	(4.7%)	(81.4%)
Other arts and humanities	48	2	0	9	37
	(100.0%)	(4.2%)	(0.0%)	(18.8%)	(77.1%)
Professional fields	35	2	1	16	16
	(100.0%)	(5.7%)	(2.9%)	(45.7%)	(45.7%)
Education	79	9	2	23	45
	(100.0%)	(11.4%)	(2.5%)	(29.1%)	(57.0%)
Other or unspecified fields	2	1	0	0	1
	(100.0%)	(50.0%)	(0.0%)	(0.0%)	(50.0%)
TOTAL	1,437	41	17	778	601
	(100.0%)	(2.9%)	(1.2%)	(54.1%)	(41.8%)

[a] Represents a 75 percent sample of total (33,727) doctorates awarded in 1972–73. See Table A-10 for an explanation of survey coverage.
[b] Includes Chicano, Mexican American and Spanish American.

SOURCE: Special analysis by NBGE of data from National Research Council, National Academy of Sciences, November 1974.

TABLE A–13 Doctoral Degrees Awarded by Field of Study, Race and Ethnic Identity, Citizenship Status, 1972–73 (Noncitizens—Temporary Visas)

		Noncitizens—Temporary Visas			
Field	Total [a]	Black	Spanish American [b]	Oriental	White
Physical sciences and mathematics	456	9	16	203	228
	(100.0%)	(2.0%)	(3.5%)	(44.5%)	(50.0%)
Physics and astronomy	162	3	5	71	83
	(100.0%)	(1.9%)	(3.1%)	(43.8%)	(51.2%)
Chemistry	132	3	5	79	45
	(100.0%)	(2.3%)	(3.8%)	(59.8%)	(34.1%)
Earth sciences	45	0	1	16	28
	(100.0%)	(0.0%)	(2.2%)	(35.6%)	(62.2%)
Mathematics	117	3	5	37	72
	(100.0%)	(2.6%)	(4.3%)	(31.6%)	(61.5%)
Engineering	382	8	9	160	205
	(100.0%)	(2.1%)	(2.4%)	(41.9%)	(53.7%)
Life sciences	413	32	27	144	210
	(100.0%)	(7.7%)	(6.5%)	(34.9%)	(50.8%)
Basic medical sciences	85	6	4	33	42
	(100.0%)	(7.1%)	(4.7%)	(38.8%)	(49.4%)
Other biosciences	106	7	5	38	56
	(100.0%)	(6.6%)	(4.7%)	(35.8%)	(52.8%)
Medical sciences	41	2	4	10	25
	(100.0%)	(4.9%)	(9.8%)	(24.4%)	(61.0%)
Agricultural sciences	177	17	14	61	85
	(100.0%)	(9.6%)	(7.9%)	(34.5%)	(48.0%)
Environmental sciences	4	0	0	2	2
	(100.0%)	(0.0%)	(0.0%)	(50.0%)	(50.0%)
Social sciences	332	20	3	82	227
	(100.0%)	(6.0%)	(0.9%)	(24.7%)	(68.4%)
Psychology	55	1	0	8	46
	(100.0%)	(1.8%)	(0.0%)	(14.5%)	(83.6%)
Economics	115	9	1	27	78
	(100.0%)	(7.8%)	(0.9%)	(23.5%)	(67.8%)
Anthropology	47	2	2	12	31
	(100.0%)	(4.3%)	(4.3%)	(25.5%)	(66.0%)
Political science, public administration, and international relations	59	5	0	21	33
	(100.0%)	(8.5%)	(0.0%)	(35.6%)	(55.9%)
Other social sciences	56	3	0	14	39
	(100.0%)	(5.4%)	(0.0%)	(25.0%)	(69.6%)
Arts and humanities	177	10	2	36	129
	(100.0%)	(5.6%)	(1.1%)	(20.3%)	(72.9%)

246

Field	Total [a]	Noncitizens—Temporary Visas			
		Black	Spanish American [b]	Oriental	White
History	39	0	0	7	32
	(100.0%)	(0.0%)	(0.0%)	(17.9%)	(82.1%)
English and American language and literature	35	3	0	6	26
	(100.0%)	(8.6%)	(0.0%)	(17.1%)	(74.3%)
Foreign languages and literature	34	1	1	5	27
	(100.0%)	(2.9%)	(2.9%)	(14.7%)	(79.4%)
Other arts and humanities	69	6	1	18	44
	(100.0%)	(8.7%)	(1.4%)	(26.1%)	(63.8%)
Professional fields	95	4 -	2	10	79
	(100.0%)	(4.2%)	(2.1%)	(10.5%)	(83.2%)
Education	189	20	3	54	112
	(100.0%)	(10.6%)	(1.6%)	(28.6%)	(59.3%)
Other or unspecified fields	3	0	0	1	2
	(100.0%)	(0.0%)	(0.0%)	(33.3%)	(66.6%)
TOTAL	2,047	103	62	690	1,192
	(100.0%)	(5.0%)	(3.0%)	(33.7%)	(58.2%)

[a] Represents a 75 percent sample of total (33,727) doctorates awarded in 1972–73. See Table A-10 for an explanation of survey coverage.

[b] Includes Chicano, Mexican American, and Spanish American.

SOURCE: Special analysis by NBGE of data from National Research Council, National Academy of Sciences, November 1974.

Appendix B: Survey Forms

EXHIBIT B-1: Demand for Minority Faculty in AAU Institutions

EXHIBIT B-2: Letter Survey of Fall 1974, First-Year Minority Enrollments

EXHIBIT B-3: National Research Council, Survey of Earned Doctorates, 1973–74

NATIONAL BOARD ON GRADUATE EDUCATION

Established by the Conference Board of Associated Research Councils

OFFICE OF THE STAFF DIRECTOR / NATIONAL RESEARCH COUNCIL / 2101 CONSTITUTION AVENUE, N.W. / WASHINGTON, D.C. 20418

October 7, 1974

TO: Executive Vice President

     The National Board on Graduate Education is currently developing
a report on "Minority Group Participation in Graduate Education." In
its recent report, <u>Federal</u> <u>Policy</u> <u>Alternatives</u> <u>Toward</u> <u>Graduate</u> <u>Education</u>,
the National Board expressed deep concern that members of ethnic and
racial minority groups are seriously under-represented in all sectors of
graduate education. Given the urgency and complexity of the issues
involved, the National Board decided to issue a separate report on this
topic, to provide a thorough analysis of various factors influencing
minority participation at the graduate level. Specific policy recommendations will be addressed to the federal government, states, graduate
institutions, foundations, and others involved in these concerns.

     One area of urgent concern is assessment of the <u>aggregate</u> numerical
requirements based on the various affirmative action plans for employment
of minority faculty developed by individual institutions under the direction
of the Office of Civil Rights, DHEW. Numerical hiring goals are specified
in each plan relative to some estimate of the availability of qualified
minority doctorates. However, reliable data on supply by discipline have
not been available. To improve our knowledge of the supply of minority
doctorates, Joseph McCarthy, Dean of the Graduate School at the University
of Washington, has requested the graduate dean of every A.A.U. institution
to provide figures on doctorates awarded to minority group persons in
each university, by discipline, for the period 1969 to 1975 (estimated for
1974-75). The results of his survey will be compiled shortly, based on a
100% response rate from the A.A.U. schools.

BOARD MEMBERS

David Henry
  Chairman
Joseph Ben-David
Herman R. Branson
Allan M. Cartter

Paul F. Chenea
W. Donald Cooke
John P. Crecine
Judith Blake Davis
Everett W. Ferrill
Martin Goland
Norman Hackerman

Hans Laufer
Sol M. Linowitz
Robert M. Lumiansky
Maurice Mandelbaum
John Perry Miller
John D. Millett
Hans Neurath

Rosemary Park
Martha Peterson
Richard C. Richardson, Jr.
Terry Sanford
Stephen H. Spurr
Robert Strotz
Frederick Thieme

EXHIBIT B-1: Demand for Minority Faculty in AAU Institutions

250

October 7, 1974
Page Two

      The National Board plans to investigate this question further.
We wish to obtain comparable figures about institutions' anticipated
employment <u>demand</u> for minority doctorates in faculty positions. Information about the demand for minority faculty will allow us to determine
whether the <u>aggregate</u> requirements for employment of minority faculty
in all A.A.U. schools, based on the sum of numerical targets in each
institutional affirmative action plan, differ markedly from the total
numbers of minority doctorates produced in these schools. If in fact
there exists a severe imbalance between the available supply and academic
demand for minority doctorates, then a strong case may be presented for
recognition by the federal government of its responsibility to assist
in increasing the pool of minority group doctorates, a financial responsibility now borne almost solely by the graduate institutions themselves.

1. <u>Information requested from your university</u>:

      We are requesting your cooperation in providing us with information,
based on your affirmative action plan, of your numerical targets for new
hiring of ethnic and racial minorities in academic faculty positions for
a three-year period. If you cannot provide these figures from an existing
affirmative action plan, we would greatly appreciate your supplying
<u>estimates</u> of anticipated employment needs for minority doctorate faculty
for a three-year period.

2. <u>Time Period</u>:

      Please report figures for the period July 1, 1974 - July 1, 1977,
or a period, preferably three-year, corresponding to that specified in
your institutional plan. Please indicate the precise time period for
which you have provided your figures.

3. <u>Definition of faculty positions to be included</u>:

      Positions to be included are tenured, tenure-track, or other
permanent faculty appointments, thereby excluding visiting lecturers,
"acting" professorial appointments, post-doctorate or other employment of
a temporary nature. These positions (professor, associate professor,

EXHIBIT B-1—Continued

assistant professor and similar ranks) would normally require a Ph.D. or other doctorate degree (such as Ed.D., D.Sc., D.F.A., D.A., D.B.A.) but excluding first professional degrees in such fields as law, medicine, dentistry, theology (J.D., M.D., D.D.S., D.Div.). Various faculty ranks (tenured and non-tenured) need not be differentiated; they may be reported as a combined figure.

4. Discipline or unit:

(a) In compiling these data we leave it to your discretion to define the discipline, field, department, school, college or other unit for which you have specified employment targets. However, we would prefer to have the information reported by disciplines or departments if readily available from your data base; or

(b) If the information is not available by discipline or department, then we ask the data be provided by the following broad fields;

> Arts and Humanities
> Biological Sciences
> Business Administration
> Education
> Engineering
> Health Professions
> Physical Sciences
> Social Sciences
> Other Fields (please specify)

If data are not available for these broad fields, we would appreciate your best estimates pertaining to your desired employment targets for minorities for these fields; or

(c) Failing all else (if you are unable to provide even estimates for these broad fields), please report total figures or estimates covering all departments in the university (excluding first professional degree holders).

5. Definition of minority groups to be included:

Please report data for each of the following minority groups if available;

EXHIBIT B-1—Continued

October 7, 1974
Page Four

American Indian:

    Persons considered to be Native Americans or of American
    Indian origin.

Black:

    Persons considered to be black Americans, Negroes, or of
    African origin.

Spanish-surnamed:

    Persons considered to be Chicanos, Puerto Ricans, Mexican-
    Americans, of Central American, or other Spanish origin.

Asian:

    Persons considered to be Asian-American, or of Chinese,
    Japanese or other Asian origin.

However, if you do not have data for individual minority groups, please
indicate your targets for (a) Asians and (b) all other minority groups
(Black, Spanish-surnamed, and American Indian). It is very important that
Asian figures be reported separately since their inclusion in a single
minority group total would obscure interpretation of the status of the
other minority groups.

6. Citizenship:

    Do you distinguish among U.S. citizens and non-citizens in meeting your
affirmative action goals? Please indicate the citizenship categories
included in the figures you are reporting to us.

7. Women:

    Although our report does not focus on the situation of women as a
separate group, several individuals and institutions have expressed interest
in obtaining similar data pertaining to women. Therefore, we are also
requesting data for women (including both minority and non-minority as a
single figure) by individual discipline, as outlined above in (3).

EXHIBIT B-1—Continued

253

October 7, 1974
Page Five

8. Currently Employed Minority Faculty:

In order to have accurate baseline information, we would like
information on the number of minority faculty currently employed as of
September 1974 by your institution. Please report these data to include
positions and disciplines as specified in (2), (3) and (5) above. Data
on women, as a separate group, already employed need not be reported.
Please indicate the percentage of employed minority faculty that holds
U.S. citizenship.

9. Methodology:

We would appreciate a very brief description of the methodology
involved in calculating your employment goals (both minority and nonminority). What factors did you consider in setting these goals?

The information which you provide to us will be treated as confidential
material with respect to the individual institutions. We will be pleased
to make our findings available to participating institutions as well as our
forthcoming report on this topic. Any other comments or suggestions you
may provide pertaining to affirmative action programs, based on your
experience, would be most welcome. Enclosed please find sample forms on
which you may report your figures. However, please feel free to use a
different format if you find it to be more convenient.

If you have any questions or wish further clarification, please
contact us immediately or telephone (collect) at (202) 389-6697. We would
appreciate receiving this information by October 31, 1974. Please include
the name, position and telephone number of the individual responsible for
reporting this information.

We believe these issues to be of critical importance to both graduate
education and the nation. We welcome your cooperation and interest in this
effort.

Sincerely,

Sharon C. Bush
Staff Associate

cc: Dr. David Henry
     Dr. Charles Kidd

EXHIBIT B-1—Continued

AFFIRMATIVE ACTION EMPLOYMENT OF NEW MINORITY FACULTY

Period _____ To _____

Page _____

| Discipline or Unit (Please Specify) | DEMAND FOR NEW FACULTY[a] | | | | | Total Minority Faculty Employed as of September 1974[b] |
	Black	Spanish-Surnamed	American Indian	Asian	Women (minority and non-minority)	
TOTAL						

NOTE: Please refer to questionnaire instructions for precise specifications for reporting data and additional information requested.
[a] (1) Include professor, associate professor, assistant professor and other faculty positions which are tenured or tenure-track. (2) Exclude faculty holding first professional degrees such as J.D., M.D., D.Div., D.V.M., and D.D.S. in law, theology, and the health professions.
[b] Include all persons of minority group status currently employed as faculty. Do NOT include non-minority women in this total.

EXHIBIT B-1—Continued

255

NATIONAL BOARD ON GRADUATE EDUCATION

Established by the Conference Board of Associated Research Councils

OFFICE OF THE STAFF DIRECTOR / NATIONAL RESEARCH COUNCIL / 2101 CONSTITUTION AVENUE, N.W. / WASHINGTON, D.C. 20418

October, November 1974

TO: Dean of the Graduate School

The National Board on Graduate Education is undertaking preparation of a report with recommendations on "Minority Group Participation in Graduate Education." This report will be addressed to the federal government, states, graduate institutions, professional societies, and others involved in these concerns. Enclosed for your information are a preliminary outline of issues and an advisory panel roster.

In developing this report, we have become increasingly concerned about indications that first-year enrollments of minority group persons (black, Spanish-surnamed, American Indian, *excluding* Asian Americans) in graduate schools have stabilized, or perhaps have even declined this Fall. I am writing to you to inquire about the situation in your institution.

1.   Did first-year Fall 1974 minority (black, Spanish-surnamed, American Indian, excluding Asian American) graduate enrollments (exclude professional schools such as law and medicine in which a first professional degree is normally awarded), (a) increase, (b) remain the same, or (c) decline? What is the first-year minority enrollment in graduate programs (master's or doctorate) in your school?

2.   If there has been a change, what was the approximate size of this change, in percentage terms, from Fall 1973 to Fall 1974.

3.   Similarly, what was the size of your applicant pool for this Fall as contrasted with Fall 1973?   (a) larger (b) same (c) smaller.

4.   Are you seeing more highly qualified, less qualified, or same quality of applicants this year as contrasted with prior years?

BOARD MEMBERS

David Henry
Chairman
Joseph Ben-David
Herman R. Branson
Allan M. Cartter

Paul F. Chenea
W. Donald Cooke
John P. Crecine
Judith Blake Davis
Everett W. Ferrill
Martin Goland
Norman Hackerman

Hans Laufer
Sol M. Linowitz
Robert M. Lumiansky
Maurice Mandelbaum
John Perry Miller
John D. Millett
Hans Neurath

Rosemary Park
Martha Peterson
Richard C. Richardson, Jr.
Terry Sanford
Stephen H. Spurr
Robert Strotz
Frederick Thieme

EXHIBIT B-2: Letter Survey of Fall 1974, First-Year Minority Enrollments

Several reasons have been advanced to account for changes in minority graduate enrollments including: (1) potential graduate students shifting to law and medicine; (2) changes in institutional recruitment efforts or availability of financial aid; (3) students accepting immediate employment instead of continuing to graduate school because of lucrative opportunities available with a bachelor's degree; and (4) general disenchantment with higher education. Could you comment briefly upon possible reasons for any significant changes in the applicant and enrollment levels in your school?

This is not intended to be a precise statistical survey; rather we hope to confirm (or disprove) our impressions about enrollment trends in a selected number of graduate schools.

Thank you for you help. We would appreciate your very prompt response, and will be glad to inform you of the results of these questions.

Sincerely,

Sharon C. Bush
Staff Associate

SCB:1dc

Enclosures

EXHIBIT B-2—Continued

257

NSF Form 558 1972
OMB No. 99-R0054
Approval Expires June 30, 1974

SURVEY OF EARNED DOCTORATES

Please Do Not Write in This Space

This form is to be returned
to the GRADUATE DEAN, for forwarding to .... Manpower Studies Branch, Office of Scientific Personnel,
National Research Council,
2101 Constitution Avenue, Washington, D.C. 20418

Please print or type.

A. Name in full: .... (7-28)
    (Last Name)   (First Name)   (Middle Name)

B. U.S. Social Security Number: CR ( )   Cross Reference:
(30-38)   Maiden name or ....
    — — — · — — · — — — —   former name legally changed

C. Permanent address through which you could always be reached: (Care of, if applicable) ....
    ....
    (Number)   (Street)   (City)
    ....
    (State)   (Zip Code)   (Or Country if not U.S.)

D. Date of birth: ....   Place of birth: ....
    (39-43)   (Month)   (Day)   (Year)   (44-45)   (State)   (Or Country if not U.S.)

E. Sex: 1 ☐ Male   2 ☐ Female   (46)

F. Marital status: 1 ☐ Married   2 ☐ Not married (including widowed, divorced)   (47)

G. Citizenship: 0 ☐ U.S. native   2 ☐ Non-U.S., Immigrant (Permanent Resident)
    1 ☐ U.S. naturalized   3 ☐ Non-U.S., Non-Immigrant (Temporary Resident)   (48)
    If Non-U.S., indicate country of present citizenship ....   (49-50)

H. Racial or ethnic group: (Check all that apply.)   0 ☐ White/Caucasian   1 ☐ Black/Negro/Afro-American
    2 ☐ American Indian   3 ☐ Spanish-American/Mexican-American/Chicano
    4 ☐ Puerto Rican-American   5 ☐ Oriental   6 ☐ Other, specify ....   (51-53)

EDUCATION

I. High school last attended: ....
    (School Name)   (City)   (State)   (54-55)

    Year of graduation from high school: ....   (56-57)

J. List in the table below all collegiate and graduate institutions you have attended including 2-year colleges. List chronologically, and include your doctoral institution as the last entry.

Institution Name	Location	Years Attended		Major Field		Minor Field	Degree (if any)		
		From	To	Use Specialties List			Title of Degree	Granted	
				Name	Number	Number		Mo.	Yr.

K. Enter below the title of your doctoral dissertation and the most appropriate classification number and field. If a project report or a musical or literary composition (not a dissertation) is a degree requirement, please check box. ☐   48
    Title ....   Classify using Specialties List
    ....   Number   Name of field
    ....   (62-64)

L. Name the department (or interdisciplinary committee, center, institute, etc.) and school or college of the university which supervised your doctoral program: ....
    (Department)   (School)   (65-80)

M. Name of your dissertation adviser: (please print) ....   (8-20)
    (Last Name)   (First Name)   (Middle Initial)

continued on next page

Please Do Not Write in This Space column entries:
1
6
7-28 NA
30-38 ss   d(__) 29
39 40 41 42 43
44 45
46 47
48 49 50
51 52 53
54 55 56 57 HS
58 59 60 UG
61 62
63 64 65 66 67 68 B
69 70 71
72 73 74
75 76 77 n(__) 77
2
6 GR
7 8 9 10 11 12
13 14
15 16 17 18 19 20 M
21 22 23
24 25 26
27 28 29
30 31 32
33 34 35 36 37 38 D
39 40 41
42 43 44
45 46 47 48 49
50 51 TO
52 53 CE-BA
54 55 BA-GE
56 57 GE-MA
58 59 MA-PHD
60 61 GE-PHD
62 63 64 TI
65-80 TA DI
3
6 7
8-20 TA

EXHIBIT B-3: National Research Council, Survey of Earned Doctorates, 1973–74

258

SURVEY OF EARNED DOCTORATES, Cont.

N. In the space in front of each source of support, indicate the approximate number of semesters you were supported by each of the listed sources during graduate school.

21 ___ NSF Fellowship	29 ___ GI Bill	34 ___ Teaching Assistantship
22 ___ NSF Traineeship	30 ___ Other Federal support	35 ___ Research Assistantship
23 ___ NIH Fellowship	(specify)................	36 ___ Educational fund of
24 ___ NIH Traineeship	31 ___ Woodrow Wilson Fellowship	industrial or
25 ___ NDEA Fellowship	32 ___ Other U.S. national fellowship	business firm
26 ___ Other HEW		37 ___ Other institutional
27 ___ AEC Fellowship	(specify)..................	funds (specify)
28 ___ NASA Traineeship	33 ___ University fellowship	....

38 ___ Own earnings
39 ___ Spouse's earnings
40 ___ Family contribu-tions
41 ___ Loans
42 ___ Other (specify)

O. Please check the space which most fully describes your status during the year immediately preceding the doctorate.

0 ☐ Held fellowship
1 ☐ Held assistantship
2 ☐ Held own research grant
3 ☐ Not employed
4 ☐ Part-time employed

Full-time
Employed in:
(Other than
0, 1, 2)

5 ☐ College or university, teaching
6 ☐ College or university, non-teaching
7 ☐ Elem. or sec. school, teaching
8 ☐ Elem. or sec. school, non-teaching
9 ☐ Industry or business
(11)☐ Other (specify) ....

(12)☐ Any other (specify)...........................(43)

P. How many years (full-time equivalent basis) of professional work experience did you have prior to the doctorate?
(include assistantships as professional experience)..(44-45)

Q. U.S. veteran status:

0 ☐ Veteran, or in service; dates of active duty from..............
(year)

to.............
(year)

1 ☐ Non-veteran

2 ☐ Not applicable (46-50)

POSTGRADUATION PLANS

R. How well defined are your postgraduation plans?

0 ☐ Have signed contract or made definite commitment
1 ☐ Am negotiating with a specific organization, or more than one

2 ☐ Am seeking appointment but have no specific prospects

3 ☐ Other (specify) ....(51)

S. What are your immediate postgraduation plans?

0 ☐ Postdoctoral fellowship?
1 ☐ Postdoctoral research associateship?
2 ☐ Traineeship?
3 ☐ Other study (specify) ....
If you check 0, 1, 2, or 3, please answer "T" and omit "U"

4 ☐ Employment? (other than 0, 1, 2, 3)
5 ☐ Military service?
6 ☐ Other (specify) ....(52)
If you checked 4, 5, or 6, please answer "U" and omit "T"

T. If you plan to be on a postdoctoral fellowship, associate-ship, or traineeship —

What is the purpose?

0 ☐ To add experience in your present field (53)
1 ☐ To change to a field different from that of the doctorate
(Please enter number of new field from Specialties List
...................) (54-56)

What is the primary source of support?

0 ☐ U.S. Government
1 ☐ College or university
2 ☐ Private foundation
3 ☐ Nonprofit, other than pri-vate foundation
4 ☐ Other (specify)
...................(57)

U. If you plan to be employed, enter military service, or other —

What will be the type of employer?

0 ☐ 4-year college or university
1 ☐ Jr. or community college
2 ☐ Elem. or sec. school
3 ☐ Foreign government
4 ☐ U.S. Government
5 ☐ State or local government
6 ☐ Nonprofit organization
7 ☐ Industry or business
8 ☐ Self-employed
9 ☐ Other (specify)
...................(58)

Indicate primary work activity with "1" in appropriate box; secondary work activity (if any) with "2" in appropriate box.

0 ☐ Research and development
1 ☐ Teaching
2 ☐ Administration
3 ☐ Professional services to individuals
5 ☐ Other (specify)
...................(59-60)

In what field will you be working?
Please enter number from Specialties List ....(61-63)

V. What is the name and address of the organization with which you will be associated?

....
(Name of Organization)

....
(Street)

(City, State)   (Or Country if not U.S.)   (64-69)

BACKGROUND INFORMATION

W. Please indicate, by circling the highest grade attained, the education of

your father:	none	1 2 3 4 5 6 7 8	9 10 11 12	1 2 3 4	MA, MD PhD	Postdoctoral	(70)
		Elementary school	High school	College	Graduate		
your mother	none	1 2 3 4 5 6 7 8	9 10 11 12	1 2 3 4	MA, MD PhD	Postdoctoral	(71)
	0	1 2 3	4 5	6 7	8 9	(11)	

Signature .... Date completed ....
(72-73)

EXHIBIT B-3—Continued

259

Right margin column codes: 21 ( ) 22 ( ); 23 ( ) 24 ( ); 25 ( ) 26 ( ); 27 ( ) 28 ( ); 29 ( ) 30 ( ); 31 ( ) 32 ( ); 33 ( ) 34 ( ); 35 ( ) 36 ( ); 37 ( ) 38 ( ); 39 ( ) 40 ( ); 41 ( ) 42 ( ); 43 44 45; 46; 47 48 49 50; 51; 52; T 53; 54 55 56; 57; U 58; 59 60; 61 62 63; V 64 65 66 67 68 69; W 70; 71; 72 73

Bibliography

Alfred P. Sloan Foundation. The Planning Commission for Expanding Minority Opportunities in Engineering. *Minorities in Engineering: A Blueprint for Action.* New York: Alfred P. Sloan Foundation, 1974.

American Academy of Arts and Sciences. "The Future of Black Colleges." *Daedalus* 100(1971):539–906.

———. "Slavery, Colonialism, and Racism." *Daedalus* 103(1974):1–179.

American Anthropological Association. *The Minority Experience in Anthropology: Report of the Committee on Minorities and Anthropology.* Washington, D.C.: American Anthropological Association, 1973.

American Council on Education. *National Norms for Entering College Freshmen— Fall 1970.* American Council on Education Research Reports, no. 5. Washington, D.C.: American Council on Education, 1970.

———. *The American Freshman: National Norms for Fall 1971.* American Council on Education Research Reports, no. 6. Washington, D.C.: American Council on Education, 1972.

American Sociological Association. "Million Dollar Minority Fellowship Program." *Footnotes,* vol. 1, no. 7. Washington, D.C.: American Sociological Association, 1973.

Assembly of Engineering, Committee on Minorities in Engineering. *Building Effective Minority Programs in Engineering Education.* Washington, D.C.: National Academy of Sciences, September 1975.

Association of American Medical Colleges. "Information for Minority Group Students." Chapter 6 in *Medical School Admissions Requirements, 1975–76, U.S.A. and Canada,* pp. 52–64. Washington, D.C.: Association of American Medical Colleges, 1975.

Astin, Alexander W. *The Myth of Equal Access in Public Higher Education.* Atlanta: Southern Education Foundation, 1975.

———, Robert J. Panos, and John A. Creager. *National Norms for Entering College Freshmen—Fall 1966.* American Council on Education Research Reports, no. 2. Washington, D.C.: American Council on Education, 1967.

261

————, Margo R. King, and Gerald T. Richardson. *The American Freshman: National Norms for Fall 1975.* Los Angeles: Cooperative Institutional Research Program, 1975.

Atelsek, Frank J., and Irene L. Gomberg. *Student Assistance: Participants and Programs, 1974–75.* Higher Education Panel Reports, no. 22. Washington, D.C.: American Council on Education, 1975.

Baeza, Mario L. "Efficiency, Equality and Justice in Admissions Procedures to Higher Education: A Constitutional Model for Resolving Conflicting Goals and Competing Claims." *Black Law Journal* 3(1974):132–161.

Baird, Leonard L. *The Graduates: A Report on the Characteristics and Plans of College Seniors.* Princeton, N.J.: Educational Testing Service, 1973.

————. "A Portrait of Blacks in Graduate Studies." *Findings,* vol. 1, no. 2. Princeton, N.J.: Educational Testing Service, 1974.

Ballard, Allan. "Academia's Record of Benign Neglect." *Change* 5 (March 1973): 27–33.

————. *The Education of Black Folk.* New York: Harper & Row, 1973.

Bayer, Alan E. *The Black College Freshman: Characteristics and Recent Trends.* American Council on Education Research Reports, no. 7. Washington, D.C.: American Council on Education, 1972.

Blackwell, James E. *Access of Black Students to Graduate and Professional Schools.* Atlanta: Southern Education Foundation, 1975.

Blake, Elias, Jr., and Henry Cobb. *Black Studies: Issues in Their Institutional Survival.* Washington, D.C.: Institute for Services to Education, 1974.

————, Linda J. Lambert, and Joseph L. Martin. *Degrees Granted and Enrollment Trends in Historically Black Colleges: An Eight-Year Study.* Washington, D.C.: Institute for Services to Education, 1974.

Bowles, Frank, and Frank A. DeCosta. *Between Two Worlds.* New York: McGraw-Hill, 1971.

Boxley, Russell, and Natanial N. Wagner. "Clinical Psychology Training Programs and Minority Groups: A Survey." *Professional Psychology* 2(Winter 1971):75–81.

Boyd, William M., II. *Desegregating America's Colleges: A Nationwide Survey of Black Students, 1972–73.* New York: Praeger Publishers, 1974.

Bracey, John H., Jr. "The Graduate School Experience: A Black Student Viewpoint." *The Graduate Journal* VIII(1971):444–451.

Branson, Herman R. "Black Students and the Elusive Doctorate." Paper prepared for the National Board on Graduate Education, 1973.

Brown, Janet, Heather Coleman, and Susan E. Posner. *Rosters of Minority and Women Professionals.* AAAS Misc. Publ. 75-1. Washington, D.C.: American Association for the Advancement of Science, 1975.

Bryant, James W. *A Survey of Black American Doctorates.* New York: The Ford Foundation, 1970.

Bullock, Henry Allan. *A History of Negro Education in the South.* New York: Praeger Publishers, 1970.

Burkheimer, Graham J., and Junius A. Davis. *A Census of Special Support Programs for "Disadvantaged" Students in American Institutions of Higher Education, 1971–72.* Princeton, N.J.: Educational Testing Service, 1973.

Cahn, Edgar S. *Our Brother's Keeper: The Indian in White America.* Mountainview, Calif.: World Publications, 1969.

Carlisle, Donald. *Master's and Doctoral Opportunity Programs at UCLA Entering Classes of 1967 through 1970–71—"The Danforth Years".* Los Angeles: University of California, August 1973.

262

Carnegie Commission on Higher Education. *Quality and Equality: Revised Recommendations.* New York: McGraw-Hill, 1970.

———. *A Chance to Learn: An Action Agenda for Equal Opportunity in Higher Education.* New York: McGraw-Hill, 1970.

———. *From Isolation to Mainstream.* New York: McGraw-Hill, 1971.

———. *Priorities for Action: Final Report of the Carnegie Commission on Higher Education.* New York: McGraw-Hill, 1973.

Carnegie Corporation of New York. *A Step Toward Equal Justice: Programs to Increase Black Lawyers in the South: An Evaluation Report.* New York: Carnegie Corporation, 1974.

Carnegie Council on Policy Studies in Higher Education. *Making Affirmative Action Work in Higher Education.* San Francisco: Jossey-Bass, 1975.

Carter, Thomas P. *Mexican Americans in School: A History of Educational Neglect.* New York: College Entrance Examination Board, 1970.

Casso, Henry J. "Higher Education and the Mexican American." In *Economic and Educational Perspectives of the Mexican American.* New York: The Weatherhead Foundation, forthcoming.

Chavis, John, Dalia Ducker, and Rita Foy. *Programs for the Academically Talented Black Student.* Atlanta: Institute for Higher Educational Opportunity, Southern Regional Education Board, December 1973.

Cobb, Jewel Plummer, and Carolyn McDew, eds. *The Morning After—A Retrospective View of a Select Number of Colleges and Universities with Increased Black Student Enrollment in the Past Five Years.* Report of a conference at the University of Connecticut, Storrs, April 30, 1973. Storrs: University of Connecticut.

College Entrance Examination Board. *Access to College for Mexican Americans in the Southwest.* New York: College Entrance Examination Board, 1972.

———. *Toward Equal Opportunity for Higher Education.* New York: College Entrance Examination Board, 1973.

———. *College-Bound Seniors, 1973–74.* Admissions Testing Program of the CEEB. New York: College Entrance Examination Board, 1974.

———. *College-Bound Seniors, 1974–75.* New York: College Entrance Examination Board, 1975.

Collins, O. R. "A Profile of Minority Graduate Students at the University of California, Berkeley: Recruitment, Selection, Fields of Study and Financial Support." Paper read at 140th Annual Meeting of the American Association for the Advancement of Science, February 28, 1974, San Francisco, Calif.

Comer, James P., and James E. Coleman, Jr. "Quotas, Race and Justice." *The New York Times,* 17 March 1974.

Council for Financial Aid to Education. *Graduate and Professional Education in the United States—1973–74 Profile.* A Special Supplement to the *Handbook of Aid to Higher Education.* New York: Council for Financial Aid to Education, July 1974.

Creager, John A. *The American Graduate Student: A Normative Description.* Washington, D.C.: American Council on Education, 1971.

Crossland, Fred E. "Graduate Education and Black Americans." The Ford Foundation, November 25, 1968, unpublished.

———. *Minority Access to College.* New York: Schocken Books, 1971.

Davis, Jerry S. "State Financial Aid Programs and Student Access," in *Financial Barriers to Equal Access in Higher Education,* pp. 27–49. Papers prepared for a Conference on Equality of Access in Postsecondary Education. Atlanta, Ga.

263

Davis, Junius A., and Anne Borders-Patterson. *Black Students in Predominantly White North Carolina Colleges and Universities.* Research Report 2. New York: College Entrance Examination Board, 1973.

DeFunis v. *Odegaard,* 416 U.S. 312 (1974).

————. 82 Wash. 2d 11, 507 P.2d 1169 (1973).

————. Brief of the Anti-Defamation League of B'nai B'rith as *Amicus Curiae.*

————. Brief for Children's Defense Fund *et al.,* as *Amicus Curiae.*

————. Brief for the President and Fellows of Harvard College as *Amicus Curiae.*

Delaney, Paul. "Black Psychologist Fighting Use of Intelligence Tests He Says Reflect White Middle-Class Values." *The New York Times,* 13 May 1975.

————. "Blacks Say Drive to Spur College Enrollment Ends." *The New York Times,* 26 March 1975.

Demsetz, Harold. "Minorities in the Market Place." *The North Carolina Law Review* 43(1965):271–297.

Educational Testing Service. *Graduate and Professional School Opportunities for Minority Students.* 5th ed. Princeton, N.J.: Educational Testing Service, 1973–74.

Egerton, John. *State Universities and Black Americans: An Inquiry Into Desegregation and Equity for Negroes in 100 Public Universities.* Nashville, Tenn.: Southern Education Reporting Service, 1969.

————. *Equality of Access in Postsecondary Education.* Atlanta: Southern Education Foundation, 1975.

El-Khawas, Elaine H., and Joan L. Kinzer. *Enrollment of Minority Graduate Students at Ph.D. Granting Institutions.* Higher Education Panel Reports, no. 19. Washington, D.C.: American Council on Education, August 1974.

————. *The Impact of Office of Education Student Assistance Programs, Fall 1974.* Higher Education Panel Reports, no. 18. Washington, D.C.: American Council on Education, 1974.

————. *A Survey of Continuing Education Opportunities Available to Nonacademic Scientists, Engineers, and Mathematicians.* Higher Education Panel Reports, no. 23. Washington, D.C.: American Council on Education, 1975.

Epps, Edgar G., ed. *Black Students in White Schools.* Worthington, Ohio: Charles A. Jones Publishing Co., 1972.

Fisher, Miles Mark, IV. "National Association for Equal Opportunity in Higher Education: Crusader for the Black College." *Civil Rights Digest* (U.S. Commission on Civil Rights) 3(1970):18–21.

Flax, Michael J. *Blacks and Whites: An Experiment in Racial Indicators.* Washington, D.C.: The Urban Institute, 1971.

Fleming, Patricia S. "Improving Federal Support for Equal Opportunity." Paper read before the Conference on Equality of Access in Postsecondary Education, Southern Education Foundation and The Ford Foundation, July 17–19, 1975, Atlanta, Ga.

Fleming, Robben W. "College Minority Admissions: Where Do We Go From Here?" Paper read before the Economic Club of Detroit, November 5, 1973.

Fleming, Virginia. "Equal Access and Student Financial Aid." Paper read before the Conference on Equality of Access in Postsecondary Education, Southern Education Foundation and The Ford Foundation, July 17–19, 1975, Atlanta, Ga.

Freeman, Richard, and J. Herbert Hollomon. "The Declining Value of College Going." *Change* 7(September 1975):24–31, 62.

Furniss, W. Todd. "Racial Minorities and Curriculum Change." *Educational Record* 50(Fall 1969):360–370.

de la Garza, Rudolph O. "A Chicano View of Graduate Education: Where We Are and Where We Should Be," in *Proceedings of the Fourteenth Annual Meeting, Council of Graduate Schools in the United States,* Phoenix, Arizona, December 4–6, 1974, pp. 77–83.

Gellhorn, Ernest, and D. Brock Hornby. "Constitutional Limitations on Admissions Procedures and Standards." *Virginia Law Review* 60, no. 6(October 1974):975–1011.

Glazer, Nathan. "Ethnic Groups and Education: Towards Tolerance of Difference." *Journal of Negro Education* 38(1969):187–195.

Gordon, Edmund W. "Programs for Minority Group Youth in Higher Education." In *Does College Matter?,* ed. by Lewis C. Solmon and Paul J. Taubman. New York: Academic Press, 1973.

―――. "Programs and Practices for Minority Group Youth in Higher Education." In *Barriers to Higher Education.* New York: College Entrance Examination Board, 1971.

Graduate Record Examinations Board. *Report on the Council of Graduate Schools— Graduate Record Examinations Board 1974–75 Survey of Graduate Enrollment.* Princeton, N.J.: Educational Testing Service, 1975.

Grebler, Leo, Joan W. Moore, and Ralph C. Guzman. *The Mexican American People.* New York: Free Press, 1970.

Hale, Frank W., Jr., ed. *They Came and They Conquered.* Columbus: Ohio State University Press, 1973.

Hall, Laurence. *New Colleges for New Students,* pp. 102–176. San Francisco: Jossey-Bass, 1974.

Hamilton, I. Bruce. *Graduate School Programs for Minority/Disadvantaged Students.* Princeton, N.J.: Educational Testing Service, 1973.

―――. "Irresistible Force Meets Immovable Object: A Study of American Graduate Schools' Response to the Black Revolution." Ph.D. dissertation, Stanford University, 1974.

Hartman, Robert W. *Financing the Opportunity to Enter the "Educated Labor Market."* Washington, D.C.: The Brookings Institution, 1974.

Harvard University. "Project Report: De Jure Segregation of Chicanos in Texas Schools." *Harvard Civil Rights–Civil Liberties Law Review* 7(March 1972): 307–319.

Heath, G. Louis. *Red, Brown and Black Demands for Better Education.* Philadelphia: Westminster Press, 1972.

Henderson, Algo D., and Natalie B. Gumas. *Admitting Black Students to Medical and Dental Schools.* Berkeley: University of California, 1971.

Henderson, Vivian W. "Blacks and Change in Higher Education." *Daedalus* 103 (1974):72–79.

Hill, Robert B. "Benign Neglect Revisited: The Illusion of Black Progress." Paper read at Annual Conference of the National Urban League, July 24, 1973, Washington, D.C.

Hills, Gerald E. *Minority Student Program Design in Graduate Business Schools: Perceptions of Administrative Personnel.* Knoxville: University of Tennessee, Center for Business and Economic Research, January 1974.

Honani, Daniel. *Native American Professional Resource Directory.* Albuquerque, N.Mex.: Southwestern Cooperative Educational Laboratory, August 1973.

Holmes, Eugene C. "A Philosophical Approach to the Study of Minority Problems." *Journal of Negro Education* 38(1969):196–203.

265

Howard, Bill. "Blacks and Professional Schools." *Change* 4(February 1972):13–16.
Hrabowski, Freeman Alphonsa. "A Comparison of Graduate Academic Performance of Black Students Who Graduated from Predominantly Black Colleges and from Predominantly White Colleges." Ph.D. dissertation, University of Illinois, 1975.
Institute for the Study of Educational Policy. Report no. 1. *Equal Educational Opportunity for Blacks in U.S. Higher Education: An Assessment.* Washington, D.C.: Howard University, 1976.
Jaffee, A. J., Walter Adams, and Sandra Meyers. *Negro Higher Education in the 1960's.* New York: Praeger Publishers, 1968.
———, and Zaida Carreras Carleton. *Some Demographic and Economic Characteristics of the Puerto Rican Population Living on the Mainland, U.S.A.* New York: Columbia University, November 1974.
Jay, James M. *Negroes in Science: Natural Science Doctorates, 1876–1969.* Detroit: Balamp Publishing, 1971.
Jencks, Christopher, and David Riesman. "The American Negro College." *Harvard Educational Review* 37, no. 1 (Winter 1967):3–60.
———. *The Academic Revolution.* Garden City, N.Y.: Doubleday, 1968.
Johnson, Roosevelt. *Black Scholars on Higher Education in the 70's.* Columbus, Ohio: ECCA Publications, Inc., 1974.
Jones, Ann. *Uncle Tom's Campus.* New York: Praeger Publishers, 1973.
Jones, Mack. "The Responsibility of the Black College to the Black Community." In *Does College Matter?,* ed. by Lewis C. Solmon and Paul J. Taubman. New York: Academic Press, 1973.
Jones, Phillip E. "Proposal for Training Institute for the Developing of Equality of Opportunity Program Administrators in Higher Education." August 1973. Unpublished.
Jordan, Vernon E., Jr. "Blacks and Higher Education—Some Reflections." *Daedalus* 104(1975):160–165.
Kilson, Martin. "The Black Experience at Harvard." *New York Times Magazine,* 2 September 1973.
King, Allan G., and Ray Marshall. *Black–White Economic Convergence and the Civil Rights Act of 1964.* Austin: Center for the Study of Human Resources, The University of Texas, 1974.
Kirp, David L., and Mark G. Yudof. *Educational Policy and the Law.* Berkeley, Calif.: McCutchan Publishing Co., 1974.
Kluger, Richard. *Simple Justice: The History of Brown v. Board of Education and Black America's Struggle for Equality.* New York: Alfred A. Knopf, 1976.
Layzer, David. "Heritability Analyses of IQ Scores: Science or Numerology?" *Science* 183(March 29, 1974):1259–1266.
Lee, John B., and Mary A. Malgoire. "The Distribution of Student Aid to Mexican American College Students 1972–73." Paper read before the National Institute on Access to Higher Education for the Mexican American, July 24–25, 1975, Albuquerque, N. Mex.
Leonard, Walter J. "*DeFunis* v. *Odegaard:* An Invitation to Look Backward." *The Black Law Journal* 3(Winter 1974):224–231.
Lepper, Mary M. "Minority Access to Higher Education: Problems, Trends and Challenges." Paper read before the National Institute on Access to Higher Education for the Mexican American, July 24–25, 1975, Albuquerque, N. Mex.
Lester, Richard A. *Antibias Regulation of Universities.* New York: McGraw-Hill, 1974.

266

Lopez, Ronald W., and Darryl D. Enos. "Chicanos and Public Higher Education in California." Report prepared for the Joint Committee on the Master Plan for Higher Education, California Legislature, Sacramento, November 1972.

McCarthy, Joseph L., and Dael Wolfle. "Doctorates Granted to Women and Minority Group Members." *Science* 189(September 12, 1975):856–859.

Mann, Peter B. *Higher Education in Black and White.* A seminar report. Washington, D.C.: American Association for Higher Education, Southeastern Regional Council, 1972.

Margolis, Richard J. "White Philanthropy and the Red Man." *Foundation News* 14(March/April 1974):13–22.

Martinez, J. V. *Directory of Spanish-Surnamed and Native Americans in Science and Engineering.* Rochester, N.Y.: 1971.

Martinez, Juan R. "Chicano Graduate Students: The Berkeley Experience." In *Proceedings of the Fourteenth Annual Meeting of the Council of Graduate Schools in the United States,* Phoenix, Ariz., December 4–6, 1974, pp. 83–98.

Miskel, Maryjane. "Minority Student Enrollment." *ERIC Research Currents.* Washington, D.C.: Educational Resources Information Center, November 1973.

Mommsen, Kent G. "Black Ph.D's in the Academic Marketplace." *Journal of Higher Education* XLV(April 1974):253–267.

Moore, William, Jr., and Lonnie H. Wagstaff. *Black Educators in White Colleges* San Francisco: Jossey-Bass, 1974.

Moses, Lincoln E. "Report to the Faculty Senate Spring Quarter, 1975." Stanford, Calif.: Stanford University, unpublished.

Muskrat, Joseph. "Thoughts on the Indian Dilemma." *Civil Rights Digest* (U.S. Commission on Civil Rights) 6(1973):46–50.

Myrdal, Gunnar. *An American Dilemma: The Negro Problem and Modern Democracy.* 2 vols. New York: Random House, 1972.

Nairobi Research Institute. *Blacks and Public Higher Education in California.* Prepared for the Joint Committee on the Master Plan for Higher Education, California Legislature, Sacramento, February 1973.

National Academy of Engineering, Commission on Education. *Symposium on Increasing Minority Participation in Engineering, Proceedings.* Washington, D.C.: National Academy of Engineering, 1973.

National Association for Equal Opportunity in Higher Education. *The National Goal of Equal Opportunity and the Historically Black Colleges, A Partnership for Leadership in the Development of a Year 2000 Plan for Parity in Education.* Summary statement. Washington, D.C.: National Association for Equal Opportunity in Higher Education, 1975.

National Association of State Universities and Land Grant Colleges, FYI, April 12, 1970. "Graduate Schools Seek Minorities." Washington, D.C.: NASULGC, 1970.

National Education Task Force de la Raza. *A Relook at Tucson: '66 and Beyond.* A report of a National Bilingual Bicultural Institute, Albuquerque, N. Mex., November 28–December 1, 1973.

National Research Council. Commission on Human Resources. *Minority Groups among United States Doctorate Level Scientists, Engineers, and Scholars.* Washington, D.C.: National Academy of Sciences, 1974.

———. *Summary Report 1974: Doctorate Recipients from United States Universities.* Washington, D.C.: National Academy of Science, 1975.

———. Office of Scientific Personnel. *Summary Reports 1971–1973: Doctorate Recipients from United States Universities.* Washington, D.C.: National Academy of Sciences.

267

National Scholarship Service and Fund for Negro Students. *Minority Youth: The Classes of 1972 and 1973.* New York: NSSFNS, 1974.

National Science Board. *Graduate Education: Parameters for Public Policy.* Washington, D.C.: National Science Foundation, 1969.

Newman, Rogers J. *The White Student Enrolled in the Traditionally Public Black College and University.* Atlanta: Institute for Higher Education Opportunity, Southern Regional Education Board, September 1973.

Nichols, David C., and Olive Mills, eds. *The Campus and the Racial Crisis.* Washington, D.C.: American Council on Education, 1970.

O'Neil, Robert M. "Preferential Admissions: Equalizing the Access of Minority Groups to Higher Education." *The Yale Law Journal* 80(March 1971):699–767.

――――. "Racial Preference and Higher Education: The Larger Context." *Virginia Law Review* 60, no. 6 (October 1974):925–954.

――――. "After DeFunis: Filling the Constitutional Vacuum." *University of Florida Law Review* 27(Winter 1975):315–342.

Parmeter, J. Thomas. "Impact of the Thirteen College Curriculum Program on Graduating Seniors: Motivational and Attitudinal Facts." Washington, D.C.: Institute for Services to Education, 1974. Unpublished.

Parsons, Talcott, and Kenneth B. Clark, eds. *The Negro American.* Boston: Beacon Press, 1967.

Patterson, Bradley H., Jr. "The Federal Executive Branch and the First Americans." *Civil Rights Digest* (U.S. Commission on Civil Rights) 6(1973):51–56.

Peterson, Roy P., and Juanita Betz Peterson. "Southern White Institutions and Black Students: A New Partnership." *Educational Record,* Winter 1974, pp. 13–22.

Pifer, Alan. *The Higher Education of Blacks in the United States.* New York: Carnegie Corporation, 1973.

President's Commission on Higher Education. *Higher Education for American Democracy.* Vol. 1—*Establishing the Goals.* Vol. 2—*Equalizing and Expanding Individual Opportunity.* Washington, D.C.: U.S. Government Printing Office, 1947.

Raspberry, William. "Divergent Perceptions of Black Progress." *The Washington Post,* 27 November 1974.

Rodriguez, Richard. "On Becoming a Chicano." *Saturday Review,* 8 February 1975, pp. 46–47.

Roizen, Judy. "Black Students in Higher Education." In *Teachers and Students,* ed. by Martin Trow, pp. 113–181. New York: McGraw-Hill, 1975.

Sawyer, G. M. "The Questions Are No Longer 'Academic.' " Paper read before the Conference on Equality of Access in Postsecondary Education, Southern Education Foundation and The Ford Foundation, July 17–19, 1975, Atlanta, Ga.

Scully, Malcolm G. "Open Admissions Students Found Staying at CUNY." *The Chronicle of Higher Education,* 25 March 1974.

Sells, Lucy W., ed. *New Directions for Institutional Research: Toward Affirmative Action.* No. 3 San Francisco: Jossey-Bass, Autumn 1974.

Semas, Phillip W. "Law Rolls Double in Decade: Women and Minorities Gain." *The Chronicle of Higher Education,* 14 January 1974.

Shinto, William. *Present Status of Asians in America and Educational Issues.* Costa Mesa, Calif.: United Ministries in Higher Education, August 24, 1974.

Smith, Michael. "The Constitutional Status of American Indians." *Civil Rights Digest* (U.S. Commission on Civil Rights) 6(1973):10–16.

Southern Education Foundation. *Small Change: A Report on Federal Support for Black Colleges, 1972.* Atlanta: Southern Education Foundation, 1972.

Southern Regional Education Board. *The College and Cultural Diversity, The Black Student on Campus, A Project Report.* Atlanta: Institute for Higher Educational Opportunity, October 1971.

Sowell, Thomas. *Black Education, Myths and Tragedies.* New York: David McKay Co., 1972.

————. "The Great IQ Controversy." *Change* 5(May 1973):33–37.

————. *Affirmative Action Reconsidered: Was It Necessary in Academia?* Washington, D.C.: American Enterprise Institute for Public Policy Research, December 1975.

Spurlock, Langley A. *Minorities in White Colleges: A Survey of Opinion from Students, Faculty, and Administrators.* Washington, D.C.: American Council on Education, 1974.

Stanford University. *The Minority Report: A Review of Minority Student Concerns in the Graduate and Professional Schools.* Stanford, Calif.: Stanford University, September 1974.

State of Connecticut Commission for Higher Education. *Equal Opportunity, Special Needs of Minorities in Higher Education and Methods of Meeting Needs.* Document no. 13. Hartford: Commission for Higher Education, February 1973.

Stuart, Reginald. *Black Perspectives on State-Controlled Higher Education: The Tennessee Report.* New York: John Hay Whitney Foundation, 1973.

————. *Black Perspectives on State-Controlled Higher Education: The Florida Report.* New York: John Hay Whitney Foundation, 1974.

————. *Black Perspectives on State-Controlled Higher Education: The Mississippi Report.* New York: John Hay Whitney Foundation, 1974.

————. *Black Perspectives on State-Controlled Higher Education: The Virginia Report.* New York: John Hay Whitney Foundation, 1974.

Taylor, Theodore W. *The States and Their Indian Citizens.* Washington, D.C.: U.S. Government Printing Office, 1971.

U. S. Bureau of the Census. Current Population Reports, Special Studies, Series P–20, no. 224. *Selected Characteristics of Persons and Families of Mexican, Puerto Rican and Other Spanish Origin: March 1971.* Washington, D.C.: U.S. Government Printing Office, October 1971.

————. Current Population Reports, Special Studies, Series P–20, no. 238. *Selected Characteristics of Persons and Families of Mexican, Puerto Rican and Other Spanish Origin, March: 1972.* Advance report, July 1972.

————. 1970 Census of Population. Subject Reports, Final Report PC(2)–5B. *Educational Attainment.* Washington, D.C.: U.S. Government Printing Office, March 1973.

————. 1970 Census of Population. Subject Reports, Final Report PC(2)–1B. *Negro Population.* Washington, D.C.: U.S. Government Printing Office, May 1973.

————. 1970 Census of Population. Subject Reports, Final Report PC(2)–1D. *Persons of Spanish Surname.* Washington, D.C.: U.S. Government Printing Office, June 1973.

————. 1970 Census of Population. Subject Reports, Final Report PC(2)–1E. *Puerto Ricans in the United States.* Washington, D.C.: U.S. Government Printing Office, June 1973.

————. 1970 Census of Population. Subject Reports, Final Report PC(2)–1C. *Persons of Spanish Origin.* Washington, D.C.: U.S. Government Printing Office, June 1973.

————. 1970 Census of Population. Subject Reports, Final Report PC(2)–1F. *American Indians*. Washington, D.C.: U.S. Government Printing Office, June 1973.

————. Current Population Reports, Special Studies, Series P–23, no. 46. *The Social and Economic Status of the Black Population in the United States, 1972.* Washington, D.C.: U.S. Government Printing Office, July 1973.

————. Current Population Reports, Special Studies, Series P–20, no. 264. *Persons of Spanish Origin in the United States.* Washington, D.C.: U.S. Government Printing Office, May 1974.

————. Current Population Reports, Special Studies, Series P-23, no. 54. *The Social and Economic Status of the Black Population in the United States, 1974.* Washington, D.C.: U.S. Government Printing Office, July 1975.

U.S. Commission on Civil Rights. *What Students Perceive.* Clearinghouse Publication no. 24. Washington, D.C.: U.S. Government Printing Office, February 1970.

————. *Mexican Americans and the Administration of Justice in the Southwest.* Washington, D.C.: U.S. Government Printing Office, March 1970.

————. *The Unfinished Education: Outcomes for Minorities in the Five Southwestern States.* Mexican American Education Study. Report II. Washington, D.C.: U.S. Government Printing Office, October 1971.

————. *The Excluded Student.* Mexican American Education Study. Report III. Washington, D.C.: U.S. Government Printing Office, May 1972.

————. *The Federal Civil Rights Enforcement Effort: A Reassessment.* Washington, D.C.: U.S. Government Printing Office, January 1973.

————. *To Know or Not to Know. Collection and Use of Racial and Ethnic Data in Federal Assistance Programs.* Washington, D.C.: U.S. Government Printing Office, February 1973.

————. *Teachers and Students.* Mexican American Education Study. Report V. Washington, D.C.: U.S. Government Printing Office, March 1973.

————. *The Southwest Indian Report.* Washington, D.C.: U.S. Government Printing Office, May 1973.

————. *Toward Quality Education for Mexican Americans.* Mexican American Education Study. Report VI. Washington, D.C.: U.S. Commission on Civil Rights, February 1974.

————. *Counting the Forgotten: The 1970 Census Count of Persons of Spanish Speaking Background in the United States.* Washington, D.C.: U.S. Commission on Civil Rights, April 1974.

————. *Twenty Years After Brown: The Shadows of the Past* (1st in a series). Washington, D.C.: U.S. Commission on Civil Rights, June 1974.

————. *Twenty Years After Brown: Equality of Educational Opportunity* (2nd in a series). Washington, D.C.: U.S. Commission on Civil Rights, March 1975.

————. *The Federal Civil Rights Enforcement Effort—1974.* Vol. III. *To Ensure Equal Educational Opportunity.* Washington, D.C.: U.S. Commission on Civil Rights, January 1975.

U.S. Congress, House, Committee on Education and Labor, and Senate, Committee on Labor and Public Welfare. *Compilation of Higher Education Laws, 1972.* Joint Committee Print. 92d Congress, 2d Sess., November 1972.

————. Hearings of the Special Subcommittee on Education. "Student Financial Assistance (Graduate Programs, State Programs, and Grants)." 93d Congress, 2d Sess., June 4–13, 1974.

270

U.S. Congress, Senate. *Toward Equal Educational Opportunity: The Report of the Select Committee on Equal Educational Opportunity.* Washington, D.C.: U.S. Government Printing Office, December 31, 1972.

U.S. Department of Health, Education, and Welfare. Office of the Assistant Secretary of Education. Federal Interagency Committee on Education. "Federal Agencies and Black Colleges." Washington, D.C.: U.S. Government Printing Office, 1971.

――――. "Task Force Report on Higher Education for Chicanos, Puerto Ricans, and American Indians." 1973. Unpublished.

――――. Office for Civil Rights. *Availability Data: Minorities and Women.* Washington, D.C.: USDHEW, June 1973.

――――. Office of the Secretary, Office for Civil Rights. *Higher Education Guidelines.* Washington, D.C.: USDHEW, October 1972.

――――. Office of Education. Task Force on the Disadvantaged and Postsecondary Education. *Recommendations for New Delivery Systems: Summary Report.* Washington, D.C.: USDHEW, 1975.

――――. *Toward the Maintenance of Quality Graduate Education in Historically Black Colleges and Universities.* A report of the Office of Education Working Conference—Meeting of Deans of Black Graduate Schools, April 1975.

U.S. Department of Labor. *Spanish-Speaking Americans: Their Manpower Problems and Opportunities.* Reprinted from *Manpower Report of the President.* Washington, D.C.: U.S. Government Printing Office, 1973.

U.S. General Accounting Office. Report to the Congress. *Problems of the Upward Bound Program in Preparing Disadvantaged Students for a Postsecondary Education.* Washington, D.C.: U.S. Government Printing Office, March 7, 1974.

――――. Manpower Administration. *A Study of Black Colleges to Determine Their Capability to Deal with the Problems of Unemployment, Underemployment, and Job Training.* Washington, D.C.: U.S. Government Printing Office, 1973.

University of California. *Developing Opportunities for Minorities in Graduate Education.* Proceedings of the Conference on Minority Graduate Education, May 11–12, 1973, Berkeley, Calif.

University of Chicago. *The Future of Education for Black Americans.* Chicago: University of Chicago Press, 1973.

University of Michigan. Center for the Study of Higher Education. *Affirmative Action: Its Legal Mandate and Organizational Implications.* Ann Arbor, Mich.: University of Michigan, March 1974.

University of Toledo. "Symposium: Disadvantaged Students and Legal Education—Programs for Affirmative Action." *The University of Toledo Law Review,* nos. 2 and 3, Spring and Summer 1970.

University of Washington. *Tomorrow's Imperative Today: Multi-Ethnic Programs—A Report from the Second Annual Conference on Special Emerging Programs in Higher Education.* Seattle, Wash.: University of Washington, November 7–9, 1974.

Urban Education, Inc. *Minority Enrollment and Representation in Institutions of Higher Education.* New York: Urban Education, Inc., 1974.

Vazquez, Hector I. "Puerto Rican Americans." *Journal of Negro Education* 38 (1969):247–256.

Walker, John H., III. *Thinking About Graduate School—A Planning Guide for Freshman and Sophomore Minority College Students.* Princeton, N.J.: Educational Testing Service, 1974.

Weaver, Warren. "Now That Marco DeFunis has His Law Degree. . . ." *Compact,* July/August 1974.

271

Weinstein, Robert. *Native Americans in Rural and Urban Poverty.* Austin: Center for the Study of Human Resources, The University of Texas, November 1973.

West, Earle H. "Editorial Comment: American Minority Groups and Contemporary Education." *Journal of Negro Education* 38(1969):185–186.

Western Interstate Commission for Higher Education/Western Association of Graduate Schools. *Graduate Education and Ethnic Minorities.* Boulder, Colo.: Western Interstate Commission for Higher Education, February 1970.

————. *A Survey of College and University Programs for American Indians.* Boulder, Colo.: Western Interstate Commission for Higher Education, 1974.

Wharton, Clifton R. "Reflections on Black Intellectual Power." *Educational Record,* Fall 1972, pp. 281–286.

Wilburn, Adolph Y. "Careers in Science and Engineering for Black Americans." *Science* 184(June 14, 1974):1148–1154.

Willie, Charles V. "Perspectives on Black Education and the Education of Blacks." pp. 231–238. In *Does College Matter?,* ed. by Lewis C. Solmon and Paul J. Taubman. New York: Academic Press, 1973.

————, and Arline S. McCord. *Black Students at White Colleges.* New York: Praeger Publishers, 1973.

Willingham, Warren W. "Predicting Success in Graduate Education." *Science* 183 (January 25, 1974):273–278.

Wright Stephen J. "Traditionally Black Colleges: A Brief Review." *ERIC Research Currents,* September 1973.

————. "Redressing the Imbalance of Minority Groups in the Professions." *Journal of Higher Education* 43(March 1972):239–248.

————, Benjamin E. Mays, Albert W. Dent, Christopher Jencks, and David Riesman. "The American Negro College—Four Responses and a Reply." *Harvard Educational Review* 37(1967):451–468.

Yoshioka, Robert B. *Asian–Americans and Public Higher Education in California.* Prepared for the Joint Committee on the Master Plan for Higher Education, California Legislature, Sacramento, February 1973.

NATIONAL BOARD ON GRADUATE EDUCATION PUBLICATIONS

Board Reports

1. *Graduate Education: Purposes, Problems and Potential,* November 1972, 18 pp.
2. *Doctorate Manpower Forecasts and Policy,* November 1973, 22 pp.
3. *Federal Policy Alternatives toward Graduate Education,* March 1974, 127 pp.
4. *Science Development, University Development, and the Federal Government,* June 1975, 48 pp.
5. *Minority Group Participation in Graduate Education,* June 1976, 273 pp.
6. *Outlook and Opportunities for Graduate Education,* December 1975, 73 pp.

Technical Reports

TR. 1. *An Economic Perspective on the Evolution of Graduate Education,* by Stephen P. Dresch, March 1974, 76 pp.
TR. 2. *Forecasting the Ph.D. Labor Market: Pitfalls for Policy,* by Richard Freeman and David W. Breneman, April 1974, 50 pp.
TR. 3. *Graduate School Adjustments to the "New Depression" in Higher Education,* by David W. Breneman, with a *Commentary by the National Board on Graduate Education,* February 1975, 96 pp.
TR. 4. *Science Development: An Evaluation Study,* by David E. Drew, June 1975, 182 pp.
TR. 5. *Graduate Education and Community Colleges: Cooperative Approaches to Community College Staff Development,* edited by S. V. Martorana, William Toombs, and David W. Breneman, August 1975, 137 pp.

Other Publications

An Annotated Bibliography on Graduate Education, 1971–1972, October 1972, 151 pp.
"Comment" on the Newman Task Force Report on the Federal Role in Graduate Education, June 1973, 13 pp.

*2284-36M
1977
5-49
C